THE INFERNAL WORLD OF BRANWELL BRONTË

Daphne du Maurier

with an Introduction
by Justine Picardie

Virago

VIRAGO

This edition published in May 2006 by Virago Press
First published in Great Britain in 1960 by Victor Gollancz

A CIP catalogue record for this book
is available from the British Library.

ISBN-13: 978-1-84408-075-5
ISBN-10: 1-84408-075-7

Typeset in Bembo by Palimpsest Book Production Limited,
Polmont, Stirlingshire
Printed and bound in Great Britain by
Clays Ltd, St Ives plc

Virago Press
An imprint of
Time Warner Book Group UK
Brettenham House
Lancaster Place
London WC2E 7EN

www.virago.co.uk

Introduction

The Infernal World of Branwell Brontë has always been the least successful of Daphne du Maurier's books in commercial terms; yet it remains as fascinating as the best of her work. When it came out in 1960, her publisher, Victor Gollancz, printed eight thousand copies — far less than was usual for his best-selling author; and though it received several good reviews (including one from Muriel Spark in the *Daily Telegraph*), the biography did not sell well, perhaps because it was so different to her more popular novels and family memoirs. This failure continued to be a source of disappointment to du Maurier: in a letter to her friend, Oriel Malet, written in October 1962, she referred to the painfulness of seeing a book that 'just gets wiped off and forgotten, no matter how good the reviews. I don't think I had any bad reviews for my Branwell, but right from the start I know old V.G. was bored by the thought of it, and he never made any effort to push it after it was published.'

That her carefully researched biography had been intended to rescue Branwell Brontë from obscurity made its lack of sales all the more maddening. As du Maurier writes in her preface, she had sought to bring 'some measure of understanding for a figure long maligned, neglected and despised' — and yet her mission to rehabilitate Branwell, the reprobate brother labelled as the drunken flop of the Brontë family, was itself thwarted.

Failure, of course, is an intriguing subject; not least for du Maurier herself. By the time she embarked upon her Branwell project, she was a famous author — *Rebecca* had not stopped selling since its instant success upon publication in 1938 — yet she was not immune to insecurities. In a letter to the Brontë scholar, J. A. Symington, who helped her with her research, she expressed her fears at being out-done by another writer, Winifred Gérin, who turned out also to be working on a Branwell biography at the same time as du Maurier. 'My novels are what is known as popular and sell very well,' she wrote to Symington, soon after she heard the news of the Gérin book, 'but I am *not* a critic's favourite, indeed I am generally dismissed with a sneer as a bestseller and not reviewed at all, so . . . I would come off second-best, I have no illusions to that.'

It was not the first time that she had felt herself to have been relegated as second-best: unkind critics had already deemed *Rebecca* an inferior *Jane Eyre*; which must have been galling, given how much she admired the Brontës, having been a passionate reader of their novels since childhood. Oriel Malet reveals in her book, *Letters from Menabilly*, that she and Daphne talked endlessly about the Brontës – and about their imaginary worlds of childhood:

> . . . the source of the Brontës' imagination, and their doom, for in adult life they were unable to break free from them. Charlotte sought refuge in the Angrian Chronicles whenever life became too much for her, and suffered agonies of guilt in consequence. Emily, untroubled by conscience, immersed herself in Gondal, the country of her mind, until inspiration failed her, and she died. 'Gondal' became our codeword for all make-believe and pretence, whether conscious or not.

When du Maurier was asked to write the introduction to a new edition of *Wuthering Heights* in 1954, she used it as an opportunity to visit Haworth, and asked Oriel Malet to accompany her and her younger daughter Flavia on the trip. The three of them spent time exploring the Brontë Parsonage, and went for long walks across the moors; and as Malet writes in *Letters from Menabilly*, du Maurier 'was becoming increasingly intrigued by Branwell (the son, predictably, interesting her more than the daughters).'

It was an astute observation: for du Maurier had always been more absorbed in her son, Kits, than her two daughters (despite the fact that she became closer to the girls as they grew up, and was adored by both of them). After the trip to Haworth, she read all of the Brontë juvenilia, and became convinced that Branwell had not received the credit he was due, from Mrs Gaskell's first, enduring biography of Charlotte Brontë, and thereafter. To that end, she wrote to J. A. Symington, one of the two editors of the juvenilia (and much else besides), saying that she was 'fascinated by Branwell and I cannot understand why Brontë research has neglected him'. Symington responded enthusiastically and du Maurier decided to embark on a serious, scholarly study of Branwell – a book that would be quite unlike any she had written before; a work, perhaps, that she hoped would be taken seriously by previously dismissive literary critics.

Margaret Forster's insightful biography of Daphne du Maurier makes it clear how important this project was:

> [it] gave her the opportunity to test herself in a way she had, in fact, always wanted to do. There was a good deal of the scholar *manqué* in Daphne, in spite of her frequent claims to have a butterfly mind. As it was, she was prepared to teach herself by trial and error . . .

And there were other reasons, too, for her fascination with Branwell. She had embarked on her research not long after her husband, Sir Frederick Browning – known to his family as Tommy – had suffered a nervous breakdown, in July 1957, a collapse exacerbated by exhaustion and alcohol consumption. By the beginning of 1958, as Margaret Forster writes, Daphne herself was also 'a little unbalanced'. Some of her fears concerned Tommy's position – he was a distinguished military commander who went on to work for the Duke of Edinburgh at Buckingham Palace:

> She began imagining that all kinds of plots were surrounding her – that Tommy was being spied on by Russians who were out to get the Royal Family, and other, similar delusions. Half the time she laughed at herself, knowing that she was being absurd, but then she would suddenly decide her fantasises were rooted in reality, and become agitated.

Her fears extended to Oriel Malet, by then living in Paris: 'She rang me several times, warning me not to go out at night alone, and to avoid all public places, such as the metro . . .'

Thus du Maurier was to write with perceptive sympathy of Branwell's breakdowns, of 'the waves of depression that engulfed him' and 'the shock to his own pride' when he, 'the brilliant versatile genius of the family', was unable to sell his paintings or publish his books. But she was also able to empathise with Charlotte's distress and irritation at her brother's slump, made worse by his drinking (du Maurier, after all, had by then nicknamed her husband 'Moper'). She quotes one of Charlotte's letters at length, written to a close friend when Branwell had come home in disgrace after losing his job as a tutor, and distracting his sister from her manuscript of *The Professor*:

> It was very forced work to address him. I might have spared myself the trouble, as he took no notice, and made no reply; he was stupefied. My fears were not in vain. Emily tells me that he got a sovereign from Papa while I have been away, under the pretence of paying a pressing debt; he went immediately and changed it at a public-house, and has employed it as was to be expected. She

concluded her account by saying he was 'a hopeless being'; it is too true. In his present state it is scarcely possible to stay in the same room where he is. What the future has in store, I do not know.

Du Maurier clearly identified with Charlotte's feelings of disillusionment and frustration: as is apparent in her letter to Symington, explaining why she had been unable to spend more time looking at manuscripts in the Brontë Parsonage Museum, because of Tommy's ill health. 'I have been in constant attendance on my husband,' she wrote, 'I feel rather like Charlotte Brontë when nursing the Rev. Brontë and finding it difficult to get on with *Villette*.' And she imagined Winifred Gérin, meanwhile, speeding ahead with her biography, unimpeded by moping men.

Nevertheless, towards the end of 1959, with Tommy well enough to be left, at last, she returned to Haworth, and hunted through manuscripts and church records. Du Maurier's investigations there contributed to the novel idea, expressed in her book, that Branwell had been dismissed as a tutor from the Robinson family not, as has been commonly held, because of an affair with Mrs Robinson, but some gross impropriety with her son Edmund, Branwell's pupil. ('It is possible that, left alone at Thorp Green with Edmund, and free from the constraining presence of his employer, he had attempted in some way to lead Edmund astray . . .') Subsequent Brontë scholars have pointed out that this has more to do with du Maurier's imaginative reworking of history than any factual evidence; and it would have made an intriguing fictional plot. But as it was, she seemed to be losing interest in her idea of Branwell as an unrecognised genius; certainly by Chapter Thirteen, when she quoted the opening lines of his poem, 'Real Rest', written when he returned home to the Parsonage in disgrace ('I see a corpse upon the waters lie, / With eyes turned, swelled and sightless, to the sky, / And arms outstretched to move, as wave on wave / Upbears it in its boundless billowy grave . . .'). The remaining lines of this poem, she then declared, 'are better left unquoted. Fantasy and laudanum were rapidly destroying what creative powers were still within him.'

For all that, du Maurier's own sustained efforts and creative powers ensured that she beat her rival to the finishing post: *The Infernal World of Branwell Brontë* came out eight months before Gérin's book. But by then, du Maurier was already feeling oppressed by another rival writer: in October 1960, just before publication, she wrote to Oriel Malet, 'I see Nancy Mitford has written a book called *Don't Tell Alfred*, and I bet it gets rave notices. It comes out the same week as poor *Branwell*, who will be chucked.'

Poor Branwell; poor Daphne. To be truthful, although I would recommend her biography of him as essential reading to any du Maurier fan, it is not the easiest of her work – weighed down, occasionally, by her anxious diligence, and also by her own increasing exasperation with Branwell's failure to live up to his original promise. At the same time, she seemed almost to admit to the impossibility of ever knowing the real truth of another's life; least of all her Branwell. As she wrote in a letter to Oriel Malet, in December 1959, it was hard to get people in Haworth to talk about the facts of the past, when they so easily wandered into the irrelevant events of the present:

If you ask me, nobody there really knows anything any more. And Miss G[érin] can sit in their cottages til she's blue in the face, she will only hear the old Gaskell stories repeated over and over again, and embroidered. Imagine a person a hundred years hence, going down to Polkerris, and asking . . . about me – I mean, what *would* they say?

Yet her biography had served its purpose, in that Branwell

came vividly alive within it; and in doing so, du Maurier seemed able to write her way out of her despair, to see a future for herself and for her husband. Tommy recovered, and their marriage was ended only by his death in 1965. She lived on for many years, until 1989, and though she did not go back to Haworth, she returned often to the Brontës, and to Gondal, the sustaining landscape of the imagination.

Close to the end of her life, when she had finally stopped writing, and needed nursing at home, one of those who cared for her was a woman named Margaret Robertson, who came from Yorkshire. Robertson discovered that the Brontës were one of the few remaining topics of conversation that would spark du Maurier into animation; indeed, she would happily talk about their novels, while denying writing some of her own. The nurse, who had some psychiatric training, came to the conclusion that 'Daphne acted towards her writing past as though it were a person who had died – she was bereaved and the grief of her loss was too terrible to talk about . . .' Talking about the Brontës, however, was the best therapy; and in that, Daphne du Maurier remained entirely true to herself.

Justine Picardie, 2005

To J. Alex Symington, compiler and editor of *The Shakespeare Head Brontë*, whose life-long interest in Patrick Branwell Brontë stimulated my own, and encouraged me to undertake the present study.

I therefore purpose not, or dream,
    Descanting on his fate,
To give the melancholy theme
    A more enduring date:
        But misery still delights to trace
        Its 'semblance in another's case.

No voice divine the storm allay'd,
    No light propitious shone;
When, snatched from all effectual aid,
    We perished, each alone:
        But I beneath a rougher sea,
        And whelm'd in deeper gulphs than he.

William Cowper, *The Castaway*

Acknowledgements

I wish to thank the Council of the Brontë Society for permission to quote from manuscripts and transcripts in the Brontë Parsonage Museum; the Keeper of the Brotherton Collection, the Brotherton Library, University of Leeds, for allowing me access to manuscripts and transcripts in his care; and the Keeper of the Department of Manuscripts, British Museum, for giving me permission to make transcripts of manuscripts in the Ashley Library. I wish in particular to thank Mr Harold G. Mitchell, Custodian of the Brontë Parsonage Museum, for his unfailing kindness and good humour in answering my questions; Joan St George Saunders for her prompt help in research and her transcription of the manuscript *Percy*; Miss O'Farrell and Mrs D'Arcy Hart for their transcription of *A New Year's Story* and *The Wool Is Rising*; Miss Brunskill for her search through the Robinson deed box; Miss Dorothy Bates for her sleuth-like activities in Sowerby and Luddenden; and above all Sheila Hodges for the great patience, sympathy and skill with which she revised and edited my completed work.

Preface

When Mrs Gaskell published her life of Charlotte Brontë in 1857, she painted so vivid a picture of life at Haworth parsonage, and of the talented, short-lived family who dwelt within its walls, that every Brontë biography written since has been based upon it.

A hundred years have gone by, the biography is still unsurpassed, but during the intervening time much has come to light about the early writings of the young Brontës, proving that from childhood and on through adolescence they lived a life of quite extraordinary fantasy, creating an imaginary world of their own, peopled with characters more real to them than the inhabitants of their father's parish. Charlotte Brontë's *Jane Eyre*, Emily Brontë's *Wuthering Heights*, Anne Brontë's *The Tenant of Wildfell Hall* were all famous novels and their authoresses dead when Mrs Gaskell came to write about them. What she did not realize was that none of these novels would have come into being had not their creators lived, during childhood, in this fantasy world, which was largely inspired and directed by their only brother, Patrick Branwell Brontë.

Neither Mrs Gaskell nor Mr Brontë suspected that under the parsonage roof there were manuscripts, written by Branwell and Charlotte, which ran into many hundreds of thousands of words — far more than the published works of Charlotte, Emily and Anne. Although, on examination, Branwell's manuscripts show that he did not possess the amazing talent of his famous sisters, they prove him to have had a boyhood and youth of almost incredible productivity, so spending himself in the process of describing the lives and loves of his imaginary characters that invention was exhausted by the time he was twenty-one.

Mr Brontë, their father, writing to Mrs Gaskell after she had published the biography of his daughter Charlotte, told her: 'The picture of my brilliant and unhappy son is a masterpiece.' He did not understand, any more than Mrs Gaskell, that the 'brilliance' existed to a great extent in his own imagination, the pride of a lonely widower in the extraordinary precocity and endearing liveliness of a boy whose supposed genius disintegrated with the coming of manhood; whose unhappiness was caused, not by the abortive love-affair described by Mrs Gaskell with such gusto, but by his inability to distinguish truth from fiction, reality from fantasy; and who failed in life because it differed from his own 'infernal world'.

One day, perhaps, all the manuscripts which poured from Branwell's pen will be transcribed, not for the Brontë student only, but for the general reader. One day the definitive biography of this tragic young man will be published. Meanwhile, many years of interest in the subject, and much reading, have prompted the present writer to attempt a study of his life and work which may serve as an introduction to both. If it brings some measure of understanding for a figure long maligned, neglected and despised, and helps to reinstate him in his original place in the Brontë family, where he was, until the last years of disintegration, so loved a person, then this book will not have been written in vain.

Daphne du Maurier
Cornwall, 1960

1

He died on Sunday morning, the 24th of September, 1848. He was thirty-one years old. He died in the room which he had shared with his father for so long, and in which, as a little boy, he had awakened to find the moon shining through the curtainless windows and his father upon his knees, praying. The room, for too many months now, had been part refuge and part prison-cell. It had been refuge from the accusing or indifferent eyes of his sisters, refuge from the averted gaze of his father, whose offer of help in dressing spelt reproach. But when he was alone again, the family downstairs and about their business, only the familiar sounds of day-by-day penetrating his solitude — the cry of a child in the road, the chiming of the church clock, the opening and closing of the garden gate as someone called upon parish concerns — then the room turned to the cold walls of a dungeon, or, worse, oppressed him with the stifling weight of a tomb beneath whose heavy stone the dead-alive know perpetual suffocation. The minutes would tick away to half-past twelve or half-past four — for the hours of day were meaningless once appetite was lost and the routine of life relinquished; and the slow cough of the clock on the stairs proceeded inexorably towards that half-choke before the hour, followed at once by the stroke from the church, with no pause or respite. Eternal reproach, eternal accusation.

I know only that it is time for me to be something when I am nothing. That my father cannot have long to live, and that when he dies my evening, which is already twilight, will become night. That I shall then have a constitution still so strong that it will keep me years in torture and despair when I should every hour pray that I might die.

The scrawl was already one year, two years old, and the friend to whom it had been written had his own troubles; besides, the very tale it told had now worn thin through constant repetition. The truth was that no one cared. No one was greatly interested. And he who had fabricated the tale itself, and now lay dying on his bed, was mortally sick of lies and subterfuge and the fantasy which had gripped him. So when an easing of despair came to him suddenly, unbelievably, on the Friday evening, continuing through the following day and night, and for the first time in months and years he was free from horror and bitterness and blight, he thought that he had been forgiven and life was to begin again.

His father knelt beside his bed and prayed. It was not torment any more, or tedium, or mockery, the useless mumblings of an old man clinging to an outworn creed, but the strong and loving voice of Papa, his first god, who had constantly cared for him and never denied him. The three women watching him had lost their adult faces. They were not Charlotte, Emily and Anne, but had become once again his playmates and his slaves, his partners in magic, his beloved genii. Genius Tallii crouched beside his pillow, Genius Annii smoothed his brow, Genius Emmii watched at the foot of the bed; one and all waited for the word of Chief Genius Brannii. He smiled at them, and glancing down at his empty hand wondered for one puzzled moment why he was no longer clasping the rough form of Sneaky, the wooden soldier who had carried many aliases but had always been himself. Then he remembered that although his own body had grown the soldier had not changed, had even shrunk, so that one day, stepped upon and spoilt, he had been swept away with the

2

household dust – or 'cliffed', as his Cornish aunt pronounced it, all useless, outgrown things being cast into the sea, down Penzance.

If the comforting brave soldier had gone to his grave, his owner at least remembered how life had been breathed into this friend of his boyhood. His father had brought home for him a present of some toy soldiers. Tearing open the box, he had run to his three sisters, and had given each of them one of the little wooden figures. Immediately the soldiers had assumed names and personalities, and round them the four children had built some of their most cherished games. Out of them, indeed, had grown the heroic figures whom the sisters later wove into their tales. The soldier whom Charlotte had dubbed Wellesley was now Rochester, lover of Jane Eyre. Parry, Emily's soldier, was Heathcliff, alone on Wuthering Heights. Anne's soldier, Ross, had become Arthur Huntingdon, whose wife fled to Wildfell Hall. Only Sneaky, his own soldier, later to become Alexander Percy, remained hidden and unknown. There was still time, though. The feeling of peace that had come to Brannii surely meant that strength and power had returned to him, and he would soon be well again. He would get up from his bed and go downstairs once more to the dining-room, taking with him the old books and sheets of paper, scored with his writing, that had grown dusty in the back room which had been his studio. Then the four of them would begin all over again, conjuring phantoms and creatures from that long discarded, loved, infernal world.

One day, he told them now, all their books would be published. One day the four of them would be famous. One day men and women would come from all over England and the world to see the place where the Chief Genius lived. Instead of smiling back at him, though, they turned their faces away as if ashamed. They were unable to speak. They could not look at him. And he thought perhaps they were still angry with him for the trouble he had caused them through the years; so contrite now, and calm, he asked forgiveness. This seemed to break their hearts. They could not bear it. Yet when he had cursed them a few days back they had been indifferent. Puzzled, he stayed silent, listening to his father's prayers, and for the first time for perhaps fifteen years or more he repeated after him the word Amen. He did not understand why this should move them, nor why – his memory swept clean of all the murky fog that had shrouded it for so long – the recollections of the happy past, the childhood jokes, the family words and phrases, even the ridiculous talk he had invented, a Yorkshire dialect spoken by holding his nose between finger and thumb, should so suddenly, at this hour of the night, bring them to tears.

One by one they crept away, to weep, perhaps, in silence or together, and out of the mist which was death (though he did not recognize it) instead of his father's bowed head he saw the face of John Brown, his friend. Then he understood. He knew the eyes too well to miss what they told him. Pouched and yielding, over-full with tears, the bags beneath them flabby in their grief, a tremor at the corner of the sensuous mouth, this was not the aftermath of yet one more hilarious carousal or post-funeral celebration. Now he knew he must soon meet his Maker face to face.

He seized the roughened hand and said, 'Oh, John, I'm dying!' But the forty-four-year-old sexton, once his ally, his familiar, his mentor and his guide, could no longer help him, as he had so often done in the past, safely leading him, in helpless laughter, past a fallen table or a tumbled chair. The tombstones John had chiselled, the flat graves they had slipped and stumbled upon together, now raised themselves outside the window like warning hands. Too many mouldering bones, mocked by the pair of them, formed themselves to the skeletons they once had been, and grinned. The lids of coffins opened. The shrouded figures sat. And John himself, instead of winking, thumbs turned down ('There goes another sinner to

4

Kingdom come!'), sat helpless by the bed and could not speak.

What, then, could the dying man believe? Where were salvation and the angels? What was his credo?

Somewhere in a forgotten drawer, dog-eared and crumpled, there was a half-page of an uncompleted manuscript. Written at white-heat, in a moment of rebellion and scorn, it had suggested a parody of prayer:

> May He protect you from the burning hill that was ready to fall upon Christians – from the stones that struck the vital breath out of holy Stephen – from the gridiron that fried St Lawrence – from the crucifixion, head downwards, that gave apoplexy to St Peter – from the roasting of Polycarp – from the impetuous pride of Tertullian – from the vanity of Athanasius – from the laughing atheism of Lucian – from the humbugs of the treachery of Judas – the plagiarisms of Virgil – the repetitions of Homer – from the fate of Alcibiades' dog's tail – from the fate of Prynne's ears – from the fate of Charles the First's head and of Oliver Cromwell's nose – from the falsehood of Palmanager and Jacob – from the impudence of Colonel Blood – from the vanity of Absalom and the young Pretender – the go-and-come virginity of Queen Elizabeth, the death of pretty Queen Mary – the hard-heartedness of Brutus, the clemency of Titus that crucified fifty Jews round the walls of their city, the charity of inquisitors-general, Malay pirates, slave-drivers – from the tender mercies of Henry 8th and George 4th, of Henry 7th and old Elwes, of Prince Rupert and the Marquis of Waterford, of Chateaubriand and Robert Montgomery, of Prince Marshal Blücher and Bernard Barston – from all these terrors, Good Lord, deliver us!

Let his friend Joe Leyland design the scroll, and his familiar John the sexton chisel the words; here surely was a quotation fiery enough from the unpublished works of Chief Genius Brannii to render him immortal. But it would be too long. Something smaller, perhaps, written while he was a boy and not spewed out in anger, would serve as epitaph.

O Thou Great Divinity, Thou only God whom my mind could ever stoop to worship, whom I have long worshipped, and whom I will forever adore. I can love, I can hate, I can feel affection, I can nourish vengeance, I can do all that these can do save feel friendship and the ties of blood . . . If men could see thee − Vitality − and leave their vain superstitions, their Eternals, their Redeemers, their Saints and Angels, they would turn and cleave to Thee, the only living and true God.

It was close on nine o'clock. Instead of prayer or challenge he said to John, 'In all my past life I have done nothing either great or good.' Then his face changed, and a convulsion like so many of those that had come upon him before seized him for the last time. His sisters came back into the room, and his father too, and when he saw his father he stumbled to his feet and died.

2

When the Reverend Patrick Brontë, wishing to know more about the minds of his six motherless children than he had hitherto discovered, placed each one behind a mask to make them speak with less timidity than before, he gave to the three sisters who survived the first blessed thrill of anonymity. To speak aloud and yet remain, as it would seem, unknown, to hide identity behind a hollow face; criticism, mockery, reproof – these things could not touch the wearer of the mask.

Not only once but many times the mask must have been produced from the father's study, but what shape it was, what size, what expression it bore, has never been disclosed. A mummer's disguise, perhaps, foolish or frightening, a relic of their father's undergraduate years at Cambridge – this might explain how such a curiosity came to be found in the parsonage of Haworth. And the children, learning that their father too had once hidden his identity in such a fashion, could have been made bold. Their father, tall and upright, who walked with dignity like the Duke of Wellington himself, this being, because of the mask, became one of them. Perhaps, wishing to put himself upon their level, he in his turn may sometimes have donned the mask and answered questions, and the voice coming from the mouthpiece, sounding grotesque, would have given a twist to the imaginations of the watching six. Here was Papa yet not Papa, here was a creature who, concealed behind the grinning head, could turn himself to giant or bogy, inducing tremors of excitement which, because they were frightening, were delicious too. Or the mask may have been a night-black highwayman's disguise, giving concealment to the eyes alone, found on the moors and handed to the parson. This would impart another twist to the game, the father becoming on the instant a Turpin or a Claude Duval, and the children, even the youngest, little scapegoat rogues.

The mask thus served its turn, as did the box of soldiers which the father later brought home for his son. Put away, or lying idle on a chair, it had no magic and was a lifeless thing; worn by one of the children, it gave instant protection from the code of everyday, so that thoughts and feelings could find release in a manner not otherwise possible. In the same way a wooden soldier, with painted face and form, when freed from its box acquired a personality of its own, and could be made the spokesman of its owner – even take upon itself the owner's moods and misdemeanours.

When the widowed father first put his children behind the mask the eldest, Maria, was ten years old, the youngest not more than four. Branwell, the only boy, would have been six or seven. The answer that he gave to his father, from behind the mask, betrayed a preoccupation with physical problems very different from the moral maxims that came tripping from the lips of his sisters.

'What,' inquired Mr Brontë, 'is the best way of knowing the difference between the intellects of men and women?' Swift as an arrow came the boy's retort, 'By considering the difference between them as to their bodies.'

How instant is the vision of a kitchen fire, and the children tubbed before it, the nurse, Sarah or Nancy Garrs, bidding them not slop the water over the floor, rubbing the boy down with a rough towel; and as the youngster stood there, glorying in nudity, his eyes darted from one to the other of his sisters, their bodies smooth and white, while he – possessing not only the red hair that he shared in common with his father but something else as well – derided them for being incomplete. The days were Georgian still, the future Queen Victoria a small child; and a homely Yorkshire nurse scrubbing her bairns before a kitchen fire in the parsonage of a moorland parish would more likely laugh with the one boy, who straddled himself with so much confidence, than cover him up and banish him to bed.

The little girls would watch with envy or distaste, depending upon their natures, but if squabbles came – which would seem likely when one small boy sought to dominate his ground, for all the world like a bantam-cock in a barnyard – Emily, his junior by a year, is the most likely to have given fight.

It is significant that it was Emily, at that time five years old, rather than Maria, aged ten, of whom the puzzled father asked advice, under cover of the mask:

'What had I best do with Branwell when he is a naughty boy?'

'Reason with him, and when he won't listen to reason, whip him.'

Branwell may have been a naughty boy that very day, and so encouraged the father, interrupted in his study by uproar, to try the mask experiment. Emily was questioned before Branwell, and her suggestion of the whip would have served as stimulant to the boy when his turn came to don the strange disguise. His reply would be a stab at her, if not at all his sisters.

'Reason with me and whip me they may,' he might have answered, 'but I've got a sharper tongue than you have, and something else to aid me into the bargain.'

The boy, born on June 26th, 1817, in Thornton, on the outskirts of Bradford, where his father was curate, quickly forgot his birthplace. But the first year at Haworth, where his parents moved when he was three, must have proved disturbing. After months of agony the invalid upstairs, whom the younger ones had barely seen during her long illness, was finally laid to rest. Mama had gone to Jesus. Jesus had called her home.

9

Since she had been in pain, and Jesus was kind, no doubt it seemed the best thing that could have happened. Already Branwell could scarcely remember the hands that had caressed him, for when someone is ill for long, and voices are hushed, and children are told to be quiet and tip-toe the stairs, she who is ill and shut away turns from a living mother into a legend.

Besides, there was always Maria. The eldest sister, having greater patience with her brother than those who were closer to him in age, and remembering very possibly a promise to 'take care of the boy', the darling of the tired, sick sufferer upstairs, taught Branwell his first letters, helped him to add, told him stories, showed him pictures, so that the child, when he was tired of capering below in the kitchen and pestering the younger ones, would go upstairs to the little room over the front door which was Maria's and Elizabeth's 'study'. Curled against the older girl, whose books and papers were strewn about the floor in glorious fashion, herself sprawling, untidy, never knowing the time of day or when to wash, he was lulled into peace and security by the sound of her voice, and knew, for the first time and so forever, the bliss of listening to someone reading aloud.

It was strange fare, too, for a small boy barely in breeches – the newpapers mostly, whatever Maria could get hold of; for, ignorant of history and geography, she could discourse on the day's affairs with a knowledge far beyond her years, making her father smile and raising her aunt's eyebrows. The death of the rector's wife would have passed unnoticed in Yorkshire, except in the family circle and the immediate parish, but the newspapers in the preceding month would have been full of the death of the unfortunate Queen Caroline and the bitter wrangles that had passed between her and the monarch who now reigned, George IV. For journalists, then as now, delighted to record royal scandals, and the names of living statesmen in far-off London would be as familiar to the boy, echoing his sister, as that of the parish clerk or the nearby sexton.

Maria became substitute for Mama who lived with Jesus. Maria made Branwell fold his hands and say his prayers. Maria gave the lead to Elizabeth and Charlotte too, and in a quiet yet definite fashion soon proved herself the strongest personality in the parsonage.

The position of the aunt, their mother's sister, who had come all the way from Cornwall to look after her brother-in-law and his children, was not an enviable one. She was in her mid-forties, no longer young. She had nursed her sister devotedly through her painful lingering disease. Proud, like every Cornishwoman, she refused to be 'kept' by her brother-in-law, but insisted on paying her way and her share of the household expenses out of her own small annuity of fifty pounds a year.

She was small, with pale brown eyes and soft brown hair, neat in her person, particularly in her ways, and the expression in her eyes, shown in an existing miniature, suggests a woman who could easily be clay in masculine hands.

Today Mr Brontë would not have agonized through the years for his dead Maria. He would not even, perhaps, have taken pen in hand two years after she had died, and written to his first sweetheart, Mary Burder, telling her that his 'ancient love had been rekindled, and he had a longing desire to see her'. No doubt he would have married his sister-in-law Elizabeth, and there is no reason to suppose that the marriage would have proved anything but a happy one.

The nineteenth-century code made this impossible. A man who took his deceased wife's sister to his bosom committed incest. At forty-four and forty-five Patrick Brontë and Elizabeth Branwell were forced to share a roof but not a bed, to exchange civilities but not endearments; and although the routine that was to last for over twenty years established itself without any apparent disagreement, that the continual proximity was trying to nerve and temper showed itself in the increasing withdrawal of the one to his study or parlour, and

11

of the other to her bed-sitting-room upstairs. Patrick Brontë, warm-hearted, even passionate, highly strung, baffled and distressed by the strange change in his dying wife, who, in his own words, after a 'life of holiness' found her mind 'often disturbed in the last conflict by the great enemy', longed for the physical comfort that a loving partner could have given him. And the lonely Cornish spinster Elizabeth Branwell, cut off from her friends and relatives and all that had made Penzance a hive of bustle and activity, certainly wondered how best she could control this slapdash Irish household, where each member, down to the baby, was an individual and a curiosity.

She must often have wished for living room and space to breathe, for less of the eternal clearing up and tidying, and fewer mouths to feed – especially with Yorkshire cooking so different from Cornish baking. And although the baby was a pet and the little Branwell had ways for all the world like cousin Tom lost long ago at sea, the older girls had difficult, stubborn tempers.

Perhaps it was their aunt who first suggested school: school discipline would straighten the rounded shoulders, tauten the poked-in backs, make headway even with the clumsy fingers that could not, or would not, hold needle and thread to her satisfaction. Measles and whooping-cough, which kept the children in bed for weeks, must have proved the final straw, with the endless meals on trays, the sitting up at night, the changing of bed-linen, the scolding of the two young servants who would not do as they were bidden, the irrepressible spirits of the boy, darting in and out of the sick-room to make his sisters laugh.

In July, 1824, Maria and Elizabeth went to Cowan Bridge, that most excellent institution for the daughters of clergymen, where, according to an apologist in after years, 'the comforts were many and the privations few'. Mr Carus Wilson, the director, who in the words of his son 'spent a long lifetime in the service of others', expressed his opinions in a volume entitled *Thoughts,* which showed only too well his belief in moderation of every kind.

'The pupils,' he explained,

are necessarily put into a very simple and uniform attire. Many of them no doubt feel it. They have unfortunately been accustomed, perhaps even to excess, in this very prevailing and increasing love of dress, for alas, clergymen's families are not exempt from the mania – not even the poorest. With me it was always an object to nip in the bud any growing symptom of vanity.

Patrick Brontë, with an income of £170 a year, had not encouraged his little daughters to preen at peacocks; but the modest fees were a godsend to one in his position. Indeed, the whole experiment seemed so successful that in September of the same year he returned with another daughter, eight-year-old Charlotte, keeping Emily, the baby and the boy at home.

Peace would seem to have come upon the household. Yet all was not quite so. There was friction below stairs, or, to be more accurate, 'out back'. Miss Branwell's 'ways' did not suit themselves to those of the two young servants, and the harassed clergyman decided that it would be better to engage an elderly woman. Tabitha Aykroyd, aged fifty-three, replaced the chattering youngsters, and proved herself to be a person of great strength of character, who could hold her own with the Cornishwoman while not falling out with her, and at the same time mother the bairns and baste them for good measure.

When Emily too was sent to school with her sisters, the long evenings at last came without disturbance, and Miss Branwell, arranging the room that had been her dear sister's with bits and pieces and knick-knacks reminding her of Cornwall, could feel some equilibrium. With Maria and the other girls out of the way her brother-in-law must have seemed closer, more approachable. He could discuss the affairs of the day without the interruption of a precocious daughter, and Miss Branwell, used to good company and conversation, could feel herself, as it were, on an equal footing. She could spare her brother-in-law's eyes by reading aloud, and make little sharp remarks on parish matters. If he was too courteous to disagree, she was spared the exchange of glances between the girls.

Branwell, at first lost without his sisters, was soon happy again, for the two adults – three of them, counting Tabby – sought to console their own loneliness by banishing his. And the middle-aged woman who knew she would never now marry, never now bear a child, petted the small boy whose ways reminded her so much of her own family, of that dear gay cousin lost at sea, and argued that without the oldest girls to spoil and pamper him, or Charlotte and Emily to dispute his small possessions, her Branwell was hardly ever naughty. He even did as he was told – or, to be more accurate, what he did do was not displeasing to the adults who adored him.

If the child seemed a little part of Cornwall to his aunt, so that in telling him about the sea, and wrecks, and the giant found entombed on St Michael's Mount she renewed her own youth, to the father he was, on the contrary, all Irish. Red-haired, quick-tempered, excitable, brimful of mischief as a bog pixie, all sunshine one minute and tears the next, to the lonely widower, still reserved and friendless in his out-of-the-way moorland parish, he was a limb from his own boyhood. Imitative as a monkey, the boy was speaking in brogue on a Monday, broad Yorkshire on a Tuesday and back to the west country on the Wednesday. He already mimicked to perfection callers at the parsonage, shaking reproof from his small shoulders with a devil-may-care grin, and indeed the light in his eye was nothing more nor less than that same glow of the clergyman's own mother, Elinor McClory (or Alice, as she was often called), God rest her soul, the prettiest girl in County Down, whose smile would tame a mad bull.

The boy was his father's shadow. He followed him to the parlour, he escorted him to the vestry, he walked with him across the moors, he helped him to clean his pistols and his gun, and learnt the use of them too. With an art that could wheedle a story out of stone, he heard how his father had at one time considered taking up soldiering as a profession. He believed he would have had the brains, he told the boy, and the capacity to plan battles; indeed, if he had become a soldier he might have risen high in his profession. Life would have been very different, he would have travelled, seen the world, but as it was . . . the Almighty had chosen differently, and He knew best.

Papa, thought the child, Papa was really three persons in one. He was the boy's father, kind, indulgent, vexed at times, the supreme male of the household, the teacher of lessons, the teller of tales when lessons were done. But he was also God's representative on earth, or here in Haworth at any rate, and once mounted in the great three-decker pulpit, with the board above it which read, 'I determined not to know anything among you save Jesus Christ and Him Crucified', his eye stern, his voice threatening, it was as though Papa became God, the embodiment of wrath. At these times Branwell thought of the Great Eruption – the word still hard to pronounce – that had happened last September, before Charlotte and Emily joined the others at school, and they had all taken shelter in a farmhouse when the terrible thing happened in mid-moor, the rumbling and the splitting of the earth as the great bog flung itself into the air. Papa had preached a sermon about it ten days afterwards, and it must have been God Himself who inspired him.

He explained first how earthquakes came about, that there were natural causes underground which produced them, the waters meeting and expanding and finally bursting to the

15

surface, and then he told them – and it seemed to Branwell that the stern voice in the pulpit spoke directly to himself in the pew below – that 'God produced earthquakes as awful monitors to turn sinners from the error of their ways, and as solemn forerunners of that last and gravest day, when the earth shall be burnt up, and the heavens shall pass away with a great noise, and the universal frame of nature shall tremble, and break, and dissolve'.

A shiver seemed to move the congregation at the awful words. No man durst look at his neighbour, and Branwell felt himself one of them, no longer 'parson's son' and a favoured being, but a backslider and a sinner, as bad as the Israelites who had been swallowed up in a pit for their evil ways, as Papa went on to explain:

'Be thankful that you are spared' – and it was not his father's voice surely, but the voice of the great Offended One.

Despise not this merciful but monitory voice of Divine Wisdom. Hear, and learn to be spiritually wise, lest the day come suddenly upon you when God will laugh at your calamity, and mock when your fear cometh; when your fear cometh as a desolation, and your destruction cometh as a whirlwind; when distress and anguish cometh upon you. The Lord is long-suffering and of tender mercy; but if sinners continue to despise his mercies and disregard his judgements, they shall at last be placed forever beyond the reach of redemption in eternal torments.

The boy crouched lower in his pew. Who then would be saved? What must he do to attain Eternal Life?

'Happy are they,' the awful voice continued,

and they only, who attend to the voice of the Holy Spirit; who deny themselves, and take up their daily cross and follow Christ. They shall have faith, which is the victory that overcometh this world – they shall come off more than conquerors over death – and, in perfect security on the last day, they shall fearlessly and triumphantly survey the wreck of universal nature, when the sun shall be turned into darkness and the moon into blood, when the stars shall fall from their orbits, and the heavens and earth shall dissolve in flames, and pass away.

A long pause from the pulpit overhead. A stifled groan from the congregation. 'And now to God the Father . . .' murmured Papa, and it was over, it was finished, the slow step descended the stairway, and Branwell, seeking in vain for reassurance from the passing surpliced figure that was his father, bent his red head over his hymn-book, joining in the words of praise and adulation to the Being who, with one mighty frown and one frightful wave of the hand, could sweep him and his sisters and everybody in Haworth to perdition.

Here was the puzzle, though. Away from the pulpit, away from the parlour, Papa was as frail as himself. Did not Branwell watch him kneel in prayer by his bed each night, asking for strength to withstand temptation? Did he not sometimes toss and turn and moan in his sleep? Did he not sometimes call upon Mary – not the mother of God, but Branwell's own dead mother Maria, who was now in two places at once, safe in the arms of Jesus, and waiting under the flagstone in the church aisle for Judgement Day?

Three in One. One in Three. God the Father was in the pulpit. God the Son was in the parlour, or might even be Branwell himself in the opposite bed. And God the Holy Ghost was not a plump white dove at all but a creeping shrouded thing, cold to the touch, who whispered, who dragged sleeping children from their blankets and sheets and smothered them underground. The shock to his security was great. He and his sisters had been spared this time, the Eruption

17

had ceased, the moor was still again. But it might not always be so. There could be danger elsewhere.

In February his fears – forgotten during the winter months – were justified. Maria was taken ill at school, and Papa fetched her home to be nursed. At first his joy was great. His sister had returned, the reading aloud would begin again, and the telling of stories. But it was soon apparent, even to the heedless boy, that Maria was too ill to tell stories, too ill to read aloud, and the old, long-discarded routine began once more – the sick-room upstairs, hushed voices, hushed footsteps, anxious unhappy expressions on the faces of the adult world.

The spring days passed, and his sister became weaker. He was not even allowed to kiss her good morning or good night. On the 6th of May, 1825, his aunt told him that Maria had gone to join Mama. She, too, was safe in the arms of Jesus. She would suffer no more. If so, why the grief? Why the worn anguished eyes of Papa? And why would not God and Jesus listen to Papa who had prayed, night after night, that Maria might be spared? 'Maria is better where she is,' they told him. But lying alone on her bed, grown shrunken and small and very pale, flowers in her lifeless hands, her eyes closed, Maria was not better where she was, Maria was worse, far worse, and once nailed in the coffin, and carried to the church and put out of sight beneath the flagstone, she would surely waken through fear of the darkness and try to push the stone, and the stone would not move.

Maria was scarcely buried when the housekeeper from the school came bringing Elizabeth home. Elizabeth was also ill, Elizabeth had to go to the sick-room upstairs, and the voices were hushed, the footsteps were soft, it all began again – and this time swiftly, as if Maria herself had come back dressed up as her younger sister. God wanted Elizabeth too. Maria had not been enough for Him. 'Is it the Holy Ghost who has come for her?' No one answered his questions. The father, in a panic, brought the other two children home. And then

18

Elizabeth, like Maria and Mama, was buried beneath the aisle. God took saints and sinner alike. The sinners were swallowed in the bog, the saints were pushed under the stones.

'She exhibited during her illness,' said the bereaved father, writing of Maria, 'many symptoms of a heart under Divine influence.'

This was his consolation. But not the boy's. Because if the heavens and the earth were to dissolve in flames and the moon turn to blood, as Papa had said in his sermon, what would happen to the bodies left behind? What would happen to Elizabeth and Maria? Where, in point of fact, *was* Paradise?

> Down, down, they lowered her, sad and slow,
> Into her narrow house below:
> And deep indeed appeared to be
> That one glimpse of eternity,
> Where, cut from life, corruption lay,
> Where beauty soon should turn to clay!
> Though scarcely conscious, hotly fell
> The drops that spoke my last farewell;
> And wild my sob, when hollow rung
> The first cold clod above her flung,
> When glitter was to turn to rust,
> Ashes to ashes, dust to dust!

The lad of nineteen, thinking more about the verse of James Hogg and John Wilson of *Blackwood's Magazine* than of the dead Maria, would continue to write line after line in this fashion. But in 1825 the sudden deaths of Maria and Elizabeth, coming as they did just before his own eighth birthday, shocked the little boy into an apprehension that would never leave him, that would for years to come fill his dreams by night, however much energy and fury he put into his day.

3

The four remaining children were told that their two sisters had died of 'consumption', or 'decline'. The words were to haunt them for life. How much truth there was in the statement will never be known. Consumption, in the early nineteenth century, was a scourge indeed; nevertheless, there is much in the history of the last few weeks of the two little girls which it is hard to explain. Why, according to Mrs Gaskell, did Maria, before she left school in February from 'ill-health', have a 'blister' applied to her side? A blister was given in those days to draw pain. And what was the mysterious and 'alarming accident' which happened to Elizabeth, whose head was 'severely cut' in consequence – so much so that Miss Evans, the mistress in charge (who later wrote to Mrs Gaskell about the incident), was obliged to take the child to her own room, 'not only for the sake of greater quiet, but that I might watch over her myself'? It has not been discovered if Elizabeth knew of the death of her sister at the time of her 'accident'. If she did, was she as shocked by death as her small brother Branwell? Did she walk in her sleep and fall?

Six years later Charlotte Brontë, telling stories to her roommates in another and a happier school than Cowan Bridge, frightened her listeners with an account of sleep-walking, making her tale so vivid that she suddenly screamed herself, and refused to continue. Indeed, for days afterwards her conscience worried her, so ashamed was she of what she had done. Could it be that she knew, and remembered all too clearly, what had happened to Elizabeth?

In 1825, back at the Parsonage, the four remaining children came closer to one another than they had been before
the double tragedy. A primitive herd instinct made them group
together – there was surely security in numbers. The two who
had been left at home, becoming small shadows of father and
aunt, gravitated to the returning Charlotte and Emily like
moths to flame: Branwell to Charlotte, Anne to Emily. The
boy had not realized how much he had missed the companionship of someone his own age. Papa was all-important, but
Papa did not 'play'. And Charlotte, a year older than himself,
with an imagination striking sparks from his, would meet his
change of mood at every turn, became adventurer or prince,
soldier or bandit, the characters they invented for themselves
depending upon the lesson of the day, the story read aloud,
the events in the daily newspaper.

Branwell, taught by his father in the parlour downstairs
while his sisters, upstairs in their aunt's bedroom, had more
simple instruction, already possessed a vocabulary unusually
wide in a child of eight. He had the quality of mind that
could read a page at a glance and commit it to memory, hear
a lesson and repeat it verbatim, store the names of persons,
places, characters, countries in a particular box in his brain
and unlock it, when he chose, without a fault in recollection,
and so astonish his company – his father in particular. Naturally
left-handed, he could write equally well with either hand, and
could even, in later years, write two letters at the same time,
one with his right hand and one with his left. Mr Brontë,
believing his son to be a prodigy, pressed him to Latin and
Greek, on top of the rest of his studies. Here was a boy, he
told himself, who was in a fair way to becoming a first-rate
classical scholar, and who, with his extraordinary capacity for
absorbing knowledge, might one day shine above his contemporaries at Oxford or Cambridge.

There was one danger. His son might prove *too* clever.
So brilliant, in fact, that the illness known at that time as

'brain-fever' might suddenly attack him. The boy was highly strung and very excitable. When too enthusiastic he seemed to reach a pitch of delight that was near to hysteria, and then as suddenly he would collapse, for no rhyme or reason, and there would be shivers and tears.

His temperament was far too nervous for school, that was evident. There must never be any question of it. Here at home the father could watch his boy, see that no harm came to him. Indeed, by having him to sleep in his own room he felt doubly certain that his son could not come to danger. He could watch his boy, even when the child slept: the high forehead, the fine Roman nose, the mass of tawny hair so like his own. It was moving, too, to realize that, being so close to him, the boy seemed at times to take on his own moods, be melancholy when he was melancholy, or gay when he felt robust.

The child was so precocious that the father in his loneliness must often have felt the need to talk to him as if they were contemporaries. Perhaps he told Branwell of days gone by, of his love for Maria his wife, for Maria his daughter, now saints in Heaven and blessedly removed from this sinful earth, though his own solitude was hard to bear, and must continue to the end of his days. Maria . . . Maria . . . The name must still have escaped his lips in unguarded moments – for it did not do to be continually reminding the living of the dead, except to let them shine as examples of grace and purity. Branwell, his left hand busy with the writing of the private magazine which he and Charlotte were editing, would not notice if the right hand scribbled Maria, or, if he did, he would be delighted with his prowess, for here was a feat that no one could achieve except himself.

The children had several games, initiated by Branwell and Charlotte together. There was the 'Young Men's Play', which had begun when Branwell was nearly nine years old, and his father had brought home for him a box of twelve toy soldiers to replace some which he had lost.

'When I first saw them in the morning after they were bought,' Branwell wrote five years later, in the note to a series of stories called *The History of the Young Men* ('young men' being the name which he had given to the soldiers), 'I carried them to Emily, Charlotte and Anne. They each took up a soldier, gave them names, which I consented to, and I gave Charlotte Twemy (i.e. Wellington), to Emily Pare (Parry), to Anne Trott (Ross) to take care of them, though they were to be mine and I to have the disposal of them as I would. Shortly after this I gave them to them as their own.'*

The *History* itself contained a fanciful account of the episode, in which Branwell, no longer a small boy in his night-shirt, was transformed into 'an immense and terrible monster', and his sisters likewise.

'His head which touched the clouds was encircled with a red and fiery halo, his nostrils flashed forth flames and smoke, and he was enveloped in a dim, misty, and indefinable robe.' Leaping down upon the wooden soldiers – now changed, in the boy's imagination, into a party of trembling and fearful young men – the monster grasped them

in his huge hand and immediately flew away. After a short time, however, he alighted at an immense palace which he entered, and conveyed them into a hall of inconceivable extent and splendour. At one end of the room were seated three beings of much the same height as himself wrapped in clouds and having flames of fire around their heads. When he entered they all stood up and inquired 'Have they come?' 'Yes,' he answered, at the same time saying 'Down before them, instantly.' The taller of the three new monsters seized Arthur Wellesley, the next seized E. W. Parry and the least seized J. Ross. For a long time they continued looking at them in silence,

*In this and other extracts from the writings of Branwell and Emily, spelling and punctuation have been corrected for the sake of ease in reading.

which however was broken by the monster who brought them there, he saying, 'Know you then that I give into your protection, but not for your own, these mortals whom you hold in your hands.'

At hearing this, Wellesley, Parry and Ross each set up a doleful cry, thinking that they were forever to be separated from their king and companions, but the three monsters, after expressing their thanks to their benefactor, assured them that they would watch over their lives and as their guardian demons wheresoever they might go. The monster first seen then seized hold of Sneaky saying, 'Thou art under my protection and I will watch over thy life, for I tell you all that ye shall one day be kings.'

Another game was 'The Islanders', in which each child chose an island and peopled it with the heroes of his choice. Branwell chose the Isle of Man, and as heroes John Bull, Leigh Hunt and the surgeon Astley Cooper.

These two games, or 'plays', as the children called them, developed finally into the 'African Adventure', where the soldiers, wrecked on the Guinea coast, fought the natives for survival, and ended by founding a colony which they partitioned into twelve kingdoms, one for each soldier. Branwell, his inventive brain on fire, drew maps to show the colony, and then proceeded to draw up a constitution and people the kingdoms with leaders, statesmen, editors – who, of course, published newspapers and magazines. He even found time to write, in the person of Young Soult, the poet of Glass-Town, capital of the now vast African colony, a two-act play in blank verse called *Caractacus*. Whatever Branwell read, whatever he was taught, whatever piece of local gossip or general news he picked up during the day, was at once sifted in his mind, discussed with Charlotte, and reproduced on paper.

They worked – or 'played', as the adults called it – in the same little nursery-study that had been Maria's. This was their domain. Here the Four Genii reigned supreme. Kings and soldiers fought and died, Statesmen were elected and fell from power, rebels rose, rebellions were quashed, and Chief Genius Brannii, waving his magic wand, his hair a fiery crest, his small eyes darting behind his spectacles – for both he and Charlotte were short-sighted – hardly taller at twelve than he had been at nine, directed and controlled this game that had become their passion, and was interrupted only by meals and lesson hours.

The early poems and stories which developed out of their games were crude, perhaps no more imaginative and no better written than similar tales by other gifted children, but the output was astonishing. The little booklets, written with a mapping pen in microscopic handwriting that only their authors could read, and neatly joined and sewn together, ran into many thousands of words. Sometimes, to make the game more secret still, Branwell used a peculiar dialect of his own, a blend of Yorkshire, Greek and Latin, which could only be spoken among the four of them, to the mystification of their elders.

The waging of war was Branwell's speciality. There must be battles and yet more battles. Blood, and mud, and death and disaster.

Between 1830 and 1832, besides the magazines and *Caractacus*, he wrote six books entitled *Letters from an Englishman*, the supposed adventures of a banker visiting Glass-Town in the African colony. The play *Caractacus*, written on June 26, 1830, when his father was ill in bed, and indeed so weak with what was presumably influenza that according to Charlotte, he 'could not rise without assistance', may have been specially composed to revive the invalid, thus pleasing him with classical talent.

Fortune, how fickle and how vain thou art,
One hour thou smil'st upon th'unhappy wretch
Who is deluded by thy tempting offers,
The next struck by thy with'ring frown he falls
Into the black abyss of hopeless woe,
Just so the sky unspotted by a cloud
Fortelleth not the dark and coming tempest . . .
O Hope, I cast my lingering eyes upon thee.
Thou art my lamp where bright but glimmering rays
Do light me on my way, when o'er Adversity's
Thorny and darksome wilderness I travel.
Nor wilt thou leave my footsteps till I gain
That broad and stormy torrent which no man
Has e'er o'ercome, Death's loud and billowy waters . . .

Possibly it was *after* reading this, and not before, that Mr Brontë was unable to rise without assistance! He would have found the *Letters from an Englishman*, had he ever been permitted to read them, even harder fare to stomach, for in these Branwell threw off classical discipline, and, though supposedly describing Africa, let his imagination run riot on Haworth moor, where he had probably scrambled the very afternoon he wrote this chapter.

From the pleasant and delightful country we had just left no trees appeared, or, if any, some huge black Scotch firs in clumps by the roadside, here and there small patches of heather on the summits of the hills, the ripe corn was exchanged for brown furze, the fresh green grass for swamps and rushes, and after a few minutes' further riding, we found ourselves entering on an immense moor which to the eye presented nothing but a ceaseless sea of heath – not a single object to enliven the dreary waste, but now and then a flock of red grouse or a savage and gigantic poacher . . . But to complete the sum of our misfortunes night was rapidly rolling down . . . and then a relentless torrent of rain and hail poured upon us like shot from a battery. Lord Charles suddenly exclaimed 'I see a light'. We looked eagerly, and indeed there was a cottage hardly a stone's throw from us. The Marquis knocked at the door. It was opened by a gigantic fellow who bolted forward and collared him.

The room was of considerable extent, and its walls hung round with guns and other peaceable instruments. The occupants were 5. The first a man nearly 8 feet high, bony, haggard, his nose and chin were hooked like the beak of a hawk, his eyes small, deep, sunk, and of a sinister, malignant expression. His face was covered with tremendous scars, particularly one which had almost cloven his chin in two   this however was partly covered by a pair of huge mustachios, and thick, bushy beard.

Not content with inventing one giant to make his sisters shiver, Branwell, who must always exaggerate, introduced four more, and in a few moments the fight was on between the two largest desperadoes.

They both showed themselves complete masters of the art, and went to work in slashing style. The first blow was aimed by Scroven, but his antagonist, parrying it with his elbow, delivered him a most tremendous stroke on the forehead which covered him in blood. Brandy was given him, upon which he rallied, laid on Naughty in good style, giving him a stinger on the throat apple, and for a long time it was doubtful which would get the victory until Naughty delivered his antagonist a closer on the collar-bone which smashed through the skin and caused the blood to stream on the ground in torrents.

Miss Branwell, quietly sewing in her bed-sitting-room next door, would wonder at the exclamations, the stifled laughter, the possible arguments of, 'It wouldn't happen like that', and 'It would . . . it would . . . I've seen them myself,' the boy's voice rising higher in excitement. Then would be the time to interfere, to tap on the wall with the admonition, 'Play quietly, now, Papa will hear you.' There would be a sudden hush, the voices sunk to a murmur, and the reading of the tale be continued in a whisper, until perhaps it would become too blood-thirsty for Anne, the youngest, and she would take refuge with her aunt, declaring, 'I don't like Branwell's play.'

The small room, six feet by four, was fine for writing, shoulders hunched and head bent over the table; but when it came to play more energetic, for demonstration of the noble art, Branwell with fists in air whirling himself into a frenzy, quarters were close, and there must have been a risk that someone would get hurt. If it should be Anne, then Emily, her champion, probably gave Branwell a taste of his own medicine. It was not flattering to his pride to have a younger sister already taller than himself, who gave as good as she got. Better, perhaps, to banish both to the kitchen, where they could listen to Tabby's stories, rather than his own.

What sport it was though, to mix sometimes with other boys, for his father permitted it, if they were well behaved and came from Sunday School. They were not always so well behaved when Mr Brontë's back was turned. A small crowd would collect together, quiet at first, then boasting and kicking each other's shins, with Branwell, on the fringe of the crowd, watching them fascinated. One half of his mind would seize the real picture, the lads laughing and shouting, squaring up for a fight in 'parson's field', as they called the few acres directly behind the parsonage. Willie Wood, the undertaker's son, and one or two others would soon be joined by an older group of young men in their twenties, egging the lads on for want of something better to do – John and William Brown, sons of the sexton, Bill Moseley, perhaps, and the Sutcliffe brothers from the nearby village of Stanbury. Then the scene before his eyes would transform itself into part of his secret game, the scramble and the jeering would come from Glass-Town, Africa, not Haworth, Yorkshire. Willie Wood and his friends were suddenly revolutionaries, an armed mass of some three hundred thousand men about to attack the Government in front of St Michael's Cathedral, under the leadership of Alexander Rogue, a 'tall man with a pale countenance, worn into wrinkles with care and anxiety. His appearance, evidently once handsome, seemed broken down by hardships and depraved habits.'

Mr Michael Heaton of Royd House, brother of Mr Robert Heaton of Ponden Hall, taking a short cut home from church, or Mr Merrall of Griffe Mill, father of four youngsters itching to fight but controlling themselves on the Sabbath – any of these gentlemen could, unknown to himself, serve for Rogue. Mr Sunderland, the schoolmaster at Stanbury, Mr Redman, the Haworth parish clerk, Mr Brown, his father's sexton, all could be turned into colonists in Africa; and when the boys dispersed, the last eye cut and the last nose blooded, Branwell would walk home with the Brown brothers, flattered by the attention of the two young men who, before dropping him at 'parson's gate' and so down the lane to their own home, chaffed the boy and showed him how to use his fists if he were attacked.

Charlotte and Emily might refuse to believe the tales he told them after these encounters with the lads from the village, but once he had acted it out before them, and written it down, the story became so true that they knew it had happened. Not only had he fought six boys and blooded them so that they ran howling for home, but he had also led a revolution. Now Alexander Rogue was none other than himself.

What might have been, what actually was, what in truth was not – how superbly the scenes would fuse in Branwell's imagination, joyous, happy and free. While in the minds of some of his contemporaries, who knew nothing of the secret game, nothing of Glass-Town and Alexander Rogue, there remained, years afterwards, only isolated incidents to tell to visitors to Haworth – the memory, for instance, of a boy with scarlet hair, in a rocking-boat at Keighley fair, one Feast day.

The drums sounded, the cymbals clashed, the horses of the merry-go-round pranced on their giddy course. As the evening lengthened, and the fairy lights were lit, and the fun grew fast and furious, one single swingboat careered in mid-sky above the twinkling booths, urged onwards, ever faster, by the boy who clung to the ropes, and who, even as the boat rose and fell again, screamed at the top of his voice, dizzy with excitement, 'Oh! my nerves . . . my nerves . . . my nerves!'

4

In January, 1831, Charlotte, now fourteen and a half, was sent to school again. Like Branwell, she was small for her age, and, as her schoolfriends told Mrs Gaskell later, 'anything but pretty, her naturally beautiful hair of soft silky brown being then dry and frizzy-looking, screwed up in tight little curls; and so short-sighted she always appeared to be seeking something. She was very shy and nervous, and she wore a dark, rusty-green stuff dress of old fashioned make, detracting still more from her appearance.'

The new school was Roe Head, near Mirfield, not twenty miles from Haworth, standing back from the high road between Leeds and Huddersfield, and the headmistress was Miss Margaret Wooler, who ran the school in association with her sisters, Miss Catherine, Miss Marianne and Miss Eliza. Not two miles away lived an old friend of Charlotte's father, the Reverend Hammond Roberson, who, with Mrs Franks of Huddersfield, a friend of Thornton days, had probably recommended Roe Head as being excellent in every respect, and quite unlike the former Cowan Bridge.

There seemed no reason for the decision to send Charlotte to school. She had grown beyond her aunt's rather moderate instruction, but she could, and no doubt did, share Branwell's lessons with their father. Teaching two clever children would not have put too heavy a burden on Mr Brontë's shoulders; indeed, competition between the pair would have spurred the boy to greater achievement.

Possibly the intensity of the writing upstairs in the old nursery had become a puzzle to both father and aunt. The children were trying their eyes and becoming round-shouldered, and the cramped, minute script would affect the legibility of their handwriting later. Besides, the very secrecy of the game could be unhealthy. The adults could not but be aware of all the strange names and places mentioned between the two as if they existed in reality, what with nods and smiles and innuendoes, a sly allusion from Charlotte, a dramatic gesture from Branwell. It would do Charlotte good to mix with other girls of her own age – all this make-believe was not 'fitty', the aunt may have declared, using an apt Cornish expression.

She may have suggested that Branwell should go to school also. But Mr Brontë was adamant. Charlotte, yes; not the boy. Highly strung as he was, he would never survive the rough treatment of boarding school. The excitability of his nature would be misunderstood; and who, in a dormitory filled with mocking play-fellows, would distinguish between dream and nightmare or, worse still, those occasional nerve tremors which were perilously like convulsions? The boy was best at home, supervised by his father.

So Charlotte departed for Roe Head. The break in companionship came hardest upon Branwell. He and Charlotte were inseparable, and now, just as their 'play' had reached a new high peak of interest, she was to be taken from him. Emily and Anne made sorry substitutes, preferring to begin a 'play' of their own – largely copied from his invention, even using the same names for their paltry characters. He consoled himself as best he could by continuing the saga of *Letters from an Englishman*, which he would send his sister every week throughout the term, thus keeping her abreast of African news.

If Aunt Branwell and Mr Brontë hoped that separation would mean a break-up of the nonsense between brother and sister, and that Charlotte, with the wider interests of school life, would put away childish things, they were mistaken. A year and a half at Roe Head gave the young authoress, who had already written as many stories and edited as many magazines as her brother, a grounding in English grammar and geography. In these, it appeared, she was woefully ignorant, in spite of having helped to colonize the Guinea coast. She also improved her knowledge of French and history, and squeezed into her retentive mind every scrap of knowledge the Miss Woolers could impart to her. Nevertheless, the 'play' was going as strong as ever. The thought of it had been her solace through many a weary school day, and, what was more, the very persons of her school-fellows and teachers could be transformed into characters in it – unknown to themselves, very naturally.

Branwell could now add considerably to his list of characters, introducing not only the inhabitants of Haworth, whom he saw every day, but also the Miss Woolers of Roe Head, who could become the wives of his commanders. Miss Margaret, Charlotte's headmistress, whose 'long hair, plaited, formed a coronet, and whose long large ringlets fell from head to shoulders', surely made an excellent Lady Zenobia Ellrington, future bride to Alexander Rogue. And Charlotte's two friends, Ellen Nussey and Mary Taylor, the first dark and quiet and gentle, the second fair, intelligent, and so pretty that the headmistress used to say she was 'too pretty to live', were ready-made heroines, only waiting to take their place upon the African shore.

They must never know, of course. Secrecy must be maintained. If anyone should ever discover about the play, read the hidden books, identify a living figure in one of their fictitious beings . . . there would be catastrophe. Charlotte impressed this upon her brother, less discreet than herself in conversation; and with a curious, half-conscious feeling that what they were inventing was somehow wrong, would be disapproved of and condemned by everyone but themselves, they called their creation 'the infernal world', as if Satan himself were Lord High Instigator.

By midsummer of 1832 Miss Branwell began to find the

education of the two younger girls beyond her. The simplest, and indeed the most inexpensive solution in the pinched household was for Charlotte to return home and put her newfound knowledge to the teaching of her sisters. This she did. The four were reunited once again. The 'play' proceeded. There was still no question of Branwell going to school. His godfather and his mother's cousin by marriage, the Reverend William Morgan, vicar of Bradford, may have suggested it, Mr Sunderland, the schoolmaster at Stanbury, may have urged it too – Mr Brontë remained firm. His son's temperament would not permit of public school. Physically, the boy was healthy. His constitution was stronger than that of his sisters. Just as there is mystery in the illness of the little girls at Cowan Bridge, so is there something unexplained in the matter of Branwell's schooling. No father, however fond, could have been quite so obstinate without some good reason which he preferred to keep as private as possible. Can the explanation be that Branwell had already begun to show symptoms of the fits which were to torment him, with ever-increasing frequency, towards the end of his life? Epilepsy, in the nineteenth-century mind associated with insanity, was a hardly mentionable affliction, one to be disguised at all costs: boarding-school, to such a boy, would be out of the question. Mr Brontë, blamed by many for indulging his only son, may have kept proud silence about an affliction which he hoped time would cure.

Meanwhile the wooden soldier Sneaky, alias Young Man Naughty, alias Alexander Rogue the rebel and pirate, was slowly developing into Alexander Percy, future Viscount Ellrington and Earl of Northangerland, the sinister and embittered individual whose many love affairs and changes of fortune were so unlike anything that could ever have happened, or was likely to happen, to a boy of sixteen. This character can only have been founded on Branwell's ideal of the heroic figure he must himself have longed to be. This Branwell was not diminutive, bespectacled, home-taught, scribbling poems and stories with his left hand: he was over six feet high, auburn-haired and handsome, leading revolutions, felling rivals with a strong right hand.

The coming of adolescence brought a change not only to the style but to the subject matter of the two secret writers. Adventure gave place to romance. War was no longer of paramount importance. Love and intrigue – illicit love, especially – brought zest to those who wrote and those who listened. Moore's *Life of Byron* opened new vistas, and old numbers of *Blackwood's* were doubtless thumbed for the 'Noctes Ambrosianae', where matters which had hitherto been absorbed for the sheer delight of reading for reading's sake took on suggestive meaning. What were the 'bad things' done by Lord Byron, and referred to – presumably with a shake of the head – by Professor John Wilson of *Blackwood's* in the character of Christopher North? Just as fruitful, in a different way, were the snatches of gossip around Haworth itself, which, involving the local gentry and manufacturers, suddenly became fraught with possibility.

Charlotte, who had experienced the fever of schoolgirl passion for each of her friends Ellen Nussey and Mary Taylor in turn, delighted to see them in the roles of anguished heroines, desperate for the passion of her own Byronic self – for the plain, intensely shy, seventeen-year-old ex-schoolgirl was none other than Arthur Wellesley, Marquis of Douro, soon to be Duke of Zamorna; though these same friends, to whom she wrote constantly from home, telling them how she taught her sisters and passed the days in a 'delightful though somewhat monotonous course', had not the slightest idea that they had changed identities not once but twice, that both had died and been revived, and one of them would perhaps become a Duchess.

Branwell, without the memory of school to whet his fancy, brought twisted touches to the collaboration – and the fact that, though most of the manuscripts are signed with Charlotte's name, much of the handwriting is Branwell's proves how close that collaboration was. Words half-digested and half-understood now scattered the pages. African maidens, seduced by colonist nobles, gave birth to monsters; heroes were no longer their fathers' sons but the result of shameful passion; illegitimacy was rife in Africa — or Angria, as the largest kingdom was now called — and not only illegitimacy but incest too. The theme that occurred frequently, both now and in later stories, was that of a married man's infatuation for his wife's younger sister. That the theme had its origin, neither in *Blackwood's* nor in Byronic literature, but in their own moorland parish, was admitted many years later by Charlotte herself, speaking to Mrs Gaskell in a moment of indiscretion. The story, connected with 'the family of a woollen manufacturer, and moderately wealthy', had, according to Mrs Gaskell, 'made a deep impression on Charlotte's mind in early girlhood'. Heard at secondhand, and misreported, the tale was not even true; but the Heatons of Ponden Hall and Bridge House, the family concerned, were to suffer many a transformation, in the course of time, at the hands of Charlotte, Branwell and Emily, too. A golden touch of imagination, combined with much romantic reading and ill-digested gossip dropping on young ears, brought the Heatons immortality.

In August, 1813, Elizabeth Heaton, youngest daughter of Robert Heaton and Elizabeth Murgatroyd, had been obliged to marry, suddenly and disastrously, a young shopkeeper from Gomersal, John Bates, who later ill-treated her. But at least he gave her baby a name, which was why Robert Heaton paid him to marry her. The poor eighteen-year-old bride endured two years of married life, and then returned home to Ponden Hall so 'much emaciated, that there seemed little hope of her recovery'. She died a year later, within a few months of her mother, and it was these two who were said to 'walk and weep in the garden, though both had long mouldered in their graves'. The brothers and sisters of the unhappy girl were married and middle-aged by the time Charlotte and Branwell and Emily heard the tale, Robert the younger living at Ponden Hall and his brother Michael at Royd House. What riches for inventive minds, what glut of material for adolescent authors!

Weaving the murky past of their father's parishioners into fictitious Angrian amours was not the only occupation of Branwell and his sisters at this time. In 1834 a passion for drawing seized them, and Mr Brontë was persuaded to engage the services of a drawing-master, a Mr Robinson of Leeds, who had studied under Sir Thomas Lawrence and had even painted the Duke of Wellington himself, a feat which must certainly have recommended him to Charlotte, alias the Marquis of Douro.

Mrs Gaskell, years later, observed that the drawing-master was 'a man of considerable talent, but very little principle'. She did not enlarge upon the subject, but the microscopic manuscripts of Mr Robinson's pupils during this period, which Mrs Gaskell never read, give much prominence to the love life of Sir William Etty, a more famous contemporary of the Leeds artist. In one of the stories he turns out to be the illegitimate son of Alexander Percy himself – offspring of a fatal love affair between Branwell's hero and an Italian countess.

The drawing-master certainly gave a fillip to imagination, and rather more besides; he encouraged in seventeen-year-old Branwell, always the first of the four to excel in any subject, an ambition to take up painting as a profession, an ambition which increased in intensity after a visit, in the summer of 1834, to an exhibition at Leeds given by the Northern Society for the Encouragement of Fine Arts.

Mr Robinson himself contributed portraits to this collection, but the exhibit that caught Branwell's eye, and the praise of the critics too, was not a painting but a piece of sculpture, a gigantic bust of Satan, modelled by a young man of twenty-three from Halifax called Joseph Bentley Leyland. Leyland had already been lauded for another colossal statue – Spartacus – which had been on exhibition in Manchester two years before. The bust of Satan was later taken to London, and the critic of the *Morning Chronicle* said of it that –

Mr Leyland has conquered the difficulties of his task with a masterly hand. The moment chosen by the sculptor is that celebrated passage in Milton's poem, known as Satan's Address to the Sun. The characteristic marks of the features are, a scornful lip, distended nostrils, and a forehead more remarkable for breadth than prominence, indicative of great mental capacity, bereft of moral principle. Mr Leyland has made his Satan a being, not fearful merely, but of that Satanic beauty which is so true to the conception of Milton.

Branwell, walking round the Leeds Gallery with the drawing-master, must have returned again and again to the bust of Satan. Here indeed was Alexander Percy, not just a figment of his own imagination, born in dreams from childhood, but cast in plaster before his very eyes, the conception of someone only six years older than himself, living at Halifax, not fifteen miles from Haworth. If Joseph Leyland had become famous at twenty-three, why not Branwell Brontë? He too could work in a studio at the parsonage, as Leyland had worked in his own home at Halifax; he would paint in oils as Leyland worked in clay, and later study in London, mix with other artists and sculptors as Leyland now did, and then return and have an exhibition at Leeds.

He may even have seen the young sculptor himself at the exhibition, and pressed his drawing-master for an introduction. Joseph Bentley Leyland, square-shouldered, dark, good-looking in a lazy, sardonic way, would have nodded briefly, giving a kind word perhaps to the excited red-haired lad, neither of them foreseeing that this was a significant meeting, the prelude to a friendship which would prove both curious and close.

Branwell, eager to find out all he could about the twenty-three-year-old sculptor, would learn from Mr Robinson that he was the son of a well-known bookseller and naturalist; that he had begun modelling in clay at sixteen; and that thanks to the patronage of a Halifax gentleman, Mr Christopher Rawson, who had a fine collection of Greek marbles, he had been able to study these until he felt himself sufficiently trained to send two original works to an exhibition in Manchester, one of the Thracian Spartacus, the other of his own greyhound. Noticed by the portrait painter Thomas Illidge, who praised his work, Leyland followed Illidge to London, and was at once taken up in artistic circles, meeting Francis Chantry, among others, and studying anatomy under the painter and writer Benjamin Robert Haydon – who had taught Constable and Landseer, and, living on the borderline of sanity for many years, was to kill himself in 1846.

Branwell went back to Haworth with his mind afire with plans for the future. His talk was now all of Leyland, of art, of London; and into the secret chronicles of their Angrian game came a new description of Alexander Percy, penned this time by Charlotte, who must also have seen Leyland's bust of Satan in the gallery at Leeds.

The expression is somewhat pensive, composed, free from sarcasm except the fixed sneer of the lip and the strange deadly glitter of the eye, whose glance – a mixture of the keenest scorn and deepest thoughts – curdles the spectator's blood to ice. In my opinion the head embodies the most vivid idea we can conceive of Lucifer, the rebellious archangel: there is such a cold frozen pride; such a fathomless power of intellect; such passionless yet perfect beauty . . . And then his eye . . . a gleam, scarcely human, dark and fiend-like . . . I felt as if he could read my soul, and had a harassing dread lest anything good might arise

39

which would awake the tremendous power of sarcasm that I saw lurking in every feature of his face. Northangerland has a black drop in his veins that taints every limb, stagnates round his heart, and there in the very citadel of life turns the glorious bood of the Percies to the bitterest, rankest gall . . .

Branwell, in the midst of his account of the foundation of the Kingdom of Angria (some twenty-three pages of crowded microscopic handwriting), makes Percy exclaim:

> Backward I look upon my life,
> And see one waste of storm and strife,
> One wrack of sorrows, hopes, and pain,
> Vanishing to arise again!
> That life has moved through evening, where
> Continual shadows veiled my sphere;
> From youth's horizon upward rolled
> To life's meridian, dark and cold.

A few months later, changing from the minute print to his natural upright hand, Branwell continued in much the same vein, making his hero survey the past, bereft suddenly of his wife Mary:

> Oh what is Man? A wretched being
> Tossed upon the tide of time,
> All its rocks and whirlpools seeing,
> Yet denied the power of fleeing
> Waves, and gulfs of woe and crime;
> Doomed from life's first bitter breath
> To launch upon a sea of death,
> Without a hope, without a stay
> To guide him upon his weary way.

Cowper's *The Castaway* had hit Branwell even harder than the sight of young Leyland's Satan, and the story of Cowper's bouts of insanity must have made him question his own fitful moods and doubts. What sin could be worse than death itself? What great betrayal brought a genius like Cowper to such a brink of horror and despair?

> Hatred and vengeance, my eternal portion,
> Scarce can endure delay of execution,
> Wait, with impatient readiness, to seize my
> Soul in a moment –

thus Cowper wrote, before one of his fits, deeming himself 'damned below Judas'.

The point was – who could be saved? Was Lucifer himself cast down from heaven by the Almighty when the world was created, and told to tempt the men and women who should people it? Was James Hogg right, in his *Memoirs of a Justified Sinner*, when he asserted that Satan could walk about disguised as oneself, committing murders and fornication, and a hapless innocent being, who had committed no crime, yet be accused of them, the world being ignorant of the fact that Satan had usurped the body?

If so, it meant that Satan could seize his right hand and master it, compelling it to write what it had no desire to write. The prospect was too hideous to contemplate. The two sides of Branwell's nature stood in balance. The one affectionate, ardent, devoted to his family and above all his father, hoping – for their sake as well as for his own – that either by writing or by painting he would prove so successful that not only they but the whole world would come to recognize his talent; the other diffident, mocking, sceptical, doubting as much in his own powers as in a Power above, and sometimes so fearful of the black abyss of Eternity that the only way to quieten apprehension would seem to be a plunge into vice and folly.

Already his belief in prayer had grown less; and that his early faith was lost is shown by his description of the death of Mary Percy, his hero's second wife, written about this time:

She, so long as her strength held out, would often desire to be placed on a sofa at a great open window, and in the glorious sunshine would gaze with a smile upon the vast expanse of foliated vegetation, which, as she said, would accompany her to the grave.

[Percy's] distressing and hopeless agony, which now he scorned to conceal, and which day after day was preying upon his heart till he had become savage and dark almost to madness, gave her thoughts of what he would be when the last hour came, and when she was gone forever.

She shuddered, and started to picture her strange, wild, wonderful husband, and she said, 'He is so far past my sight that I have never seen the depths of his character. Oh, I do not think in the world there lives, or has ever lived, a man of so mighty a spirit and with so utterly unrestrained and unrestrainable a mind. He can never be bent or taught. I see it, but I do not know what his course shall be, or where it will end. Is he to live on, year on year, in his dark and dreaded melancholy, which I have seen darker than I dare tell?'

And at other times she would waste herself in tears of bitterness over her children, whom she would never see again, and who in all the storms and dangers of life would be tossed and threatened without a mother, or any knowledge of one. She pictured them in distress and sickness, but there was none to help, and the heart of this dying mother yearned in vain towards those who thought not of her, and who she felt would, if they lived, look on her grave as if no mother lay buried there . . .

'Oh, Alexander, the place whither I am hastening,

though unseen, is indeed awfully near. But there is something which still chains me. You are here, and I cannot bear to leave you. I know now that you cannot believe what I am certain is true – that you think me about to decay and perish forever. You have had given you such a mind that you could not fail under any circumstances to drink to its dregs the cup of sorrow. I dread to think of the deeds into which I see you entering. For them we may be parted for ever!'

What was all this to her husband? Why, unmixed torment. He was certain that what she said was a bright delusion; that an hour, perhaps, would reduce her to a corpse without life and spirit hereafter. He felt certain that under any circumstances they must part forever. That heart that was filling with black fierceness towards men, and defiance towards the visionary heavens, could make no promise of life without condemning sin. His arms were around her, her head was on his shoulder, and all he could say was with the parting embrace 'O, Mary, Mary, a long, long farewell.'

Mary was dead. He seemed completely withered and silent. All the days that had been, the being that was gone, the thoughts, the voices, the scenes that were as if they had never been, all rushed back to his mind with overpowering directness. And he leant over the chill white wasted corpse till, numb with torture, his eye and his mind seemed to receive no impression. He spoke to no one, never raising his eyes, never dropping a single tear.

A magnificent horse stood near, ready for mounting. He was attired in a travelling cloak of mourning black.

'Now then,' he said, 'now then, thou art gone, Mary . . . There is a long journey of life before me, and yet through all the wild turmoil that I shall pass through, however long I live, there shall be no voice of thine to lighten me. Till now, whatever was my misery, thou, Mary, wert the star that seemed to rise above me. Had'st thou never been alive, I should not now be alive; whilst thou lookedst always to me for guidance, I knew it was myself who leaned on thee. But here is the end of all these feelings. Here I feel that the wild visions of Heaven and a hereafter must be laid aside. What is there? Real death! Nothing but the body hidden in its coffin, dead and buried here beneath me, fast festering to decay. Through all, I know, Mary, that I have lost thee; and how can I feel a breeze of joy when ten, twenty years to come I shall have to say. "But thou art dust, Mary, now – gone long before – and I, while memory is fading and the past is sinking into nothing, shall know, as I do now, that I shall Never, Never See Thee More."'

The horse was mounted, and with fiery speed its rider urged it far from these agonizing remembrances, and away from Percy Hall.

Sir, – Having an earnest desire to enter as a probationary student in the Royal Academy, but not being possessed of information as to the means of obtaining my desire, I presume to request from you, as Secretary to the Institution, an answer to the questions –

Where am I to present my drawings?
At what time?
    and especially
Can I do it in August or September?

This draft of a letter is scribbled on the back of a piece of paper containing three poetical fragments. There is no date, and it is impossible to say whether a final letter was written and sent. Two clues show that the time must have been the early summer of 1835. The first of them is a letter from Charlotte to her friend Ellen Nussey, dated July 2nd of that year, saying that she was to return to Roe Head as a teacher, taking Emily with her as a pupil, and that Branwell was to go to London, where it was hoped that he would be placed at the Royal Academy. The second clue is a letter from Mr Brontë four days later, written to his old friend Mrs Franks of Huddersfield, telling her that 'It is my design to send my son to the Royal Academy for Artists in London'.

Two months later, Branwell would appear not yet to have left for London, for on September 7th his father wrote to the drawing-master at Leeds, Mr Robinson, thanking him for his 'great kindness towards my son', and continuing, 'if all be well, Branwell hopes to be with you on Friday next, in order to finish his course of lessons.'

Branwell most likely did exactly this; went to Leeds, took his last lesson – as he thought – and set out for London and the Royal Academy. The rest is mystery. Whether Branwell submitted his drawings, whether they were not advanced enough for him to be admitted as a pupil, has never been discovered: no letters on the subject exist in the archives of the Royal Academy.

Branwell's only expenses would have been his board and lodging, and inquiries must have been made about this before setting forth for London. Tuition was then, as it is today, entirely free, for the annual exhibitions at the Royal Academy pay for the drawing school. Students are accepted on merit. They are obliged to show some ten works of their own choice, and drawings 'from life' should be included. The standard was, and always has been, high. All these facts Mr Robinson would himself have known. He is unlikely to have allowed a pupil of his to submit drawings unless he was sanguine about his success.

Charlotte's letters from Roe Head to her friend Ellen Nussey never speak again of Branwell's possible tuition at the Royal Academy, and Miss Nussey herself, years later, when questioned by Mrs Gaskell, said, 'I do not know whether it was conduct or want of finances that prevented Branwell from going to the Royal Academy. Probably there were impediments of both kinds.'

Branwell himself had turned eighteen. He was not shy like his sisters. He had plenty of self-confidence. Earlier that summer he had been secretary to the local Conservative Committee during a contested election for the West Riding of Yorkshire, the two opponents being John Stuart-Wortley, 2nd Baron Wharncliffe, and Viscount Morpeth, and he appears to have impressed everyone with his powers of conversation, and – an additional asset in committee work, perhaps – the ability to write with both hands at the same time.

Branwell undoubtedly went to London; but whether he was escorted by his father, by Mr Robinson, or by John Brown, who was now sexton at St Michael's, Haworth, and at thirty-one was becoming a man of some importance in the small community, remains unknown. Mr Robinson would seem to be the most likely. The art teacher would have known that Joseph Leyland was living in London at that time, lodging with William Geller, the mezzotint engraver, hard at work on his life-sized statue of 'Kilmeny', the sinless maid of whose fate Branwell and his sisters must have read a hundred times in James Hogg's famous *Queen's Wake*. Leyland, too, admired James Hogg, and had been inspired by the spotless maid who walked out one day and fell asleep, awaking in a land where no rain fell and no wind blew,

> a land of vision, it would seem,
> a still, an everlasting stream,

a country of the spirits, who kept her seven years, until she begged to be allowed home once more, to warn her people of what would befall them, how their fair cities would burn and their streets run blood. The knowledge that Leyland was in London would have been enough to draw Branwell there, in excitement at the thought that 'the fair Kilmeny' could be cast in plaster as well as the head of Satan.

There is the evidence of one man, happening to be in London at that time, who was said to have seen Branwell Brontë at the Castle Tavern, Holborn. This gentleman, called Woolven, later a ticket collector on the Leeds and Manchester Railway, said that he met Branwell for the first time at the tavern, apparently alone, and was much impressed by the boy's 'unusual flow of language and strength of memory'; so much so that 'the spectators made him umpire in some dispute arising about the dates of certain celebrated battles'.

No word, though, about what had happened at the Royal Academy . . .

Branwell himself, writing *The Adventures of Charles Wentworth* nearly a year later, on May 28th, 1836, has this to say:

It was a bright and balmy May morning, so throwing himself back on the seat, he was shortly swept away in a world of thinking, the text of his ideas being that all this stirring expedity to the mightiest city of the world, where he was to begin real life, had not created one half or one quarter the excitement and pleasure he had always fancied in it. Now this, he thought, was always looked to by me as one of my greatest fountains of happiness, and when I found the stream of pleasure running drier and drier I comforted myself with the idea that as I approached twenty-one I was nearing the great spring where all my thirst would be gratified. But what is it which for a year or two has been whispering in my ear – Happiness consists in Anticipation . . .

Next, he recollected what his advisors had told him, when they saw him, in expectation of an ample fortune falling into his arms, give himself up to idleness and go about doing nothing and caring nothing but building air castles for the adornment of his future life.

'Now,' they said, 'you can never have real happiness without working for it. Exertion is the nutshell which holds pleasure, crack it, and it can be found. Otherwise never. Again, the harder the shell, the better the nut.'

My first argument leads me to the conclusion that I shall have nothing to reward my exertion. Then why should I labour? There are plenty of paths in this life. Which shall I take? Only they all require walking to get on them. But I have it now. Life is a downward journey; all concur in saying it carries us downhill.

Therefore, as men move on in life they are always

tending there. And I cannot remain on the summit of childhood, for time comes wafting past, seizes my hand, and hurries me along, whether I will or not. I'll go across life sideways and never down.

And later:

All day Wentworth had been walking about object-less, but given up to impressions made from passing scenes, never staying to eat or drink nor attending to personal appearance, but with a wildish dejected look of poverty-stricken abstraction. His mind was too restless to stop and fully examine anything. He was going about striking sparks from his mind. He felt that want, that restless uneasy feeling with which rest is torment, and ease begets stupor. The flashes of feeling which were constantly scintillating thrilled his soul, and he cared and thought of nothing more.

Before him stretched docks, and shipping, and merchandise, and the blue boundless sea . . .

Did Branwell Brontë fail to pass into the Royal Academy schools; or did the 'flashes of feeling' and the 'restlessness' which beset Charles Wentworth herald, in the eighteen-year-old boy, an attack of epilepsy?

There was silence for ever more in Haworth about Branwell's visit to London.

In December of that same year the editor of *Blackwood's Magazine* received an impassioned letter from a correspondent in Haworth saying: 'Sir, Read what I write. And would to heaven you could believe it true, for then you would attend and act upon it. I have addressed you twice before, and now I do it again.' The writer went on to praise James Hogg, who had died earlier in the year and John Wilson, explaining how as a child '*Blackwood's* had formed his chief delight', and that he felt 'no child before enjoyed reading as he did, because none ever had such works as *The Noctes, Christmas Dreams, Christopher in his Sporting Jacket* to read.' He continued:

Now, sir, to you I appear writing with conceited assurance; but I *am not*; for that I know myself so far as to believe in my own originality; and on that ground I desire of you admittance into your ranks. And do not wonder that I apply so determinedly; for the remembrances I spoke of have fixed you and your Magazine in such a manner upon my mind that the idea of striving to aid another periodical is *horribly repulsive*. My resolution is to devote my ability to you, and for God's sake, till you see whether or not I can serve you, do not so coldly refuse my aid. All sir, that I desire of you is – *that you would in answer to this letter request a specimen or specimens of my writing, and I even wish that you would name the subject on which you would wish me to write.*

Had the writer ended his letter then, perhaps he would have had a reply. But the last paragraph must have proved his undoing.

Now, sir, do not act like a commonplace person, but like a man willing to examine for himself. Do not turn from the naked truth of my letters, but *prove me* – and if I do not stand the proof, I will not further press myself upon you. If I do stand it – why – You have lost an able writer in James Hogg, and God grant you you may gain one in
                                        Patrick Branwell Brontë.

The letter was thought amusing enough to file in the archives of *Blackwood's*, but not to answer.

The Royal Academy was barred to Branwell. *Blackwood's* did not want him as a contributor. There was nothing for it but to continue the history of Angria, and fill page after page with second-rate verse.

One consolation to bruised pride was that Emily, now seventeen and the tallest of the family, with 'the eyes of a half-tamed creature', had been so shaken by school regulations and lack of privacy that she had not endured Roe Head for more than three months. Anne had taken her place, and Emily was now back at home to share the days with Branwell. They read and discussed the more horrifying tales of James Hogg, where ghosts arose from the grave to become brides of mortal men, doctors discovered elixirs of love and charmed not only men and women but bulls as well, and the Baron St Gio, the man without a conscience, murdered an heiress and her family, whose bleeding bodies a stable-lad threw into a ditch.

Charlotte had never cared for the more lugubrious side of Hogg, but it was chosen fare for Emily, and as she and Branwell walked over the moors – for she was a great walker, and jumped the bogs and ditches without caring how wet she became – they would vie with one another as to who could produce the more fearful fantasy, the more desperate character, each one bearing a resemblance, of course, to some real person in the neighbouring farms – old Jonas Sunderland, perhaps, up at Top Withens, who worked a hand-loom with his wife, or Jonas Pickles, who lived at the Heights with his three daughters, and once kept thieves with blackened faces at bay for two hours with a hatchet.

They came to know every inch of Haworth and Stanbury Moors, during these months when Charlotte and Anne were at school, sometimes walking as far west as Hebden Bridge and Heptonstall, or north across Jackson's Ridge to Wycoller. Each lonely farmstead would hold a story – a slice of truth from Heaton legends, or a drama reminiscent of the fantastic tales of James Hogg. Down at Rush Isles, for instance, Betty Heaton had married her step-brother John Shackleton (the complexities of inter-marriage fascinated Branwell and Emily),

51

Betty's father William himself being the youngest son of a thrice-married father. What cousinly attraction or rivalry kept them apart from the Heatons of Ponden Hall? And why did John Murgatroyd Heaton, oldest brother of the unfortunate Elizabeth who had been seduced at seventeen, embezzle five hundred pounds from his father's estate and die, aged twenty-four?

Down at Sladen Beck, below Bottoms Farm, a child had been found dead in their own time; and if they skirted the Ponden lands, crossed the high road to Colne and trespassed by Two Laws farm, they might catch a sound from poor Bill, who, rebuffed by his sweetheart when he was thirty years old, in 1817, the year Branwell was born, had gone to his room, measuring nine feet by six, and lain there in bed ever since, the window closed, never uttering a word. Folk said he had to roll over to eat his meals, for his legs had become so contracted and drawn to his body that he could no longer move them in the four-poster bed, and when the crumbs fell on the blanket he licked them where they lay.

Nearer home and passing Sowdens, now a farm but a parsonage in days gone by, they would speculate upon the personality of Parson Grimshaw, who had lived there for twenty years, and so scared the Haworth congregation with his sermons about hell-fire that they used to jump out of the public-house windows and run for their lives if they saw him coming. During a service he would leave the church to see if any truant members of the congregation were idling in the churchyard, and if they were he would drive them back into church like a drover herding cattle. No one was permitted to walk in the fields on the Lord's day: Parson Grimshaw walked out himself to scatter them. Once a man who was guilty of adultery was standing in a shop in Haworth, and Parson Grimshaw, observing him, explained: 'The devil has been very busy in this neighbourhood. I can touch the man with my stick who lay with another man's wife last night – the end of

52

these things will be death, the ruin of body and soul for ever.'

Papa at least, brother and sister may have agreed, did not behave like that. Perhaps it had served Parson Grimshaw right when his son Johnny, aged twelve, inherited Ewood over in Midgley from his grandfather, and did as he pleased. It was a curious thing how the sons of parsons so often went to the bad. Gossip said that Johnny Grimshaw drank himself to death two years after his father died. 'Once tha' carriest an angel, but now tha' carriest a devil,' he cried as he rode his father's horse into a lather. Emily must have felt sympathy for Johnny's young sister Jane, sent away to school at Kingswood, near Bristol, and dying there when she was only thirteen, from home-sickness, perhaps, or yearning for the freedom of the moors – who could tell?

Together brother and sister gazed up at the dark windows of Sowdens, where the Grimshaws had lived, wondering, perhaps, whether Johnny and Jane had been by when their evangelical father received 'the glorious vision from the seventh heaven'. Parson Grimshaw had told John Wesley, 'Two under my own roof are just now under true conviction, one a girl of about eighteen years, and the other a boy about fourteen, and I hope my own little girl between ten and eleven years old.'

Emily, however, was not always free to roam the moors, or scribble poems and stories in the 'study' upstairs; she had to give Tabby a hand in cooking, and practise that wretched hemming under the eyes of Aunt – the latter a penance only made bearable by tales of Cornish Tristan. So Branwell would take himself off, and wander across to the churchyard to talk to John Brown, who, as worshipful Master of the Haworth Three Graces Lodge, was trying to persuade him into Freemasonry.

It was, John assured him, very much of a secret society, with strange rites and solemn initiation ceremonies, and a Brother to guard the door so that no one entered; and if you ever broke your oath and told an outsider what happened within the Lodge – John made an expressive gesture with his hand across his throat.

To Branwell's father, John Brown would express his enthusiasm for Freemasonry in rather more guarded language. It would give the lad an interest, he must have urged, keep him up to the mark, stop him from fretting his heart out over the disappointment he'd had in London; and so Mr Brontë gave his consent to Branwell's instruction.

On February 1st, 1836, Branwell was proposed and accepted, and on February 29th – leap year making the day stand out with double significance – he was initiated as a member of the Three Graces Lodge. He was not yet nineteen – the usual age for acceptance being twenty-one – and the ceremony of initiation was an emotional experience for anyone. First, Branwell had to be prepared in an antechamber. Here the Brother acting as steward divested him of all money and metal and bared his left breast, his right arm and his right knee, with the right heel slip-shod. Then he was blindfolded, and a rope put round his neck and a sword pointed to his bare breast. He was led past the Tyler or Outer Guard, of the Lodge door, who announced his approach with three knocks. The Inner Guard gave the alarm, and the Tyler answered that 'a poor candidate was there in a state of darkness, coming of his own free will and accord and also properly prepared, humbly soliciting to be admitted to the mysteries and privileges of Freemasonry'.

Branwell was permitted to enter, and was made to kneel down before the Worshipful Master – John Brown – while the blessing of Heaven was invoked on the proceedings. He was then conducted round the Lodge for the view of the Brethren, and finally presented by the Senior Warden to the Worshipful Master, who put him through a catechism far more stirring than any he had learnt at his aunt's knee. He was commanded to kneel and place his right hand on the Bible, while with his left hand he supported the point of a compass to his bare breast. The solemn vows followed, the pledge of secrecy:

I further solemnly promise, that I will not write those secrets, print, carve, engrave or otherwise delineate them . . . so that our secrets, arts, and hidden mysteries may not become improperly known through my unworthiness.

These several points I solemnly swear to observe, under no less a penalty, on the violation of any of them, *than to have my throat cut across, my tongue torn out by the roots, and my body buried in the sand of the sea at low water mark, or a cable's length from the shore, where the tide regularly ebbs and flows twice in twenty-four hours*; or the more efficient punishment of being branded as a wilfully perjured individual, void of all moral worth, and unfit to be received in this . . . or any other warranted lodge . . .

He was then told to kiss the Bible, and the Worshipful Master asked him what was the predominant wish of his heart. 'Light,' the candidate answered; whereupon the Junior Deacon removed the bandage from his eyes.

At last Branwell could see the serious faces of the men he passed in Haworth every day, now solemnly arrayed as Brethren, and John, his friend, so curiously and fearfully changed in his capacity of Worshipful Master – surely the Grand Inquisitor himself stepped out of the Middle Ages.

The various rites were explained to him, and he was taught the secret 'grip', or token of an Entered Apprentice. Finally he was presented with the gauge, the gavel and the chisel, and, having first been allowed to dress himself once more, he returned thanks for his initiation and was placed to the west, or opposite the Master.

The long lecture followed, then a catechism on the three

55

clauses, and finally, the ceremony ended, the Lodge was formally closed 'in perfect harmony' by the Senior Warden, in 'the name of the great Architect of the Universe, and by the command of the Worshipful Master'.

Then the Brethren were at liberty 'to enjoy themselves with innocent mirth, but carefully to avoid excess, and to avoid immoral or obscene discourse'. If the Steward of the Spirit Cupboard made punch on that leap year evening, Branwell no doubt abstained, being a member of the Haworth Temperance Society.

When he came away from that upper room in the house on Newell Hill his mind was alive with images. He could still feel the sword at his naked breast, the cable round his throat and the bandage about his eyes; but if he ever dropped one hint to Charlotte or Emily that appalling fate awaited him.

It made the bond between him and John much closer, though. Now that he had been initiated he felt himself a man, strangely superior to his sisters, and superior too to his father, who would never learn what rites were carried out, what vows were uttered.

From that first evening of initiation Branwell advanced rapidly in the craft, and by April 25th he was raised to the rank of Master Mason, being instructed in the signs of joy and exultation and the five degrees of fellowship. How stimulating it must have been to receive a stroke on the forehead from John, as Worshipful Master, to lie down, shamming dead, and then be raised by John, bringing him foot to foot, knee to knee, breast to breast. It would have given him a feeling of comradeship shared yet secret. John as Worshipful Master shone with a blaze of power and glory; he was no longer Papa's sexton but something much bigger, more exciting, a sort of demi-god . . . or was it demon?

Exciting, too, to exchange private signals with him in the vestry, in front of Papa who did not know what they meant, but continued talking solemnly about church business; or to walk past the post-office and meet the saturnine John Heaton from Well Head, and give him the sign of exultation and have it acknowledged!

These things made up for the disappointment of continuing silence from the editor of *Blackwood's*, who had not even had the courtesy to return his long poem 'Misery', sent on April 8th, now torn to shreds and lying, no doubt, in some Edinburgh dustbin.

> All Dark without, All Fire within,
> Can Hell have mightier hold on sin?

Now was the moment, perhaps, to create a bloody revolution in the infernal world, and have Alexander Percy, Earl of Northangerland, banish his son-in-law, Arthur Zamorna, King of Angria (alias Charlotte imprisoned at Roe Head), two thousand miles away to the rocks of Ascension Isle. The revolution launched, there would be time to paint again — never mind the Royal Academy — fit up as a studio the small back bedroom where he now slept alone, and persuade John to dress up in his Sunday best and have his portrait painted, his leonine head and shoulders backed by an evil storm.

6

Branwell's literary output, between the ages of nineteen and twenty-one, was fantastic. The complete history of the kingdom of Angria in nine parts, including several long stories and many poems, covers sheet after sheet of manuscript, all in microscopic handwriting. These manuscripts, scattered as they are today, and housed in various collections throughout the country, might – after years of study – give the patient reader some idea of this extraordinary conception.

Here was this imaginary colony, situated where we should find Ghana and Nigeria today, founded by the original soldier adventurers when Branwell was eleven or twelve years old; then split into kingdoms, united into an empire, given a written constitution and an army, its geography and population noted in minute particular, relief maps drawn, military and political history recorded, the life stories of the individual leaders, with their personal appearance, qualities, failings and emotions, all described in detail; the whole a gigantic fantasy conjured up in the imagination of a brother and sister who were constantly separated by the sister's school term, and neither of whom had any personal experience of the world outside their own small neighbourhood.

Those manuscripts of Branwell's which have been transcribed, the poems and stories which have been printed, show no outstanding literary merit. Manner and style are crude, the events described betray the young author's naïve preoccupation with gambling and dissipation, the most deadly sins, perhaps, to a boy brought up by a Methodist aunt and an evangelical father. Nevertheless, although many a poet and novelist scribbles in adolescence, foreshadowing maturer work to come, not many found a colony and people it, as this boy and his sister founded Angria, so shaping its history and the lives of its people that to its creators the colony became a living entity.

In August, 1836, Branwell, for the purpose of reference, summarized the early life of his hero, Alexander Percy, intending to expand it later.

This child, in the first years of his life, was a beautiful angelic looking being with golden hair and blue eyes, and a musical voice, and of a soul capricious, passionate, indulged, and bent with amazing devotion towards the science of music, for which he discovered a passion in his earliest infancy that only strengthened as it grew into a soul-wrapping sort of Idolatry. He lived in music, and when disengaged from his grand pursuit he wandered about or laid himself down for hours on hours in the stately park or girdling woods beneath the glorious skies of an African summer afternoon. The rich luxuriance of nature, the deep blue of heaven, the gold and brightness of the clouds, the dazzling effulgence of the sun, filled his unreasoning but sensitive spirit with a delight which he could not express or attempt to name. It was the same when he accompanied his mother to her cottage on the shores of the Atlantic, where, seated on her lap, he would gaze for hours at the wide waltzing waving sea; the same at night when he stole out of the crowded and dazzling rooms of his father's hall to look at the moon or stars in the midnight sky. It was that feeling too which led him to be for ever talking about religion, the Bible, and heaven; or wishing that to go there he might die; but with opening youth came other feelings too; a most ungovernable spirit withal, passionate and resentful, embroiling him constantly with his hard, heartless and bilious looking father, but throwing him straight away into the acquaintanceship and paths of the drunken drover old Robert Sdeath, whose hardened soul being fired on him would not leave him, but drew him on from one thing to another till even his noble but indulgent mother could not shut her eyes to the excesses of her darling son.

While still in his teens Alexander married the Lady Augusta Romana di Segovia, a beautiful but unscrupulous lady, who subsequently arranged that Sdeath should murder her husband's father for the sake of the estate which Alexander would then inherit. The lady herself was subsequently dispatched with poison, and Alexander married

Mary Henrietta Wharton, daughter of Lord Georg Wharton of Alnwick, Nigrita . . . a young and lovely creature, with a generous heart and quick warm feeling, with an imagination that spoke in the centre of her eyes, and a heart that could hardly last without friends and friendship round it.

When she died of consumption Alexander, his heart broken, 'commenced a run of hollow heartless dissipation', and was imprisoned for treachery against his superior officer. Threatened by his creditors and by the husband of a lady whom he had seduced, in despair he decided to leave the shores of his native Africa.

But once out on the open sea his active unprincipled mind began to speculate upon some method of retrieving his broken fortunes. Piracy with his men and means seemed the likeliest way. By crossing the Atlantic northward into the seas of Europe he entered the lawless and bloody trade, taking and cruelly destroying vessels, till his name the 'Rover' became a terror of the sea. Coasting along S. America and thence to the West Indies, he tracked back again towards Norway, through the British seas into the Mediterranean, and finally, almost exhausted with melancholy and restless as Cain, he ordered the vessel home under Sdeath and landed alone on the Coast of Sidon. How he wandered through Palestine, or how he returned toward Africa, is not known, for he will never tell it, but in 1824 he appeared on a sudden at Percy Hall before his brother and his child after an absence of six dark and bloody years.

The outlines of the history of his infernal world completed, Branwell, still far from weary of its wars and rivalries, reviewed the many pages with the idea of describing in greater detail the highlights of his hero's career. Alexander Percy, ex-Rogue, now Earl of Northangerland, was by this time a man past middle age, thrice married, with two sons whom he detested, a daughter, Mary Henrietta, Duchess of Zamorna, whom he adored, and an illegitimate daughter by a French mistress; though this illegitimate daughter, Caroline, does not appear in the Angrian series much before 1838 or 1839.

'If Alexander Rogue looked like Satan, the prince of darkness,' Branwell wrote of his jaded hero,

Lord Northangerland looked like Lucifer, Star of the Morning. And the sneer was here before me too, but it was changed from what I had seen before. It was a sneer of calm contempt at himself and nature, not of fierce hatred of his enemies and mankind. I acquit this man of any feeling whatsoever for man or nation, or the welfare of any state or kingdom. I acquit him of kindly affection to society and happiness. I could not call him cold and icy stoical: say rather, hot as flame . . .

To kill off this being who so possessed his creator was out of the question. Nor must he be allowed to fade into old age. Branwell's answer was to return to Percy's youth and describe him through the eyes of a discarded mistress, telling the tale, in prose and verse, of how Harriet O'Connor, later Harriet Montmorency, wife of Percy's friend and ally, left husband for lover, was deserted by Percy and died.

Hitherto Branwell had always written through the character of Percy himself, or as Charles Wentworth, Angrian poet and historian, or the nobleman Baron Richton; now, as the artless and passionate young Harriet, he described in verse not only the pangs and anguish of adulterous love but the torment of religious doubt succeeding it. The switch in sex is interesting.

Fragments of Angrian tales, suggestions in poems, all give tantalizing hints of this Harriet, who met Percy when he was paying court to his first wife, the Italian Augusta di Segovia. At one moment Percy and Harriet even appear to be rivals in love for Augusta, an emotional state of affairs foreshadowing life in present-day Chelsea rather than nineteenth-century Haworth.

The death of Harriet's older sister Caroline was to launch Branwell into a series of poems which, showing the influence of *Blackwood's* John Wilson combined with his own memories of his sister Maria, might be read aloud to both his aunt and his father without fear of disapprobation.

> They came – they pressed the coffin lid
> Above my Caroline,
> And then, I felt, for ever hid
> My sister's face from mine!
> There was one moment's wildered start –
> One pang remembered well –
> When first from my unhardened heart
> The tears of anguish fell:

That swell of thought which seemed to fill
The bursting heart, the gushing eye,
While fades all *present* good or ill
All else seems blank – the mourning march
Before the shades of things gone by.
The proud parade of woe,
The passage 'neath the churchyard arch,
The crowd that met the show.
My place or thoughts amid the train
I strive to recollect, in vain –
I could not think or see:
I cared not whither I was borne
And only felt that death had torn
My Caroline from me.

The poem describing Harriet's fall from grace is in a different key from the account of her subsequent desertion by Percy. It seems clear that there must have been a time-lag between the writing of the two poems. The account of Harriet's desertion begins thus:

At dead of Midnight, drearily
I heard a voice of horror say
'Oh God, I am lost for ever!'

After many lines imploring the Almighty for pardon, and wondering whether 'fires infernal' will hold her down in 'hideous pains', it continues:

Oh, I led a life of sinning,
At her beck, whose soul was sin;
Yet my spirit ceased repining
If a look from him 'twould win!
Bright that band with hellish glory
Circling round Augusta's throne,

Dark those hearts whose influence o'er me,
Led me in and lured me on! –
All their Mirth I knew was hollow,
Gain and guilt their path and aim,
Yet I cared not what might follow –
Deaf to warning, dead to shame.
What to me if Jordan Hall
Held all Hell within its wall,
So I might in his embrace
Drown the misery of disgrace!

Many lines further on poor Harriet admits that 'faces blushed to name her name, and silence hushed the adulterer's shame', and that:

Three short words might speak her lot –
Fallen, Forsaken, and Forgot!

Despite the absurdity of some of the verse, the reader feels a sense of regret that so much has been left unsaid. Jordan Hall, the abode of the wicked Lady Augusta di Segovia, which 'held all Hell within its wall', must have whipped its creator to a high pitch of excitement; while the wicked Augusta herself was surely a forerunner of Emily's Augusta, fatal heroine of her Gondal saga, begun that very year.

There can be no doubt that Branwell and Emily, during the time when Charlotte and Anne were at Roe Head, collaborated in ideas, if not in actual incidents or verse. One of the earlier Angrian tales, 'A Leaf From An Unopened Volume', attributed to Charlotte and now in the library of A. Edward Newton, contains so many names used later by Emily in her Gondal poems that it may indeed be a contribution by the younger sister to the Angrian series.

This story, dated 1834, concerns the second generation of the Angrian dynasty. The names of the Duke of Zamorna's sons and daughters – the Archduke Julius (later Emperor), the Archdukes Adrian and Alexander, and the Princess Irenë – and her maid of honour Zorayda, who played the guitar, are too reminiscent of Emily's later creations not to leave the reader with a strong impression that when Emily began her Gondal saga she did so as an off-shoot from Angria.

Emily's and Branwell's poems, during the year 1837, also have lines that suggest close collaboration.

Emily: O God of heaven! the dream of horror,
            The frightful dream is over now;
            The sickened heart, the blasting sorrow,
            The ghastly night, the ghastlier morrow,
            The aching sense of utter woe.

Branwell: 'O God!' – she murmured forth again,
            While scarce her shattered senses knew
            What darkness shrouded from her view –
            'Oh, take from me this sick'ning pain!
            That frightful dream, if t'was a dream,
            Has only wakened me to die;
            Yet death and life confounded seem
            To inward thought and outward eye!'

Life at the Parsonage, and at Roe Head too, would seem about this time to have struck a note of discord. Religious doubts were seizing all four young Brontës at once. Charlotte, still torn between her friends Ellen and Mary, had written to the former: 'I wish I could live with you always . . . If we had but a cottage and a competency of our own I do think we might live and love on till Death without being dependent on any third person for happiness', and later in the same year, in December of 1836: 'If I could always live with you and daily read the Bible with you, if your lips and mine could at the same time drink the same draught from the same pure fountain of mercy, I hope, I trust, I might one day become better, far better, than my evil wandering thoughts, my corrupt heart, cold to the spirit and warm to the flesh, will now permit me to be.'

Certainly gentle Ellen Nussey knew nothing of Jordan Hall and its delights. The fervour of Charlotte's letters betrayed the fever within, the guilty knowledge that in a few weeks' time she would be home for the holidays, free to indulge herself in the amours of her hero Zamorna and his new mistress. The infernal world would have her in grip again.

During the Christmas holidays of 1836–37 both Branwell and Charlotte endeavoured to atone for the secret delight that filled them when they were writing the Angrian stories by composing and revising laborious verse, in the belief that, if it were ever to win recognition, it must set a high moral and religious note. Poets they were determined to be, rather than story-tellers, verse could be sent to Mr Wordsworth and Mr Southey for criticism, but seduction and passion must remain hidden from any eyes but their own.

Charlotte wrote to Southey and Branwell to Wordsworth, Branwell enclosing a long poem describing the infant Percy asleep, before he had fallen from grace. In his letter he explained: 'What I send you is the prefatory scene of a much longer subject, in which I have striven to develop strong passions and weak principles struggling with a high imagination and acute feelings, till, as youth hardens towards age, evil deeds and short enjoyments end in mental misery and bodily ruin.' He was alluding, of course, to his whole Percy saga, and a word of encouragement from the greatest English poet of the day would no doubt have set him to work upon a more polished version of what he hoped would be an epic poem longer than Wordsworth's *Prelude*. He received no answer. His letter disgusted the ageing poet, who told Southey that it contained 'gross flattery and plenty of abuse of other poets'. In fairness to Branwell this letter, often reproduced, must be quoted again. It was dated January 19th, 1837.

Sir – I most earnestly entreat you to read and pass your judgement upon what I have sent you, because from the day of my birth to this nineteenth [actually twentieth] year of my life I have lived among secluded hills, where I could neither know what I was or what I could do. I read for the same reason that I ate or drank; because it was a real craving of nature. I wrote on the same principle as I spoke – out of the impulse and feelings of the mind; nor could I help it, for what came, came out, and there was the end of it. For as to self-conceit, that could not receive food from flattery, since to this hour not half-a-dozen people in the world know I have penned a line.

But a change has taken place now, sir; and I am arrived at an age wherein I must do something for myself; the powers I possess must be exercised to a definite end, and as I don't know them myself I must ask of others what they are worth. Yet there is not one here to tell me; and still, if they are worthless, time will henceforth be too precious to be wasted on them.

Do pardon me, sir, that I have ventured to come before one whose works I have most loved in our literature, and who most has been with me a divinity of the mind, laying before him one of my writings, and asking of him a judgement of its contents. I must come before someone from whose sentence there is no appeal; and such a one is he who had developed the theory of poetry as well as its practice, and both in such a way as to claim a place in the memory of a thousand years to come.

My aim, sir, is to push out into the open world, and for this I trust not poetry alone; that might launch the vessel, but could not bear her on. Sensible and scientific prose, bold and vigorous efforts in my walk of life, would give a further title to the notice of the world;

and then again poetry ought to brighten and crown that name with glory. But nothing of all this can ever be begun without means, and as I don't possess these I must in every shape strive to gain them. Surely, in this day, when there is not a *writing* poet worth a sixpence, the field must be open, if a better man can step forward.

Once again Branwell had made a slip. The phrase 'not a writing poet worth a sixpence' condemned him in the eyes of the elderly Wordsworth. Apart from this, the letter was sincere and well expressed. The nineteen-year-old boy then described what manner of poem he was enclosing, and ended:

Now, to send you the whole of this would be a mock upon your patience; what you see does not pretend to be more than the description of an imaginative child. But read it, sir; and as you would hold a light to one in utter darkness – as you value your own kindheartedness – *return* me an *answer* if but one word, telling me whether I should write on, or write no more. Forgive undue warmth, because my feelings in this matter cannot be cool; and believe me, sir, with deep respect,
Your really humble servant,
P. B. Brontë.

It would not have cost Wordsworth five minutes to acknowledge the letter. One word of encouragement, the poem perhaps unread, and the boy would have faced the year with at least the hope of breaking through into what must have seemed to him an impenetrable world. No answer came. Neither from Wordsworth, nor from the editor of *Blackwood's*, to whom Branwell had also written ten days before. It is very evident that he had no sense of judgement where either his own work was concerned, or that of established poets. The slackest, most sentimental lines in the poems of others were taken as the criterion of what should be; he could not distinguish between the worst of Wilson and the best of Cowper.

The poem that he sent to Wordsworth contained such lines as:

> Oh, how I could wish to fly
> Far away through yonder sky,
> O'er those trees upon the breeze
> To a paradise on high!

A Sunday School child of seven could have done better. Possibly this was, in fact, the effort of Branwell at a much earlier age – perhaps inspired by Mr Brontë's *Cottage Poems* – put away in a drawer, and revised with the mistaken idea that this sort of stuff would appeal to the Lakeland poet.

Somewhere among the same pile of manuscript, had Branwell delved a little further, he would have found a piece of his Angrian prose.

> Why, listen, and know what refined vengeance is. I'd have him whole, sound and hearty, upright on his pins and standing at one end of a table. I'd have him see what me and Simpson had been doing yesterday, no, the day before yesterday; a darkish room, but enough light to see ill with; a table, I say, and us beside it; the wind and rain blowing a racket without, and not a soul around to care for Him! Yes, Him I say (exalting his voice to a discordant screech), His son, his eldest son, holding him in his arms as if he were going to baptise him; the priest at hand with a right red iron in his paws; whereon, we stand, and here we go, have at it; then in goes the iron, first into one eye and then into the other, hissing and searing to the brain. Off I ships the pitch cap and we shakes him to the skies – this is the way my boys; this is the torment . . . Bring him out to make sport for the Philistines – Maew, Maew . . .

What a relief for Branwell to submerge in the infernal world after striving to please Mr Wordsworth! If he were not Percy or Quashia, Percy's Ashantee ally, he could turn himself into the comparatively new character of Henry Hastings, reeling home through the streets of Rosses town after a night of debauchery and drunkenness. "'The coach of Hell!" cried I, "Lend me a hand, Who-hoop! And now, off as if Daddy were at th' back of us!'"

The swing from violence to exultation, and back to despair again; an icy December crippling poor Tabby so that the girls had to do the work of the house . . . Branwell, choosing his piece of bathos, perhaps written months or years before, to send to Wordsworth, had not the discernment to pick out the scrap he had scribbled a few days previously, on January 13th, 1837, looking from the snow-bound parsonage to the white graves below.

> However young and lovely round
> Fresh faces court my frozen eye,
> They'll only desecrate the ground
> Where fairer forms corrupting lie;
> And voices sweet and music's thrill,
> And laughter light as marriage strain,
> Will only wake a ghostly chill,
> As if the buried spoke again.
> All – all is over, friend and lover,
> Need never seek a refuge here,
> Though they may sweep my heart strings over,
> No music will awake the ear.
> I'm dying away in dull decay,
> I feel and find the sands are down,
> The evening's latest lingering ray
> At last from my wild Heaven has flown.
> I feel and find that I am cast
> From hope, and peace, and power, and pride,

> A withered leaf on autumn's blast,
> A scattered wreck on ocean's tide.

Morbid, possibly, a word ill-chosen here and there, but surely better verse.

Mr Brontë and his sister-in-law have both been blamed for intolerance, and for creating an atmosphere of religious gloom at the parsonage. The truth would seem otherwise. Neither sisters nor brother ever blamed father or aunt for their own passing moods of despondency. Ellen Nussey, loved and favoured visitor to the house, remembered only 'Miss Branwell being lively and intelligent, reading to Mr Brontë in the afternoons, finishing their discussions on what they had read when we all met for tea. The social life of her younger days she used to recall with regret; she gave one the idea that she had been a belle among her own home acquaintances. She took snuff out of a very pretty gold box, which she sometimes presented to you with a little laugh, as if she enjoyed the slight shock and astonishment visible in your countenance.'

Here was no Methodist dragon, frowning on high spirits, but a little lady who, though past her sixtieth birthday in 1837, believed herself the equal in culture of her nieces and nephew, and whose Georgian manners may well have had a smack of that eighteenth century which had seen her heyday. Where else but from their aunt did Charlotte and Branwell learn of balls and socials, the quizzings with eye-glasses, the tappings with a fan, that figured so largely in the Angrian world of romance?

It was conscience that brought Charlotte time and again to the verge of breakdown: fear that teaching and the infernal world were incompatible, guilt because her attraction towards Ellen Nussey, Mary Taylor and Mary's irresistible younger sister Martha – the piquant and fascinating 'Patty' – tempted her to transform them into Zamorna's bride and mistresses. Branwell was too close to Charlotte to remain unaware of his sister's pangs of conscience. The pretty Mary Taylor made an exquisite peg on which to hang Mary Henrietta Percy – Alexander's daughter and Zamorna's bride – and how stimulating to invent an illegitimate younger sister Caroline (not the Caroline of the poem already quoted), who would have 'Patty' Taylor's imperious lovable ways. Term-time would pass all the more quickly for Charlotte if he waved the magic wand.

Branwell's trouble was not conscience but frustration. Frustration that at twenty he was still without the means of earning his living, that the home education of which his father was so proud had fitted him for nothing. Too late now for university. Too late now for the Royal Academy. The editor of *Blackwood's* would not grant him an interview. How in heaven's name was he to use the talents he believed himself to possess?

Tradition has it that about this time he went for a term as usher in a school, and that he left because the boys 'ridiculed his downcast smallness'. The school has never been named. The story awaits confirmation. It was Emily who in the autumn of 1837 tried her luck away from home, teaching at Law Hill School near Halifax and staying there, according to Ellen Nussey, a grim six months.

The desire to earn money and thus win some measure of independence must have driven her to this step, which was so uncongenial to her nature; nevertheless, Law Hill cannot have been the hard labour it was thought to be. Too many poems written during those six months suggest moments of creative fever; and the headmistress, Miss Elizabeth Patchett, described in Mrs Chadwick's *In the Steps of the Brontës* as 'a very beautiful woman of forty-four wearing her hair in curls, a skilled horsewoman, whose daily walks with the girls were a prized recreation', surely afforded some measure of interest and amusement to the hard-worked Emily, if only in her letters home.

Anne, unhappy with asthma – that complaint so often

associated with anxiety – and her own religious doubts at Dewsbury Moor, whether Miss Wooler's school had removed from Roe Head, suffered more, perhaps, than her loved sister at Law Hill. Anne's consolation would be the memory of the thirty-four-year-old Moravian minister of religion, the Reverend James La Trobe, who during an illness at Roe Head had visited her several times, bringing a message of gentle hope and comfort very different from the stern creed taught at home.

Branwell had no such clerical support. Dissenting ministers were not for him, unless they could be made sport of in an Angrian tale. The Reverend Moses Saunders and the Reverend Winterbotham, Baptist preachers at Haworth, made glorious copy from time to time, and his fellow-brethren in the Three Graces Lodge, some of them also fellow-Conservatives, could be turned into Angrian revolutionaries fighting and drinking in the wilds of Africa, without ever being a whit the wiser. The red-haired, bespectacled 'parson's son', Patrick to the village, with his book-learning and his ability to write minutes with both hands, was certainly an addition to the monthly Lodge meetings; but that every word and every action on the part of members and brethren was quietly recorded at the back of 'Patrick's' mind, to be used in some Angrian tale the instant he got back to the parsonage, was something that Messrs. Hartley, Garnett, Sutcliffe, Heaton and the other gentlemen would never know. Even the local doctor would not escape notice, but must play his small part in an Angrian beer-house scuffle.

Branwell held the post of secretary to the Three Graces Lodge from June 12th to December 11th, 1837, writing the minutes on each occasion as well as acting as organist (in other words, playing the piano). During this time he possibly had more fun mocking the brethren on paper back at home than he did at the gatherings themselves. For once the awe and the freshness had worn off the Lodge meetings, the imp in his

73

brain that gibed at all things dignified and sober could only have despised those fellow brethren who looked upon the meeting as a second Sunday school. The best part of the proceedings, no doubt, was when the Steward of the Spirit Cupboard produced refreshment, and John Brown, Worshipful Master, temporarily relaxed from his exalted position and made the company split their sides over Haworth's past.

But even John, who could make anyone's blood freeze in their veins when he had the mind, with his tales of coffins opening, and people buried alive, and shrouds displaced; who persuaded Branwell to spend a night alongside curate Hodgson in a haunted double-bed that heaved under its occupants, so frightening Branwell that he ran home to the parsonage in his night-clothes – even John, with his rough humour and warm personality, could not discuss the things that really mattered: books, poems, pictures, music, life.

There was no one of Branwell's intellectual level in Haworth, when his sisters were away and his father was in no mood to sympathize. Almost certainly Mr Brontë would have discouraged Branwell from attempting to break into the literary or artistic worlds, on the grounds that there was no money to be made in either, except under rich or noble patronage. Better, he must have said, that his son should teach, like his sisters, or follow his own calling and go into the Church.

When the old generation talked in this fashion there was only one thing to do – ignore the advice. A fellow-student who had studied under Mr Robinson of Leeds told him he was wasting his time and talent trying to work in a bedroom studio at the parsonage. He ought to live in rooms in Bradford, and get introductions to people, who would sit for him and pay for their portraits.

Easy enough for Thompson to talk. How was Branwell to raise the funds? There was always, of course, his aunt . . . His aunt might possibly make some financial arrangement with her cousin by marriage, the Reverend William Morgan of Christ Church, Bradford, Branwell's godfather. After all, she wanted him to have a successful career as much as anyone. He must do credit to her name.

Whether it was indeed his aunt who backed him, or Mr Morgan himself, or both, the upshot was that some time in 1838 Branwell achieved one of his ambitions. He had not had anything accepted by *Blackwood's Magazine*, but he did become a lodger with Mr and Mrs Kirby of Fountain Street, Bradford, renting a room which he used as a studio, and returning home to the parsonage for weekends.

He was twenty, and it was the first time – save for the fruitless visit to London – that he was sleeping away from home, away from his father. It was the start of independence, the beginning, so he hoped, of a successful artistic future, and a break, however temporary, with the claims of the infernal world.

Branwell's attempts to earn his living as a portrait painter in Bradford lasted some twelve months. Little of his work survives today. The most familiar portrait, that of his three sisters, which hangs in the National Portrait Gallery, must have been painted at home, as well as the profile of either Emily or Anne hanging beside it. Sentiment and tradition give this lovely profile to Emily, but the resemblance to the figure of Anne in the group would suggest otherwise.

It is a moving experience to look upon these portraits. The viewer senses that he is an intruder, standing on the threshold of Haworth parsonage. The faded colouring only enhances the curious dream quality of these three faces looking out upon the world from the canvas; gazing, it would seem, upon the infernal world of their own creation rather than the walls of Branwell's studio-bedroom.

Close inspection of the group has lately shown that what was thought to be a pillar is, in reality, the painted-out head and shoulders of the artist himself. The broad high forehead, the hair puffed at the sides, the line of coat and collar, all are there. Perhaps Branwell did not consider that he had done his own face justice, and in a fit of irritation smudged himself into oblivion.

A second group existed once, with Branwell standing between his sisters, holding a gun in his hand. There must have been a third group too, from which the sensitive profile portrait of Emily or Anne was torn. This group is said to have been destroyed by Mr Nicholls, Charlotte's husband, who did not think it did his wife or her sisters justice. That he was artistically at fault is proved by the surviving profile in the National Portrait Gallery.

Other drawings of the sisters surely graced the parsonage once. An artist models from his family again and again. Branwell would have drawn his father, his aunt, even the faithful Tabby. There is no trace of any such sketch today.

A few portraits have been rescued for posterity, and now hang in Branwell's old room at the Parsonage museum. Those of John and William Brown hold pride of place. These two, before the recent changes at the Museum, used to hang in Mr Brontë's bedroom, one on either side of the fireplace. They had not then been restored, but were just as Branwell left them, with the picture of William half-finished. Once again, to a layman's eye they appeared impressive. These two men, passed over by all biographers of the Brontë sisters as merely the sexton and his brother, persons of humble origin and small importance, stood out here as living figures of Branwell's infernal world. The Worshipful Master of the Three Graces Lodge held his ground with dignity, despite the threatening storm in the background; the eyes could rebuke when they pleased, the mouth purse itself to command. Yet what weak, facile sentiment lurked behind those eyes, what fleshy self-indulgence when the mouth relaxed, what corpulent and easily-prevailed-upon, sensuous charm.

William was different. No vivid colouring here, no stormy background. Before restoration the total impression was of a jaundiced yellow, and the embittered eyes and taut cruel mouth suggested a man who, away from his Sunday best or his masonic duties, would, in some shadowed corner of the church where pick-axes and digging tools and barrows were stored away, impart to 'parson's son', in his tender years, the cruder facts of life. He was, in point of fact, just nine years Branwell's senior.

These two portraits have lately been restored, William's portrait has been 'finished' – and the magic has gone.

The portraits of Mr and Mrs Kirby, Branwell's host and hostess from Fountain Street, Bradford, show a genius for satire on the part of the mocking lodger. Mrs Kirby stares from her frame in disapproval, the large frilled bonnet emphasizing in delicious fashion the prominent drooping nose and tucked-in chin, while Mr Kirby, humourless and suspicious, has the set expression of one who, reluctantly sitting for his likeness, does so for the first and last time.

Miss Margaret Hartley, their niece, who lived with them, completes the trio. She appears to be a young woman of about the artist's age. She is far from ill-looking; indeed, she has a certain charm. What Branwell thought of her it is impossible to say, but Miss Hartley herself (later Mrs Ingram) declared in after years, when biographers of Charlotte had traduced the Brontë brother as already a drunkard in his 'teens, that young Mr Brontë, during the twelve months when she knew him in Bradford, 'was steady, industrious and self-respecting'. She would not have known if she provided inspiration for any Angrian writings. It seems possible, for her parents were dead, and a young girl bereaved would have made good fare for Branwell's pen.

Mrs Kirby herself had two children. One of them, according to a friend of Branwell's, 'a beautiful little girl, was his special favourite. At his frequent request she dined with him in his private sitting-room, her pleasant smiles and cheerful prattling always charming him.'

Branwell had a gift for children which his sisters did not share. As he did not have to teach them, but only paint them, his patience and good nature stood the test. In after years, the small boys to whom he gave handfuls of pennies in the street at Haworth remembered him with gratitude – not only his generosity, but also his sense of fun, his love of a practical joke. He gave one of his self-portraits to a favourite lad from Haworth Sunday School, telling him, slyly, that the portrait was of Sir Robert Peel. It was not until the boy got home that he discovered Branwell had been playing a trick on him. This same boy remembered Branwell showing him the private room at the Three Graces Lodge, perhaps as an antidote to Sunday School. As to the self-portrait, it has vanished, along with the one of Mrs Kirby's little girl.

The young artist in Fountain Street must have charged Mr and Mrs Kirby for their portraits, but relatives and friends usually expected their sittings to be free. Although the cost of bed and board was paid for by the Reverend William Morgan, with his aunt probably contributing, Branwell would still have to find money for clothes and bare necessities. The scattering of pennies to the children of Haworth does not suggest that he was frugal. The tall hat, the black vest, the raven-grey trousers, the little rattan cane, all described in one of the Angrian stories by Charlotte, tongue-in-cheek, give hints of a young man who wished to please and appear to some advantage. Prospective Bradford sitters, manufacturers and mill-owners, would not give their custom to someone down-at-heel. Branwell would need to seek his clients in hostelries like the George Hotel, the haunt not only of the wealthy businessmen of the day but of a coterie of minor poets and painters. Among them was John James, later a historian of the district, but at this time clerk to a Bradford solicitor. He was the friend of Robert Story, Yorkshire poet and schoolmaster, well known locally for his enthusiasm in the Conservative cause.

Leeds, Halifax and Bradford all had their 'bards' who contributed to the newspapers. One of them was William Dearden, who wrote under the pseudonym of William Oakendale, the 'bard of Caldene'. He was a classical school-master by profession, and had married a Cumberland girl who was herself so proficient in Greek and Latin that they wrote their love letters to one another in these languages. William Dearden, some fifteen years senior to Branwell, may have met him at about this time, when he was teaching at Keighley grammar school, and it has been suggested that the original of the Caroline in Branwell's poem, written in 1837, was indeed William Dearden's cousin of that name, who had died ten years before of typhus fever. Any character, living or dead, served as fuel to Angrian fire.

One thing is certain. The name Caroline was something of an obsession, conscious or unconscious, with both Branwell and Charlotte. Caroline Vernon was the name of Percy's illegitimate daughter, Caroline Helstone was one of the two heroines in Charlotte's *Shirley*, and a dead Caroline is mourned in yet another of Branwell's poems, *The Wanderer*. Poetically, the reason for the obsession could be the rhythmic quality of the name itself, and nothing more significant. The agonized Harriet, Caroline's sister and Percy's discarded mistress, found that it rhymed very suitably with 'decline' when she was striving to forget adulterous shame in memories of her dead sister. As for the name Harriet, it was borne not only by Percy's mistress but, in real life, by eighteen-year-old Harriet Robinson from Stanbury, who in a year or two was to marry one of Branwell's boyhood friends, Hartley Merrall of Springhead, near Haworth. Young Hartley himself, alternating between Bradford and his father's mill, two years Branwell's junior and a lively companion, might very well have served, at some time or other, as a model for the Angrian Hector Montmorency who married the Harriet of Branwell's poem.

While he was in Bradford, or possibly just before he went there, Branwell was at last to meet the young sculptor whom he had for so long admired at a distance, the sardonic and temperamental Joseph Leyland. According to Leyland's brother Francis, William Dearden took Branwell over to Halifax, where the sculptor was at that time working on a group of African bloodhounds. When this group was exhibited later in London, it was pronounced by the *Art Journal* as 'unsurpassed by any sculpture of modern time'. The model for these animals was Leyland's own bloodhound, which had escaped from a travelling circus and attached himself to the sculptor, actually dying on the stand when Leyland was casting him in clay. The sculptor, writing about it later, said:

> I looked, and saw him raise himself upon his haunches, and endeavour to crawl towards me − it was his last effort, for looking up into my face he licked my hand and died. Believe me, I shall never forget the dying look of that bloodhound; and the grief I yet feel, when I think of him, is more like what I felt for a human being than a dog.

Dearden wrote a poem on the hound's death, which was published on July 25th, 1837.

A group of African bloodhounds, the model for which died tragically at his master's feet − here was a scene that might have stepped straight out of Angrian history! And the sculptor himself, only twenty-six years old but already praised by all the art critics of the day, friend of many famous London artists, with the promise of an outstanding career before him, seemed to the aspiring Branwell everything that he himself would like to be. He was, in fact, another Alexander Percy, with his biting tongue, his scorn of religion, his contempt for those who disagreed with him, his decision to work only when it pleased him and damn the consequences, whether debt or failure, his generosity to his artistic friends, his ability to drink them under the table, his powerful, heavily built frame, his dark eyes, his mocking expression − these qualities combined to make the sculptor as full of potential charm and danger to Branwell as the Satan Leyland had cast in clay three years before.

Leyland also called himself a poet − another bond. And he too had lost, in infancy, a small brother and sister older than himself. Branwell, whose few friends hitherto had been the brethren of the Three Graces Lodge, and boyhood acquaintances like Hartley Merrall, found Joseph Leyland romantic fare.

It was stimulating to walk into the George at Bradford, and glimpse Joe Leyland talking to Edward Collinson or Richard Waller, the one a poet, the other a portrait painter, and have Leyland beckon him over for an introduction. Or, better still, to call with Dearden at the sculptor's studio in Swan Coppice, Halifax, sit there awhile and watch him work, and drink with him afterwards at the Union Cross down the alley-way, never disclosing the fact that back at home in Haworth he was a member of the Temperance Society. To drink nothing would be to lose face. A tot of rum or a noggin of gin harmed nobody; besides, it set his brain working, fired his imagination, and he knew he would be twenty times more witty and amusing after a drink or two than if he sat sipping ginger wine like a teacher in Sunday school.

They shared the same literary tastes. Joe Leyland, who had sculptured Kilmeny, would quote James Hogg and *The Queen's Wake*, only to be capped by Branwell, who would recite line after line from *Pilgrims of the Sun*, describing the strange flight of Cela and Mary Lee, as well as passages from Hogg's more gruesome tales into the bargain. This, Branwell thought, was living at last. Halifax was better than Verdopolis (the new name for Glass-Town), Leyland more Lucifer-like than Percy, Earl of Northangerland, and himself – well, here was the puzzle, he could turn himself at will into any Angrian character he pleased. But Leyland returned to London, to exhibit his bloodhounds, and Branwell, back in Fountain Street, painting either the Reverend William Morgan or Mrs Kirby, neither of whom could have inspired him with anything but mild contempt, wondered whether after all he had chosen the right profession.

Both sitters sat from kindness – or could it be pity? Nobody seemed to want their portraits painted, or not, at least, if they had to pay for the pleasure. The trouble was that he would start a portrait, and then it would not please him; or suddenly, in the midst of it, all interest went. The faces of reality turned to fiction. Mr Kirby in flesh and blood would never have the vitality of Percy, so why waste paint on him? Branwell's friends and acquaintances had an uncomfortable habit, unknown to themselves, of turning into Angrian characters, and he himself, while trying to behave like Branwell Brontë, the promising young portrait-painter, was forever considering the world and those about him with the jaundiced, cynical eye of Alexander Percy.

This latest Percy, who had behind him half a lifetime of experience of women and their ways, made an excellent double into whose exalted frame Branwell could slip at will and find himself at ease. The insignificant Brontë, bespectacled and small, who had not grown an inch since he turned fourteen, vanished with the flick of an eyelid, and Alexander Percy, a positive danger to female society, stood in his place; so that taking tea with Mrs Thompson, wife of his artist friend, became a mild excitement instead of sixty minutes' discomfort. Mrs Thompson, did she but know it, was judged with an appraising eye; the polite young man who sat before her, balancing a teacup and saucer, could strip her in seconds. And not only Mrs Thompson; any maiden, wife or widow who walked the streets of Bradford or anywhere else would fall an easy prey to Percy, had he the mind to take them.

This dual existence must have enabled life to be lived with greater enjoyment. The snubs and slights received by a young man endeavouring to make his way into a wider circle need not even be felt. Alexander Percy gave the snubs. His was the withering glance, the scorching tongue. The knowledge that he could at will assume this second personality must have become a source of secret delight to Branwell, and an ever-present remedy to pain.

Meanwhile, the financial rewards of portrait-painting were slow to come, and he had not given up hope of finding his way into print. If William Dearden was able to get his work published, there was no reason why Branwell should not succeed some day himself. So laying down brush and palette he would take up his pen again, and because 'Oakendale, the bard of Caldene' talked Greek to his wife, and had some local success, Branwell, with his usual lack of judgement, thought the schoolmaster's style must be better than his own, and worthier of imitation – if imitation was a necessity – than anything written by Shakespeare or Keats.

Dearden's *Death of the African Bloodhound* and *The Star Seer, in Five Cantos* were surely, Branwell decided, models of excellence. Not only that – they had actually been published, a fact which carried more weight with him than anything else. A quotation from the *African Bloodhound* shows what a modest place Dearden held in the rank of even minor poets.

> Tis stilly night, and on the good old Town –
> The autumnal moon, resting her silvery orb
> On the white rondure of a fleecy cloud,
> Fair sultaness of Heaven, serenely smiles . . .

Leyland's bloodhounds might grace a London gallery, but Dearden's epitaph upon them would not long be thumbed by a reverent reading public.

> Peace to thy ashes, noble brute! thy death
> To poor humanity reads a lesson loud
> Of faithfulness unswerving. Would that all
> The art of sculpture doth embalm,
> Were worthy of thy praise – deserved the meed
> Of immortality conferred on thee!

Peace to thy ashes, noble Dearden! The bard of Caldene little guessed, as he penned his tribute to the African hounds, that a hundred years later his only claim to fame would be that, sitting in the Cross Roads Inn, between Keighley and Haworth, he had – so he declared – heard Emily Brontë's brother read aloud part of *Wuthering Heights*.

William Dearden does not mention the date of this memorable occasion, which will be discussed in greater detail in Chapter Eleven. According to tradition it took place in 1842, but there is one curious clue which might suggest an earlier date. Dearden, writing of the incident in a letter to the Halifax *Guardian*, said that a contest had been arranged between himself and Branwell Brontë. Each was to write a poem, composed specially for the occasion, and set in some period before the flood. Joseph Leyland was to act as judge. But Branwell, according to Dearden, got his manuscripts mixed, and brought the opening chapters of a novel in mistake for the poem which he had written, and had called *Azrael*, or *Destruction's Eve*. The point of interest is that *Azrael*, far from being freshly composed in the summer of 1842, had at that date already been in existence some four years. It was originally written, according to Branwell's own Notebook, on April 30th, 1838, and transcribed on May 12th of the same year. Therefore if the literary encounter took place in 1842, Branwell had a poem back home at the parsonage which exactly fitted the occasion. If, on the other hand, he did specially compose *Azrael* for the meeting with Dearden – as the terms of the contest stipulated – then the encounter must have taken place in the early summer of 1838, when Branwell was in his Fountain Street lodgings.

The Wanderer was first written in the summer of the Bradford period, on July 31st, and revised and sent to *Blackwood's* in September, 1842. A long and tedious poem, once thought to be by Emily, it tells how a serving officer, many years absent in India, returns to find himself and his home changed, and his lost sweetheart a shade.

Yet Branwell, when he forgot to copy the bard and wrote in the person of Percy, as he had done the year before in *Percy's Last Sonnet*, came nearer to writing well than he gave himself credit for:

Cease, Mourners, cease the sorrowing o'er the Dead,
For if their life be lost its toils are o'er,
And woe and want shall visit them no more;
Nor ever slept they in an earthly bed
Such sleep as that which lulls them dreamless held
In the true chambers of the eternal shore,
Where sacred silence seals each guarded door.
Oh! Turn from tears for these thy bended head
And mourn the Dead alive, whose pleasure flies
And life departs before their benighted eyes,
Yet see no Heaven gleam through the joyless gloom.
These only feel the worm that never dies,
The quenchless fires, the horrors of the tomb.

During his year at Bradford he spent his weekends at Haworth. The parsonage once more rang with sound and life when all three girls were there. Emily and Anne were back home again now, Emily – according to Ellen Nussey – having survived her six months at Law Hill, while Anne had left Dewsbury Moor as early as Christmas, 1837, for reasons of ill-health. Perhaps it was the youngest sister's breakdown that decided Emily to quit teaching under 'the skilled horsewoman' Miss Patchett.

Charlotte was still teaching at Miss Wooler's school, but by the end of May, 1838, she too was home again, having abandoned her post after 'weeks of mental and bodily anguish not to be described'. The fact that she plunged at once into an Angrian romance, in which the now aged Percy, Earl of Northangerland, discusses his mistress and his illegitimate daughter, Caroline, with his son-in-law Zamorna, husband of his legitimate daughter Mary, shows how easily Charlotte could throw off care once she was steeped again in the infernal world.

'Where is Louisa now?' [the father-in-law, Northangerland,
enquires of Zamorna, speaking of the discarded mistress].
'Is she still in your custody?'

'Yes, safe enough – I keep her at a little place on the
other side of the Calabar . . . Why do you ask me so
particularly? Surely you're not jealous, old Puritan?'

Small wonder Charlotte told her friend Ellen: 'A calm and
even mind like yours cannot conceive the feelings of the shattered wretch who is now writing to you.' If Ellen should ever
discover the appalling licence of the world below . . . but the
minute handwriting made every manuscript safe. Nor would
Mary Taylor and her young sister Martha – the entrancing
Patty – ever know, when they stayed at the parsonage a few
days later, that Mary's 'lively spirits and bright chatter' and
'frequent flushes of fever', and Martha, 'chattering as fast as
her little tongue can run, and Branwell standing before her,
laughing at her vivacity' – all described in a letter to Ellen –
would, the instant they left Haworth, send brother and sister
rushing to their manuscripts in an ecstasy of creation, both
intent on making nineteen-year-old Martha not only the
offspring of illicit love but the prey of her dissolute brother-
in-law Zamorna.

Branwell was sometimes torn between turning Charlotte's
friends into Angrian heroines and introducing characters not
known to his sister. His prowess with a gun, after all, brought
him invitations to join shooting parties of a rough and ready
kind. Also, there were certain farmhouses, scattered here and
there on Haworth and Stanbury moors, whose occupants were
either brethren of the Three Graces Lodge, like the saturnine
John Heaton of Well Head, or – and this could be capital fun
– members of one of the local brass bands, with the Heatons
of Ponden rivalling the band of the Merrall boys. One house
in particular seems to have taken Branwell's fancy. Whether it
was indeed Ponden Hall, home of Mr Robert Heaton, or one

87

of the three farmhouses some distance away in mid-moor, known as Low, Middle and Higher Withens, it would in any case appear, from Branwell's description, to be the same house, part manor, part farm, that his sister Emily was to describe as Wuthering Heights. Branwell, in a sketch dated December, 1837, had called it Darkwall, its owner William Thurston and its owner's wife, inevitably, Maria.

The farthest house was one which stood on the highest level of the far pasture land, with large black walls and mossy porch and a plantation of gloomy firs, one clump of which − the oldest and the highest − stretched their horizontal arms above one gable like the Genii of that desolate scene. Beyond this house its long-built walls made a line with the November sky, and the path across them led on to an interminable moor, whose tracks might furnish a long day's sport after snipe or heathcock. But no birds flew near the house except the linnets twittering by hundreds on some wet old wall, and yet despite its loneliness this house was of no common note in the extensive parish, and half the fireside tales of times gone by were sure to take 'Darkwall' for their scene, and its owners for their subject.

At the time when the narrative opens Mr Thurston, who 'was more addicted to vice than virtue', had been absent from home for some time; but he was shortly expected back, and his wife was in the kitchen preparing 'a kingly supper' for her spouse and his cronies.

Suddenly a clatter was heard outside, heralding the arrival, not of Mr Thurston, but of 'a man of such uncommon height attired in short green frock, white cord breeks, and top boots, with a white broad brim on his head, and immense orange whiskers on his face'.

The newcomer was, needless to say, none other than Alexander Percy himself.

'Now, my girls,' he said, 'let me see your lady as soon as you can.'

And therewith he strode to the fire, standing with his back towards it on the hearth, and placing his hat on a table. The servants crowded together, giggling to note the celebrated man, and he looked a noble fellow enough with his superb white forehead and head of auburn curls and cheeks so richly haloed, though their marked lines of dissipation and the athwart glance of his eyes took somewhat from the gazers' admiration, and left a sensation akin to fear. She who had done his bidding returned to usher him into a parlour, but he swore he was not so loath to leave them, and began a verbal salute that made them hardly know where to look for smiling, till the door opening hushed them, and Mrs Thurston entered, who, now dressed with wreathing curls and snow white neck and shoulders, looked as handsome as she before had looked ladylike. Each warmly advancing shook hands and, 'By God,' he said. 'I could not have thought to see my little Maria so much improved by time, it spoils all that I know but it has mended thee . . .'

The brief description of Darkwall, and the arrival of Alexander Percy upon the scene – after which the manuscript breaks off abruptly – is chiefly remarkable for the naïveté of the writer. Here was Branwell, aged twenty and a classical scholar, writing with fair narrative power but with a lamentable ignorance of punctuation and spelling, and now and then betraying an ingenuousness that would be expected in a child of twelve. This suggests that his home upbringing and his sister's company had indeed brought him to an age of

89

maturity in a state of almost childlike innocence. The rough quips of village cronies, the coarse humour of moorland acquaintances, both had left him untouched. He knew no more of 'life' at twenty than he had done at ten, and his 'dissipated' hero was a little boy's image of what a bold, bad man should be.

The poem *Azrael*, or *Destruction's Eve*, which has already been mentioned, was intended to be sterner stuff than the Percy narrative. This was the rebellion of Man before the Flood. It opened with Noah standing before Methuselah's grave, calling on men to turn away from Sin, and Repent! Repent! Noah had barely finished his exhortation when he was interrupted:

> And one arose – upon whose face,
> Passions and crime had left their trace,
> Contending with a tameless pride
> That Man and God alike defied.

Branwell called his rebel Azrael (the Masonic symbol for 'Perfect Intellect', and also the Muslim Angel of Death), but once again he was, of course, Percy under another guise. Azrael protested against Noah, Jehovah, Fate and all tradition, and called on mankind to follow him rather than listen to the threats of an angry God.

The story hardly matters, or the verse either. *Azrael* is interesting because it is Branwell shouting the inevitable young man's challenge to accepted thought and accepted teaching, to his aunt's hymn-book and his father's sermons, to the spectre of death and disease lurking around the corner, which no amount of prayer could evade. The vision of Marah, Azrael's dying wife, who appeared suddenly to warn him of the approaching flood, was not only Mary, warning the young Percy of the dangers of an evil life, but also the spirit of the dead Maria, Branwell's oldest sister, whose shadow was forever lurking in that Haworth grave, rebuking the boy who would forget her.

Maria . . . Mary . . . Marah . . . Branwell could no more escape from the phantom that pervaded his dreams than he could banish his second self; at twenty he was still asking the question he asked at eleven – where to . . . which way . . . which hand, my right or left?

> We say this world was made by One
> Who's seen or heard or known by none.
> We say that He, the Almighty God
> That framed Creation with a nod,
> His wondrous work so well fulfilled
> That – in an hour – it All rebelled!
> That though he loves our race so well
> He hurls our spirits into Hell –
> That though He bids us turn from sin
> He hedges us with tempters in –
> That though He says the world shall stand
> Eternal – perfect – from his hand,
> He's just about to whelm it o'er
> With utter ruin – evermore!
> And all for deeds that we have done
> Though he has made us every one!
> Yes, WE – the image of his form!
> We! The dust to feed the worm!

The poem breaks off abruptly with Azrael pledging Moloch in a glass of wine – Moloch, the harsh god who commanded men to sacrifice that which they cherished most dearly.

The poem remained incomplete. Perhaps Branwell did not consider it worth finishing. It was enough to throw down the gauntlet to the voice of authority, heard in his father's pulpit, symbolizing a faith which he himself no longer held and a way of life he had no wish to follow.

8

A copy of *Modern Domestic Medicine*, by Thomas John Graham, M.D., was one of Mr Brontë's most thumbed books. Notes in his handwriting cover the margins, the most profuse being found on those pages relating to the digestive organs. For Mr Brontë was a martyr to dyspepsia. It is instructive to learn that he found bicarbonate of soda 'very injurious', and was of the opinion that brown bread was irritating and heating to delicate, sensitive stomachs. He also noted that people should sleep with their heads to the north, and should make water once in three or four hours, neither more nor less. Three ounces of white poppy heads and half-an-ounce of elder flowers was good for piles – in short, the 'dear saucy Pat' to whom Cornish Maria Branwell had written in 1812 had become, through widowed loneliness, a hypochondriac.

There is also mention of wine, including sherry and madeira, at twenty-six to thirty shillings a dozen. This is unexpected, for Mr Brontë was president of the local Temperance Society. Perhaps there is some connection between the reference to wine and the letter which he wrote in October, 1838, to Mr Milligan, a surgeon at Keighley, thanking him for some antidote, the nature of which is not specified:

> I have taken your prescription, and after due time, and after having fairly weighed the effects, I can from my own experience (which I judge to be the best authority) honestly assert, that nothing received from the hands of any medical gentleman has ever done me more good ... I have frequently thought that you might have

wondered why I was so *particular* in requiring your signature – the truth is, I wished to have *Medical Authority* for what I might do, in order that I might be able to counteract (under providence) the groundless, yet pernicious, censures of the weak, wicked and wily, who are often on the alert to injure those who are wiser and better than ourselves.

Mr Brontë continued to express his thanks, but gave no hint of the nature of the remedy he had found so beneficial. The phrasing of his letter suggests that, like St Paul, he may have been advised to take a little wine 'for his stomach's sake', and feared that this might attract adverse comment. After all, the wine had to be bought, Haworth was a small place, and it is difficult to keep such things secret.

Significant for a different reason is his underlining, in the volume of *Modern Domestic Medicine*, a remedy for intoxication. '12 drops of pure water of ammonia, taken in a wineglass of milk and water, repeated in ten minutes and again in half-an-hour.' A note in Mr Brontë's hand says: 'Cold water may answer best. B.' The text continues:

> Dr Plet relates the case of a young man of nervous and irritable constitution who on the 22nd of January, 1822, became so violently drunk that he did the most indecent things, and broke everything he could get at. When Dr Plet saw him he was armed with a knife and running at his parents, with his eyes glaring and his mouth foaming. 12 drops of water of ammonia were given him in a glass of sugar and water, and he was calmed immediately, ashamed and confused at his conduct.

The vicar of Haworth notes: 'Only some little effect, only a small quantity, well diluted. B. 1837.' One can assume from this that at some time – or perhaps more than once – during

1837 the drops of ammonia, 'well diluted', were indeed applied: not to himself, very naturally, but possibly to an overexcited Branwell. If the vicar took wine for his stomach's sake the son must have been aware of the fact, and did the same – though for a less innocuous reason. The Temperance Society knew him no more. When a young man has reached his majority, as Branwell did in June, 1838, he will not be dictated to by a retiring, elderly parent.

Someone slept ill within the parsonage walls, though whether it was Branwell, Emily, Charlotte, Anne or even Mr Brontë himself the volume of *Domestic Medicine* does not reveal. The only hint is the 'B. 1838' beside the heading *Nightmare*. The note reads:

> Dr McNash, who has written very ably on the philosophy of sleep, has justly described the sensation of nightmare as being the most horrible that oppress human nature – an inability to move during the paroxysm – dreadful visions of ghosts, etc. According to Dr Buchan people, when oppressed with the nightmare, moan in their sleep, and should be awakened.

Did Mr Brontë, a night-shirted figure, candlestick in hand, go to the back bedroom where his son lay sleeping on May 14th of that year, the date scribbled in Branwell's hand beneath a poem expressing the agony of Harriet?

> O Percy! Percy! *where* art thou? –
> I've sacrificed my God for thee,
> And yet thou wilt not come to me! . . .
> Methought I saw a sudden beam
> Of passing brightness through the room
> Like lightening vanish – Percy, come!
> Leave me not in the dark; t'is cold,
> And something stands beside my bed –

Oh, loose me from its icy hold
That presses on me! Raise my head –
I cannot breathe! . . .

Mr Brontë knew nothing of Harriet, nothing of Azrael, angel of Death – transcribed two days before – nothing of a story called *Wuthering Heights*, later to be read aloud at the Cross Roads Inn, but perhaps existing even now in a first draft which Branwell had been permitted to see:

. . . My fingers closed on the fingers of a little, ice-cold hand! The intense horror of nightmare came over me; I tried to draw back my arm, but the hand clung to it, and a most melancholy voice sobbed, 'Let me in – let me in!' . . . As it spoke, I discerned, obscurely, a child's face looking through the window. Terror made me cruel; and finding it useless to attempt shaking the creature off, I pulled its wrist on to the broken pane, and rubbed it to and fro till the blood ran down and soaked the bedclothes; still it wailed, 'Let me in!' and maintained its tenacious grip, almost maddening me with fear . . . 'Begone!' I shouted. 'I'll never let you in, not if you beg for twenty years.' 'It is twenty years,' mourned the voice, 'I've been a waif for twenty years! . . .'

No panacea for those dreams now; the damage had been done long since, in childhood. The unconscious fears of the sleeping Branwell filled the parsonage with phantoms, the dread of premature disease and death conjuring up the spirit of the lost Maria who wandered in eternity, haunting her brother all his life.

Terror vanished with the day. Poems could remain unfinished, manuscripts be cast into a drawer, paintings left to dry upon the easel. Life was all important – visiting new scenes, meeting new people, forgetting all the ghosts which came by night. Activity was what Branwell most desired.

The whole world was changing. He could not impress the fact strongly enough upon his father and aunt. The invention of the steam engine, the coming of the railway, had altered, was in the process of altering out of all recognition, the face of the countryside. Soon no one would travel by road at all, but go by train from one end of the country to the other. This would not greatly affect the older generation; but for the young, for people like himself, it meant new opportunities, new ventures, a social revolution and nothing would ever be the same again.

No doubt such talk was received quietly at the parsonage. Neither Mr Brontë nor his sister-in-law had any desire to travel, either by coach or rail. Their attitude must have been exasperating to Branwell. Movement excited him – the hiss of steam, the power of engines, the talk of engineers employed upon construction. It was lively, it was new, it belonged to the future. In 1839 he talked less of his painting. His enthusiasm was all for the railway. Whenever opportunity could be found he would go over to Hebden Bridge or Todmorden and watch the work in process, for the line from Manchester to Leeds was to pass through the Todmorden valley.

The canal running from Littleborough to Todmorden and passing Sowerby, Luddenden Foot and Hebden Bridge was the chief means of transport for stores and material to be used in the construction of the railway. Every day barges travelled to and fro, anchoring for the night very often in the cul-de-sac, or 'basin', at Luddenden Foot, when the bargees would spend their evenings at the Woodman, the Weavers Arms or the Anchor and Shuttle. These men fascinated Branwell. They were a law unto themselves, rowdy, rough, coarse, but of fine physique; these were the people he would prefer to draw and paint; not dull, drab creatures like Mr and Mrs Kirby.

Bargees – or 'boaties', as they were called – cared for nothing and no one. They were travelling gypsies, drinking, fighting, laughing. Their way of life was crude, but it was free. Branwell felt at ease with them. They did not know that he was 'parson's son' from Haworth; they did not ask who he was, they did not care. All they saw was a little red-haired chap who glanced up at them from behind his spectacles and smiled. They welcomed him aboard their barges. He showed no side. He made them laugh. This, Branwell must have thought, was even better than the George at Bradford; because in the George, or at the Union Cross in Halifax, the poets he met had succeeded in getting their poems published and the artists had sold their pictures, while he, Branwell, was still an apprentice and a nonentity in their eyes. With the boaties it was different; he would feel anonymous, secure. The knowledge, too, that his father would disapprove, would be shocked and possibly horrified, would have been an added stimulant. Since university and the Royal Academy had been denied him, it was best to go to the opposite extreme, to mix with men like these, who cared nothing for intellect, who worked with their hands.

Back at home things became quieter than ever. Anne, with silent determination, took a post as governess with a Mrs Ingham, of Blake Hall, Mirfield. No one could dissuade her from so doing. The youngest Brontë had a strong will beneath the quiet façade. The desire to earn her living, and so spare her father's purse, was synonymous with freedom. A month or so later Charlotte also tore herself away from the insidious delights of Caroline Vernon in love with her own brother-in-law, and took a temporary post as governess with a Mrs Sidgwick of Stonegappe.

The eldest and the youngest were earning money. The other two were not. Emily, brushing the carpet, sweeping the stairs or peeling potatoes in the kitchen under Tabby's eye, was as insulated from intrusion as a hermit crab.

No – there was something in his face,
Some nameless thing they could not trace,
And something in his voice's tone,
Which turned their blood as chill as stone.
The ringlets of his long black hair
Fell o'er a cheek most ghastly fair.
Youthful he seemed – but worn as they
Who spend too soon their youthful day . . .

Her private world held no terrors for her. Any dark nameless ghost was welcome.

Branwell had quitted Mrs Kirby's rooms in Fountain Street. No rich client, desirous of having his portrait painted, had appeared. Twelve months' residence in Bradford had little to show beyond a heap of canvasses, most of them unfinished, which he might just as well give away to the sitters as expect payment for; the rest could be stacked against a wall in the studio back-bedroom.

He was twenty-two in June, 1839, and at that age Joseph Leyland had modelled Spartacus and shown it at the Manchester Exhibition. But Branwell had not had Leyland's opportunities, including the patronage of rich people like the Rawsons of Hope Hall, Halifax. No, something would turn up. He would sell a portrait yet, or have a poem published; meanwhile, it was summer, and he amused himself by going about the countryside, and, best of all, taking a trip to Liverpool, perhaps by barge, with young Hartley Merrall and one or two others, where they enjoyed themselves so much that they stayed longer than they intended, and Branwell, in his excitement, ran short of funds.

Sight-seeing, with a bunch of companions, was what Percy would have done with Montmorency and O'Connor. Going into St Jude's church, where the evangelical Hugh McNeile was preaching, and watching the famous preacher shake his fist at Popery and the wicked wiles of Rome, was an echo of what these Angrian friends had done in an earlier manuscript, when they visited the Wesleyan chapel in Slug Street and Percy himself had dressed up as the Reverend Ashworth.

The forty-four-year-old Irish preacher McNeile was the draw of Liverpool, his opposition to the church of Rome a byword, but most delightful of all – to Branwell and his mocking friends – was the tirade against the celibacy of the Romish priesthood, which spelt 'the degradation of men, the anguish, and agony and ruin of women, and the deliberate murder of little children'. The subdued 'Hear, hear!' would not be heard, but the stifled laughter might, and Branwell, scribbling notes from the sermon to send to his father, must have nudged his friends to silence, and thought what a superb parody could be made of the whole affair in some future Angrian tale, with Percy and Co, dolled up in sable attire, and St Jude's transformed into Sanctification Chapel.

'What happens,' thundered the Reverend McNeile, 'when the Papal system mars the lovely process of marriage? O, what but unsubdued passions, uncontrolled conduct, baseness and degradation, a woeful blank in the happiness of our race, a dismal eclipse of the soft radiance of Christianity, in the lurid, the blood-stained horrors of Antichrist!'

'No Popery!' was a famous Evangelical cry. Branwell was used to it at Haworth, but sometimes he thought of his Irish grandmother, who was born a Catholic and changed her faith on marriage, and he may have wondered if it was his Papist Irish blood that made him ridicule Protestant ranters.

What else Branwell and his friends did in Liverpool besides visit St Jude's church remains obscure. The sea and the docks on Merseyside must have proved a great attraction. So much so, perhaps, that according to Leyland's brother Francis, who was not of the party, 'an attack of tic compelled him [Branwell] to resort to opium, in some form, as an anodyne, whose soothing effect in pain he had previously known'.

This may have been the tale in after-years. An attack of tic drove de Quincey to laudanum – Branwell would have read this in de Quincey's *Confessions*. The same remedy soothed frayed nerves, and was a common panacea for diarrhoea and coughs. More significant still, it was said to ward off consumption.

Branwell may have taken his first dose of laudanum for any of these reasons. The fear of a convulsive attack seizing him in Liverpool, as it possibly had done in London four years before, would be enough to send him to the nearest pharmacy. His father noted in the volume of *Domestic Medicine* that *tic douleureux* are French words signifying a 'painful convulsive fit', and they should be pronounced 'tic doolaros'. In those days opium could be obtained with the utmost ease for a few pence. Anything that dulled pain, or the apprehension of pain, and stimulated the imagination too, was likely to attract Branwell; besides, the very fact that opium had inspired Coleridge and de Quincey gave the drug a romantic flavour. If de Quincey could take fifty-three ounces of laudanum on one of his peak days, then it could not harm Branwell to take three. It was something that would not be noticed at home, either. It was different from drinking.

The *Pharmacological Basis of Therapeutics*, a more modern work than Mr Brontë's volume of *Domestic Medicine*, reports that 'the vast majority of addicts are persons classified as neurotic or constitutional psychopathic inferiors, and addiction is only one manifestation of their fundamental personality defect . . . The drug provides an escape mechanism from reality, a way of release from the failures and disappointments of everyday life, a means of bridging the gap between ambition and accomplishment.'

To a boy of twenty-two who had not passed through the Royal Academy schools or painted the picture of the year, whose poems were refused by *Blackwood's*, whose letters to Wordsworth remained unanswered and who still passionately desired to believe in his own genius, laudanum – with its ten per cent of opium – spelt liberation.

Here was a way to fulfilment without effort. A nagging conscience became numb. And, most wonderful of all, nightmares turned to dreams, the Erinyes to the Eumenides, the reproachful warning Marah to a clinging Proserpine. Henceforth Branwell would know where to turn when doubt and disappointment sounded in his father's voice, when his aunt asked for the twentieth time if he had sold a picture, when Charlotte, blunter still, inquired his plans. How brighter far than hers the colours and the images of his infernal world!

Back in Haworth Branwell painted young Hartley Merrall's portrait – perhaps a gift to his bride Harriet – and as a finishing touch decorated the four corners of the canvas with the names of Bach, Mozart, Haydn and Handel. This was a tribute to his friend Hartley, who, like his three brothers, was a keen musician.

For a time the talk was all of Liverpool. Branwell's enthusiasm was infectious. The family must go – his father, his aunt, the girls; nobody had lived if they had not seen Liverpool. But inevitably, as always with the hesitant projects of the older generation, interest faded. His father was too busy – he was still waiting for a curate to replace Mr Hodgson, his previous assistant – and no doubt his aunt felt that the house could not be left in Tabitha's charge. As for the girls, the girls would all have had their own excuses. Emily would not go without Anne, and Anne was due back at Mrs Ingham's. Only Charlotte, escaped from her temporary post with Mrs Sidgwick, was free for a holiday, and she, of course, preferred to go off to Bridlington with Ellen Nussey.

Branwell could go nowhere. July in Liverpool had emptied his small exchequer. He could not even afford to send a couple of sovereigns to poor Mrs Robinson, widow of his old art master at Leeds, as an acknowledgement – so he told his artist friend Thompson in a letter – of the kindness with which I was treated by her and our poor Master. But I am going to Leeds I believe shortly, and then I hope to be able in some degree to help one whom too many – I am afraid – have injured. Indeed, it astonished me when I read the hints contained in your letter, though I need not have wondered for this world is all rottenness . . .

The note concluded with an irritable word for Mrs Kirby, who expected him to go to Bradford to varnish her portraits. 'Mrs Kirby's name is an eyesore to me – what does the woman mean? How can I come paddling to Bradford with my wallet on my back in order to varnish her portraits . . .' This letter from Branwell is dated August 14th, 1839. No later letter exists to explain the reference to Mrs Robinson. The art master and his ill-treated widow fade from view. Nor did Branwell take up any appointment in Leeds, which his letter suggested he may have had in mind.

Leyland, the sculptor, was back in Halifax, which made that town even more interesting than Bradford. He had found fame in London, but not stability. He took a studio at the back of No 10, The Square, and with a cynical disregard for his own artistic reputation advertised the premises as:

Halifax Marble Works,
Square Road,
J. B. Leyland, Sculptor.
Monuments, busts, tombs, tablets, chiffonier slabs and all kinds of marble work used in the uphol-stery business, made to order. A variety of marble chimney pieces on view, cleaned, repaired, or set up.

If Joseph Leyland, darling of the critics, could not make a living out of sculpture, then nobody could blame an unknown artist, Branwell decided, for failing after twelve months in Bradford.

On October 14th a large exhibition was opened at the national school in Sowerby Bridge, on behalf of the Mechanics' Institute, to which Leyland contributed a head of his beloved lamented African bloodhound and a bust, The Lady of Kirklees, inspired by a poem of his and Branwell's indefatigable friend, William Dearden. Branwell, with Leyland and his friends, went to the exhibition, where a heterogeneous collection of objects had been assembled, from a sword said to have been Napoleon's to Wesley's wig. The big names of the neighbourhood graced the occasion: the Priestleys of White Windows, the Rawsons of Haugh End, John Crossley of Scaitcliffe Hall, barrister, and inheritor, through his Lockwood mother, of all the Ewood lands once held by poor Johnny Grimshaw. The 'gentry', transformed into fictitious guise in many an Angrian tale, could now be observed at closer quarters. Mixing with them, though a little apart, of course, would be Joseph Leyland's humbler friends, landlords William Haigh and Jackson from the Craig Vale and White Horse Inns, and the hostess from the hostelry at Heptonstall.

It was a happy way to spend an autumn day: starting off from the coach's stopping-place, the Swan Hotel at Halifax, halts for refreshment along the seven-mile stretch of road at both Sowerby Bridge and Luddenden Foot, thence back again to Halifax, Leyland and his friends to No. 10, The Square, and Branwell to pick up his Haworth coach at the Wheatsheaf Inn.

It was no way, though, to earn money. Winter was approaching. Leyland had commissions to fulfill, only half finished and already past delivery date, and Branwell had to face the fact that unless he accepted the post of tutor which had been proposed to him, and which at least gave him the chance of seeing the Lakeland country he had always hoped to visit, home of Wordsworth, Southey and Hartley Coleridge, he would be obliged to spend the winter of 1839–40 kicking his heels in Haworth without a penny in his pocket.

Charlotte, writing three days after Christmas to Ellen Nussey, said:

> One thing, however, will make the daily routine more unvaried than ever. Branwell, who used to enliven us, is to leave us in a few days to enter the situation of a private tutor in the neighbourhood of Ulverston. How he will like it or settle remains to be seen; at present he is full of hope and resolution. I, who know his variable nature, and his strong turn for active life, dare not be too sanguine.

9

Branwell's own impressions of life with Mr Robert Postlethwaite of Broughton House, Broughton-in-Furness, are given in a letter to John Brown which he wrote on March 13th, 1840, and which so amused the Worshipful Master of the Three Graces Lodge, and his brother William, that it was treasured in the Brown family until a few years before William's death in 1876, when it disappeared. The letter has been quoted many times as proof of Branwell's shocking character. It must be quoted again, not only because it gives clues to individuals who have escaped notice, but because it is entertaining for its own sake.

Old Knave of Trumps,
    Don't think I have forgotten you, though I have delayed so long in writing to you. It was my purpose to send you a yarn as soon as I could find materials to spin one with, and it is only just now that I have had time to turn myself round and know where I am. If you saw me now, you would not know me, and you would laugh to hear the character the people give me. Oh, the falsehood and hypocrisy of this world! I am fixed in a little retired town by the sea-shore, among wild woody hills that rise round me – huge, rocky, and capped with clouds.
    My employer is a retired county magistrate, a large landowner, and of a right hearty and generous disposition. His wife is a quiet, silent, and amiable woman, and his sons are two fine, spirited lads. My landlord is a respectable surgeon, and six days out of seven is as drunk

as a lord! His wife is a bustling, chattering, kind–hearted–soul; and his daughter! – oh! death and damnation! Well, what am I? That is, what do they think I am? A most calm, sedate, sober, abstemious, patient, mild–hearted, virtuous, gentlemanly philosopher, the picture of good works, and the treasure–house of righteous thoughts. Cards are shuffled under the table–cloth, glasses are thrust into the cupboard, if I enter the room. I take neither spirits, wine, nor malt liquors. I dress in black, and smile like a saint or martyr. Everybody says, 'What a good young gentleman is Mr Postlethwaite's tutor!' This is fact, as I am a living soul, and right comfortably do I laugh at them. I mean to continue in their good opinion. I took a half year's farewell of old friend whisky at Kendal on the night after I left. There was a party of gentlemen at the Royal Hotel, and I joined them. We ordered in supper and whisky–toddy as 'hot as hell'! They thought I was a physician, and put me in the chair. I gave sundry toasts that were washed down at the same time, till the room spun round and the candles danced in our eyes. One of the guests was a respectable old gentleman with powdered head, rosy cheeks, fat paunch, and ringed fingers. He gave 'The Ladies' . . . after which he brayed off with a speech; and in two minutes, in the middle of a grand sentence, he stopped, wiped his head, looked wildly round, stammered, coughed, stopped again and called for his slippers. The waiter helped him to bed. Next a tall Irish squire and a native of the land of Israel began to quarrel about their countries; and, in the warmth of argument, discharged their glasses, each at his neighbour's throat instead of his own. I recommended bleeding, purging, and blistering; but they administered each other a real 'Jem Warder', so I flung my tumbler on the floor too, and swore I'd join 'Old Ireland!' A regular rumpus ensued, but we were tamed at last. I found myself in bed next morning, with a bottle of porter, a glass, and a corkscrew beside me. Since then I have not tasted anything stronger than milk-and-water, nor, I hope, shall, till I return at mid-summer; when we will see about it. I am getting as fat as Prince William at Springhead, and as godly as his friend, Parson Winterbotham. My hand shakes no longer. I ride to the banker's at Ulverston with Mr Postlethwaite, and sit drinking tea and talking scandal with old ladies. As to the young ones! I have one sitting by me just now – fair-faced, blue-eyed, dark-haired, sweet eighteen – she little thinks the devil is so near her!

I was delighted to see thy note, old squire, but I do not understand one sentence – you will perhaps know what I mean . . . How are all about you? I long to hear and see them again. How is the 'Devil's Thumb', whom men call —, and the 'Devil in Mourning', whom they call —? How are —, and —, and the Doctor; and him whose eyes Satan looks out of, as from windows – I mean —, esquire? How are little —, —, —, —, 'Longshanks', and the rest of them? Are they married, buried, devilled and damned? When I come I'll give them a good squeeze of the hand; till then I am too godly for them to think of. That bow-legged devil used to ask me impertinent questions which I answered him in kind. Beelzebub will make of him a walking-stick! Keep to thy teetotalism, old squire, till I return; it will mend thy old body . . . Does 'Little Nosey' think I have forgotten him? No, by Jupiter! nor his clock either. I'll send him a remembrancer some of these days! But I must talk to someone prettier than thee; so good-night, old boy, and

Believe me thine,

The Philosopher.

Write directly. Of course you won't show this letter; and for heaven's sake, blot out all the lines scored with red ink.

The letter, dashed off so gaily by a carefree Branwell, was shown to all of Haworth; or at least to that portion of Haworth society which would foregather, after the Three Graces Lodge had been closed in perfect harmony in their Masonic rooms, in the 'snug' at the Black Bull, under the benevolent eye of the landlord 'Little Nosey'.

That the Worshipful Master did blot out the lines scored with red ink is evident from the surviving copy of the letter, but a list of the members of the Three Graces Lodge for the year 1840, which was in existence until a few years ago, gave one 'esquire' among them. He was John Heaton.

John Heaton, woolcomber, aged twenty-three when he became a member of the Lodge in 1830, was one of the many Ponden Hall cousins scattered around the Worth valley among the acres known as Dean Fields. According to a tithe list for 1840, he held twenty-four acres at Well Head on Oakworth moor, with one brother at Upper Pitcher Clough and another at Slippery Ford. Sheep Hole and Silver Hill, Old Snap and Throstles Nest – all were Heaton holdings, the very names lyrical enough to set imagination on fire. If Branwell's 'esquire', whose 'eyes Satan looks out of, as from windows', inspired Nelly Dean's description of Heathcliff's eyes, 'that couple of black fiends, so deeply buried, who never opened their windows boldly, but lurk glinting under them like devil's spies', then Heathcliff's identification with John Heaton becomes possible.

As to the rest – the Devil's Thumb, the Devil in Mourning, Longshanks and the bow-legged devil – a freemason perhaps could wrestle with the symbolism; but the Mosleys, Toothills, Akroyds, Greenwoods, Blands and Ropers who figure among the old lost minutes of the Three Graces Lodge would doubtless have recognized themselves in 1840. So would 'Prince William of Springhead', either a Merrall or William Cockcroft Greenwood, son of Joseph Greenwood, J.P., and Parson Winterbotham, Baptist minister of West Lane chapel, Haworth, since 1831.

The evening in the Royal Hotel, Kendal, sounds so like Percy on a spree with O'Connor and Montmorency that doubt enters the mind whether the event can ever have taken place, except in Branwell's imagination. Would a young tutor risk getting drunk the night before he entered upon a situation, and in a town where his employer might be known? So much was wishful thinking, so much parody, so much high spirits born of doubt. Percy did all these deeds in fantasy: he wore the laurel wreath and waved the wand, he was villain, king and hero, and he bore the brunt of the blame when things went ill, just as a wooden soldier once committed the many sins a small boy did not dare.

Success with women was one of Percy's greatest boasts. From the day when the young Alexander knelt at the feet of Augusta, who was to become his first wife, until the time when the ageing Earl of Northangerland traded his mistress to his son-in-law, Percy's only moments of freedom from female entanglements were on the battlefield. Branwell, sitting in the same room as the daughter of the Broughton surgeon with whom he lodged, would remember the small attempts at gallantry which had hitherto seemed successful: an arm to Ellen Nussey, a duet with Mary Taylor, laughter at the irrepressible 'Patty', polite exchanges with Mrs Kirby's niece during the painting of the portrait. Now, on his own for six months, more completely separated from home than he had ever been at Bradford, some slight attempt at conquest must be made.

Charlotte, in a letter to Ellen Nussey some eight months afterwards, said: 'Did I not once tell you of an instance of a relative of mine who cared for a young lady till he began to suspect that she cared more for him and then instantly conceived a sort of contempt for her? You know to what I allude. Never as you value your life mention the circumstances – Mary is my study – for the contempt, the remorse, the misconstruction which follow the development of feelings in

109

themselves noble, warm, generous, devoted and profound, but which, being too freely revealed, too frankly bestowed, are not estimated at their real value.'

That the scornful, strong-minded Mary Taylor should ever have had a penchant for Branwell seems unlikely, but both Charlotte and Branwell, obsessed with sex in Angria, lived out their fiction in real life. A glance from Mary would have amounted, in the eyes of both brother and sister, to a declaration.

It is significant that the opening narrator of *Wuthering Heights*, Mr Lockwood, describes sentiments identical with those of Branwell at Broughton-in-Furness, and in Branwell's own particular style. Lockwood says:

> While enjoying a month of fine weather at the sea-coast, I was thrown into the company of a most fascinating creature; a real goddess in my eyes, as long as she took no notice of me. I 'never told my love' vocally; still, if looks have language, the merest idiot might have guessed I was head over ears; she understood me at last, and looked a return – the sweetest of all imaginable looks. And what did I do? I confess it with shame – shrunk icily into myself, like a snail; at every glance retired colder and farther; till finally the poor innocent was led to doubt her own senses, and overwhelmed with confusion at her supposed mistake, persuaded her mamma to decamp. By this curious turn of disposition I have gained the reputation of deliberate heart-lessness; how undeserved, I alone can appreciate.

Branwell, like young Mr Lockwood, was bold on paper, certainly in the letter to John Brown, and perhaps in letters to his sisters at the parsonage. Whether he was also bold in person, vis-à-vis the surgeon's daughter, has yet to be proved. Tradition has it that his appointment with Mr Robert Postlethwaite, J.P., terminated in June, 1840, 'at his father's wish'. Mr Brontë presumably did not wish it to get about

110

Haworth that the magistrate had asked him to remove his son, who, 'imbibing too freely', according to Postlethwaite tradition, had not proved himself the best of all possible influences upon his young sons John and William.

Whatever Branwell's conduct as tutor at Broughton House, and whatever sighs and glances passed between him and the surgeon's daughter in the house where he lodged – surely less satisfactory than those relaxing moments experienced in the barges on the Todmorden canal – Branwell's main desire, to make himself known to Hartley Coleridge, at Nab Cottage, on the banks of Rydal Water, came to fulfilment during his employment with Mr Postlethwaite. The letter that he wrote to the poet on April 20th, enclosing his second *Harriet* poem, as well as two translated Odes from Horace, was in much the same vein as that with which he had approached Coleridge's neighbour Wordsworth, though written perhaps with more modesty and care.

Sir,—

It is with much reluctance that I venture to request, for the perusal of the following lines, a portion of the time of one upon whom I can have no claim, and should not dare to intrude; but I do not, personally, know a man on whom to rely for an answer to the question I shall put, and I could not resist my longing to ask a man from whose judgement there would be little hope of appeal.

Since my childhood I have been wont to devote the hours I could spare from other and very different employments to efforts at literary composition, always keeping the results to myself, nor have they in more than two or three instances been seen by any other. But I am about to enter active life, and prudence tells me not to waste my time which must make my independence; yet, sir, I love writing too well to fling

111

aside the practice of it without an effort to ascertain whether I could turn it to account, not in *wholly* maintaining myself, but in *aiding* my maintenance, for I do not sigh after fame and am not ignorant of the folly or the fate of those who, without ability, would depend for their lives upon their pens; but I seek to know, and venture, though with shame, to ask from one whose word I must respect: whether, by periodical or other writing, I could please myself with writing, and make it subservient to living.

I would not, with this view, have troubled you with a composition in verse, but any piece I have in prose would too greatly trespass upon your patience, which, I fear, if you look over the verse, will be more than sufficiently tried. I feel the egotism of my language, but I have none, sir, in my heart, for I feel beyond all encouragement from myself, and hope for none from you.

Should you give an opinion upon what I send, it will, however condemnatory, be most gratefully received by,

Sir, your most humble servant,
P. B. Brontë.

The first piece is only the sequel of one striving to depict the fall from unguided passion into neglect, despair, and death. It ought to show an hour too near those of pleasure for repentance, and too near death for hope. The translations are two out of many made from Horace, and given to assist an answer to the question – would it be possible to obtain remuneration for translations such as these from that or any other classical author?

Hartley Coleridge, to his eternal credit, must have answered, for Branwell, in a letter written on June 27th, the day after his birthday, reminds the poet of the delightful day he had spent in his company at Ambleside.

Hartley Coleridge, eldest son of Samuel Taylor Coleridge, and one of the least-known and most intriguing figures in English literature, would have been at this time forty-three. A child of brilliant promise, idolized by his parents, loved by Wordsworth, Southey and indeed all who knew him, he gave signs, on adolescence, of so acute a sensibility, so nervous and highly strung a temperament, that although he survived school, entered university, and obtained a fellowship at Oriel, the breakdown, when it came, was half-expected; the father, although he had not bequeathed insanity to his son, had bred a being who could in no way face reality, who shrank from pain, who could not open a letter without trembling, and who was constitutionally incapable of leading a normal life.

The erratic swing from extravagant hilarity to deep melancholy, increased by bouts of heavy drinking, made it impossible for him to hold his fellowship; he was obliged to forfeit it, to the shame and sorrow of himself and his family. Here was a neurotic who was saved from suicide or some other form of violent outburst by an ability to spill excessive emotional energy on paper.

His poems, at their worst, would shame the bard of Caldene. His sonnets, at their best, can compare with Shakespeare's. This strange, lovable near-genius was so far from being able to fend for himself that, after some painful years of struggle to be a schoolmaster, he retired to Grasmere, where he was cared for by a farmer's widow until she died. He then lived with another young farmer and his wife, later moving with them to Nab Cottage, Rydal Water, where he ended his days.

Hartley Coleridge's book of poems, published in 1833, his contributions to *Blackwood's Magazine*, and his series of 'Yorkshire Worthies' would have been read and enjoyed by Branwell before ever he took his post as tutor at Broughton-in-Furness. Indeed, the sonnet written with a backward glance at childhood would seem such an echo of Branwell's own sentiments that it is curious the boy did not approach Hartley

Coleridge originally, rather than waste his efforts as a letter-writer upon the elderly Wordsworth.

> Long time a child, and still a child, when years
> Had painted manhood on my cheek, was I;
> For yet I lived like one not born to die;
> A thriftless prodigal of smiles and tears,
> No hope I needed, and I knew no fears.
> But sleep, though sweet, is only sleep, and waking
> I waked to sleep no more, at once o'ertaking
> The vanguard of my age, with all arrears
> Of duty on my back. Nor child nor man,
> Nor youth, nor sage, I find my head is grey,
> For I have lost the race I never ran:
> A rathe December blights my lagging May;
> And still I am a child, tho' I be old,
> Time is my debtor for my years untold.

One of the strangest things about Hartley Coleridge was his appearance. He was barely five feet high, and – there must have been some congenital cause for this – when he was quite young his thick dark hair turned white, and he walked with the gait of an old man. This touching, shuffling creature, with his dark lustrous eyes, who loved all animals and little children, who sometimes, in his absent-minded fits, would wander from his cottage home and forget to return, alarming the friends who cared for him, was one of the few established writers ever to encourage Branwell in the hope that he might some day win a small place for himself in literature.

No record, alas, exists of their conversation that day by Rydal Water, or of what the older man thought of Harriet, Augusta, Percy and the sins of Jordan Hall; but surely at some moment in their time together Branwell would have discovered that he and Charlotte were not alone in their infernal world, that, long before Angria had been created at Haworth, the dream continent of Ejuxria had become real to the young Hartley Coleridge; that islands, countries peopled with statesmen and generals, had had their existence in his mind from boyhood through adolescence into manhood, and were perhaps still, to the prematurely aged man of forty-three, more vivid and real than the shepherds on the fells.

His brother Derwent, writing of Hartley's childhood 'play' after his death, said:

A spot of waste ground was appropriated to his use. This was divided into kingdoms, and subdivided into provinces, each of the former being assigned to one of his playmates. A canal was to run through the whole, upon which ships were to be built. A tower and armoury, a theatre and a 'chemistry-house' (under which mines were expected to be formed) were to be built, and considered common property. War was to be declared and battles fought between the sovereign powers . . . and he had a scheme for training cats, and even rats, for various offices and labours, civil and military.

His usual mode of introducing the subject was – 'Derwent, I have had letters from Ejuxria,' then came his budget of news, his words flowing on in an endless stream, and his countenance bearing witness to the inspi- ration – shall I call it? – by which he was agitated.

This resemblance to the Angrian and Gondal 'play' of the Brontës is uncanny; and the discovery of a mutual obsession would forge an instant bond of sympathy between twenty- two-year-old Branwell and the poet of forty-three. The urge that had driven Hartley Coleridge to drinking, and to what must have seemed to his friends an aimless existence in the hills among simple people, was surely the same flight from reality that drove Branwell deeper, year by year, into the infernal world. Here he was master, here he controlled his puppets, and here the inordinate ambition which, both in himself and in Hartley Coleridge, fought to overcome a sense of inferiority could best be satisfied, where it could meet no challenge. Better to be lord and master of Angria and Ejuxria than measure oneself against superior brains; better to converse with shepherds and boaties, a little god and an accepted friend, than be worsted in an encounter, not only with intellectuals, but with the more common-place minds of day-by-day as well.

One of the favourite Ejuxrian 'plays' of the young Hartley was the tale of Scauzan, a subtle and intellectual villain, and Scauzan's father, a giant, who was continually outlawed and persecuted by his son. The significance of this fantasy – Hartley's unconscious resentment against the genius of his father, which he could never hope to equal – is obvious, although Hartley's brother Derwent, speaking of the childhood game, was unaware of its meaning.

Similarly, Branwell's Angrian hero must surely have had some deep-seated, if unconscious, inspiration in his own father. Into the character of Alexander Percy, with his dead wife Mary whom he could not forget and a beloved daughter of the same name, can be read not only Branwell himself but also his father. Branwell the child, asleep in Mr Brontë's room, the unknowing medium for his father's loneliness and frustration, worked out in fantasy the rebellions of them both, bringing to fruition the dreams and ambitions that had never, would never, achieve reality.

Today, Branwell Brontë and Hartley Coleridge, alike in so much, possessing the same weaknesses, fated indeed to die within a few months of one another with minds and bodies wasted from the same cause, could have sat by Rydal Water and hammered out the reason for their deep-seated fears, and perhaps even helped one another to find some alleviation of their trouble. In the spring of 1840 Hartley Coleridge could only shake Branwell by the hand and wish him luck, advise perhaps on his reading matter, and suggest that he should continue with

116

his translation of the Odes of Horace. He may not have felt qualified to judge the introspective Harriet, with her doubts of the Almighty, her longing for her lover Percy despite her adulterous shame. A young man who had written so many lines *as* a young woman, rather than *about* one, might have seemed singular even to an eccentric like Hartley Coleridge.

And Branwell, waving farewell to the hunched, white-haired figure by the lakeside, would not consider for one moment that the poet's tragedy was similar to his own, that although Coleridge was a known and respected figure in the literary world he still represented failure, both as man and as poet, and that those melancholy eyes, those trembling hands, conveyed a warning to Branwell not to sink too deeply into his infernal world, lest the myriad oceans should engulf him, just as Hartley Coleridge had been drowned in the Ejuxrian sea. The note scribbled years before, when he was seventeen, at the conclusion of an Angrian manuscript, might have served as a further reminder, had he possessed the intuition to interpret it: 'That night I dreamt I saw Angria devouring Percy . . .'

The conversation, that spring day on Ambleside, was mainly literary: this is born out by the letter Branwell sent to Hartley Coleridge after he had returned to Haworth. He had already, from time to time during the past few years, amused himself by translating Odes from Horace; now, encouraged and inspired by Coleridge's own translations, Branwell had completed the entire contents of the First Book, with the exception of Ode XXXVIII – a note beneath the number explaining why: 'This ode I have no heart to attempt after having heard Mr H. Coleridge's translation, on May day, at Ambleside.'

His letter to the poet said:

Sir – You will, perhaps, have forgotten me, but it will be long before I forget my first conversation with a man of real intellect, in my first visit to the classic lakes of Westmorland. During the delightful day which

I had the honour of spending with you at Ambleside, I received permission to transmit to you, as soon as finished, the first book of a translation of Horace, in order that, after a glance over it, you might tell me whether it was worth further notice or better fit for the fire.

I have – I fear most negligently, and amid other very different employments – striven to translate two books, the first of which I have presumed to send you, and will you, sir, stretch your past kindness by telling me whether I should amend and pursue the work or let it rest in peace?

Great corrections I feel it wants, but till I feel that the work might benefit me, I have no heart to make them; yet if your judgement prove in any way favourable, I will rewrite the whole, without sparing labour to reach perfection.

I dared not have attempted Horace but that I saw the utter worthlessness of all former translations, and thought that a better one, by whomsoever executed, might meet with some little encouragement. I long to clear up my doubts by the judgement of one whose opinion I should revere, and – but I suppose I am dreaming – one to whom I should be proud to inscribe anything of mine which any publisher would look at, unless, as is likely enough, the work would disgrace the name as much as the name would honour the work. Amount of remuneration I should not look to – as anything would be everything – and whatever it might be, let me say that my bones would have no rest unless by written agreement a division should be made of the profits (little or much) between myself and him through whom alone I could hope to obtain a hearing with that formidable personage, a London bookseller.

Excuse my unintelligibility, haste, and appearance of presumption, and —

Believe me to be, Sir, your most humble and grateful servant,

P. B. Brontë.

If anything in this note should displease you, lay it, sir, to the account of inexperience and *not* impudence.

It was a mistake, perhaps, to dismiss as worthless the efforts of Cowley, Pope, Dryden, Congreve and many other previous translators of Horace; and, too, a fault in taste and judgement to mention the word 'remuneration', with the suggestion that profits should be shared, the older poet tipped, as it were, for his courtesy in furthering the cause of one unknown (a common mistake among many would-be writers), but Hartley Coleridge would seem the last man in the world to take offence.

Whether he answered the letter, what advice he gave, Branwell did not disclose. His translations from Horace remained unpublished until 1923, when the late John Drinkwater had them privately printed by the Pelican Press. Mr Drinkwater said in his introduction:

They are unequal, and they have many of the bad tricks of writing that come from out of some deeply rooted defect of character. But they also have a great many passages of clear lyrical beauty, and they have something of the style that comes from a spiritual understanding, as apart from mere formal knowledge, of great models.

In conclusion, John Drinkwater said:

I do not wish to advance any extravagant claim for this little book, but I think it adds appreciably to the evidence that Branwell Brontë was the second poet in his family, and a very good second at that . . .

119

The reader who has no Latin can only appreciate a translation from that language on its own merits. The Odes of Horace were written for other audiences, and to suit different tastes. It would throw light on Branwell to know which, among the thirty-seven that he translated, gave him the most pleasure. The IVth, *To Sestius*, would seem to come nearest to a reflection of his own moods and fancies.

Rough winter melts beneath the breeze of spring,
Nor shun refitted ships the silenced sea,
Nor man nor beasts to folds or firesides cling,
Nor hoar frosts whiten over field and tree;
But rising moons, each balmy evening, see
Fair Venus with her Nymphs and Graces join,
In merry dances tripping o'er the lea;
While Vulcan makes his roaring furnace shine
And bids his Cyclops arms in sinewy strength combine.

Now let us, cheerful, crown our heads with flowers,
Spring's first fruits, offered to the newborn year,
And sacrifice beneath the budding bowers,
A lamb, or kid as Faunus may prefer:
But – pallid Death, an equal visitor,
Knocks at the poor man's hut, the monarch's tower;
And the few years we have to linger here
Forbid vain dreams of happiness and power,
Beyond what man can crowd into life's fleeting hour.

Soon shall the night that knows no morning come,
And the dim shades that haunt the eternal shore;
And Pluto's shadowy kingdom of the tomb,
Where Thee the well-known dice may never more
Make monarch, while thy friends the wine cup pour;
Where never thou mayest woo fair Lycidas,
Whose loveliness our ardent youth adore:

Whose faultless limbs all other forms surpass,
And, lost amid whose beams, unseen all others pass.

Branwell's comparative success with Hartley Coleridge had inspired Charlotte to send one of her Angrian romances to Coleridge's neighbour Wordsworth, the locality changed from Africa to Yorkshire to give the tale more semblance of reality, but she received a snub for her pains. The elderly poet told his correspondent, who had signed her story 'C.T.', that he could not make out whether the writer was an attorney's clerk or a novel-reading dressmaker. In short, she was not encouraged to continue. Charlotte laid aside her pen for the time being, but no damping criticism could quench for long the smouldering fire of that restless imagination, forever seeking outlet in some form or other, and this summer in particular weaving romance into the person of her father's new curate.

The most interesting thing about the Reverend William Weightman, beloved of all biographers because by tradition he sent the parsonage into a flutter, flirting with the girls, their friends and all the young ladies in the neighbourhood, besides being of a most amiable and kind-hearted disposition, is the fact that during his first few months as curate he was called – behind his back, very naturally – 'Miss Celia Amelia'. Even in her letters to Ellen Nussey, that most eager – though hardly perceptive – of friends, Charlotte alluded to the curate as 'she' and 'her'.

Branwell returned from Broughton-in-Furness to find this delightful newcomer *persona grata* in his father's home, exchanging valentines and drawings with his sisters, and sitting for his portrait to Charlotte dressed in his 'varsity gown, taking care to point out the exquisite silk material from which it was made. Who can wonder that the ex-tutor, straight from the proximity of the surgeon's daughter, should write:

When you, Amelia, feel like me
The dullness of satiety,
You will not smile as now you smile,
With lips that even me beguile . . .

At last somebody had turned up in Haworth who would make the dining-room at the parsonage a counter-attraction to the 'snug' at the Black Bull. Unfortunately, the prospective curate William Weightman flitted to Ripon at mid-summer to prepare for his ordination, and from there to Appleby and Crackenthorp, and was away at least six weeks. Once more Branwell found himself at a loose end. The Book of Odes was finished, but nobody cared to publish it. The paintings remained unsold in the studio back-bedroom. Tutoring had proved an error, teaching was not his forte. His exchequer was low, though, and he must somehow earn his living. What better way than to enter the service of the Leeds and Manchester railway? Work on it was progressing fast: soon the link-up would be completed, and the eastward-bound train from Manchester would come thundering past Todmorden through the Calder valley. There was more life down the line than there was at home, and before long Sowerby Bridge would be a busy junction, with trains running east and west. There would be work in plenty for ambitious, enterprising young men of character who believed in progress and the dawn of a new mechanical age.

Whether Branwell himself found a situation; whether strings were somehow pulled by a Mr Fletcher, whose portrait he had painted, and who had influence with the waterways in the Calder valley; or whether his friend William Dearden, who lived at Brockwell, Sowerby Bridge, was able to put in a word for him, a post on the Leeds and Manchester railway was in fact found. At the end of September, 1840, Branwell became a booking-clerk at Sowerby Bridge station.

10

There is no record of what Mr Brontë thought of his son's new venture: any letters he may have written on the subject were not kept. Like many other parents, he was silent about his daughters' achievements until after they were dead and one of them was famous: he was consistently silent about his boy. His only known comment on Branwell refers to the time when the plan for the Royal Academy had failed: in a letter to Mrs Gaskell, written after he had read her life of Charlotte, he told her that 'the picture of my brilliant and unhappy son ... is a masterpiece'. That he was devoted to Branwell is plain from Charlotte's letter to W. S. Williams when her brother died: 'My poor father naturally thought more of his *only* son than of his daughters', and: 'Branwell was his father's and his sisters' pride and hope in boyhood, but since manhood the case has been otherwise.'

If Charlotte had been doubtful of the success of the tutorship at Broughton-in-Furness, she was equally dubious about the railway undertaking. Telling the news to Ellen Nussey as a half-joke that did not quite come off, she wrote:

A distant relative of mine, one Patrick Boanerges, has set off to seek his fortune in the wild, wandering, adventurous, romantic, knight-errant-like capacity of clerk on the Leeds and Manchester Railroad. Leeds and Manchester, where are they? Cities in a wilderness – like Tadmor, alias Palmyra – are they not?

The allusion to an oasis in the Syrian desert which reached its zenith in the first or second century A.D. under a Queen Zenobia was not likely to convey much to Ellen. Charlotte perhaps had picked up the reference from Branwell himself, for Percy's third wife was called Zenobia.

She considered that the brilliant brother whom she loved, the pride and hope of the family, should have achieved something with his brains by this time. He was twenty-three. His friend Joseph Leyland had exhibited at Leeds, Manchester and London at his age. Local poets without a quarter of Branwell's talent had their work in print. There had been so much talk, always, of what he would become, and now ... a booking-clerk.

In fairness to Branwell, the post must have had prospects. A clerkship on the railway in 1840 must have seemed as promising to a young man then as a position in an atomic energy centre would today. To ignore the railway was to ignore progress, to close an eye to the future. There was money to be made in the railways, and the post of booking-clerk at a small station might lead to a better-paid and more important job in one of the large towns like Manchester or Leeds. Branwell, if he did well, could be earning a comfortable income in ten years' time, with leisure in his spare hours for writing.

These were the arguments Branwell must have put to his family, and they were no doubt accepted as reasonable. What Charlotte would fear was lack of steady purpose, the swing of mood, the high spirits – so infectious in boyhood – which reached a peak and dropped to zero, when, if no one was by who understood, the result might be calamitous. It seemed to her, as the oldest, the planner of the family, that some measure of self-support must be obtained for all four of them. Their father was sixty-three. His health might fail at any time. If the worst should happen, if he should die, they would have to leave the parsonage to make way for his successor. This would be the moment when a brother should become head of the family and help to support his sisters.

124

The Taylor brothers were already hard at work for fear of this contingency. Their father Joshua, the jovial, stirring personality whose republican sympathies, and ability to speak French like a Frenchman, had often cast him as hero in Charlotte's Angrian romances, was now a sick man, and likely to die at any time. The Taylor brothers would never permit Mary and Martha to go out as governesses, which both Charlotte and Anne were to do again the following year. Martha would probably marry, if she found anyone to suit her; but Charlotte did not consider marriage by any means every girl's answer. Independence was the goal – for herself, for her sisters and above all for Branwell. He must, wherever he worked, develop a sense of responsibility.

Branwell, lodging at the Pear Tree Inn, just above Sowerby Bridge station, and close to Brockwell, where the Deardens lived, found a sense of responsibility difficult to acquire when his immediate superior lacked this very quality. The station-master was famous for drinking ten pints of beer, one after the other, before he started his morning duties; and with the Pear Tree so handy and the Royal Oak just up the hill – besides the Old Wharf Inn and the Navigation Inn near the canal – a contest soon developed between station-master and booking-clerk as to who had the greater capacity.

The 'offices', too, were far from comfortable. The station was in its infancy; stone buildings were considered 'frills', and Branwell and his superior were housed in wooden cabins. The 'up' and 'down' trains made the excitement of the day, and when the station-master stepped out to have another pint of beer, leaving the booking-clerk in charge, Branwell had little to do but stare up at White Windows, the great three-storied house on the hill which dominated the whole of Sowerby. It was the dwelling of Mr George Priestley, to whom the poor inhabitants would doff their hats and curtsy whenever the carriage rolled by, coachman and footmen resplendent in sky blue livery and crimson vest.

The glories of White Windows were not for a booking-clerk. The hospitality of Mr George Richardson, the 'wharfinger' of the bridge, in charge of the wharf and all the business of the canal, was nearer; here was the true life of Sowerby Bridge. The new chugging trains from Normanton lacked colour beside the barges, carrying everything from coal to timber, from wheat to wool; and the boaties themselves were more fascinating than engine-driver, fireman and guard.

When Branwell was off duty and the weather was fine, he would walk along the tow-path by the canal, or climb from the valley to the moors, or, better still, he would visit Halifax, only two-and-a-half miles away, and call upon Leyland. Here he could believe himself an artist once more, watching the sculptor at work on a group of five warriors intended for exhibition at Manchester. Perhaps Wilson Anderson would wander in, who painted landscapes and kept a beer cellar, and Joe Drake, the carver and gilder. Later they would visit the Talbot, the Cock, the Commercial or the Rose and Crown, where Drake had his premises. The point was to go where the landlord – or landlady – allowed 'tick', for all four were invariably short of money.

Leyland, of course, was the giant among small fry. His friend Illidge in London told him he was wasting his talent in the provinces, but already inertia was creeping upon him, time was slipping by, he had too many humdrum orders he must finish before thinking of London again. It was simpler to forget work and debts, and drink at the Talbot instead, amusing himself with the obvious hero-worship of young Branwell Brontë.

Whether drink alone was the cause of Leyland's slow decline, or whether he, like Branwell, took opium in some form as an experiment and became an addict, no record shows. That studio in No. 10, The Square, was the setting for bravado and strange dreams. A curious fate hung upon Leyland's work. His group of warriors was smashed in transit from the

Manchester Exhibition to its new home at Gisburn, Lord Ribblesdale's house; his Theseus lost its hands and feet, and another monument years later crashed to pieces. Today there is no trace of Spartacus or Satan. The one-time favourite of the critics is unknown. Some flaw in the material may have caused his work to crumble, but the fault was in the sculptor too; like his own Spartacus he began, at this time, to soften and decay.

It was in 1841 that Leyland's brother Francis – who, like their father, was a painter and bookseller – met Branwell for the first time at Sowerby Bridge, and some forty-odd years later described him thus:

The young railway clerk was of gentleman-like appearance, and seemed to be qualified for a much better position than the one he had chosen. In stature he was a little below middle height. He was slim and agile in figure, yet of well-formed outline. His complexion was clear and ruddy, and the expression of his face, at the time, lightsome and cheerful. His voice had a ringing sweetness, and the utterance and use of his English was perfect. Branwell appeared to be in excellent spirits, and showed none of those traces of intemperance with which some writers have unjustly credited him about this period of his life.

My brother had often spoken to me of Branwell's poetical abilities, his conversational powers, and the polish of his education; and, on a personal acquaintance, I found nothing to question in this estimate of his mental gifts, and of his literary attainments.

The description suggests that respectable Mr Francis was not taken to the Navigation Inn on the wharf to meet the boaties, nor was he invited to enter a beer-drinking contest with the station-master. Leyland, the sculptor, and Brontë, the booking-clerk, knew how to behave in front of family, and because of it Francis defended both men to the end of his days.

Branwell's 'prospects' on his appointment had been six months as booking-clerk at Sowerby Bridge and then promotion. Promotion came, but not what his family had expected. He was moved two miles down the line to Luddenden Foot. True, he was his own boss, and his position that of station-master, as he was careful to point out, though to be more truthful he shared his duties with that same Mr Woolven whom he had met for the first time at the Castle Tavern, Holborn, London, some six years before. Luddenden Foot was not a junction, like Sowerby Bridge. The duties were not arduous. The trains were few. It was farther still from Halifax and Leyland's studio. But the canal ran close, and the Basin was near. Here the barges moored, and the boaties who stopped overnight to make merry in The Woodman or the Weavers Arms were prodigal of hospitality. So were George and William Thompson, who owned the corn-mill by the canal, and James Titterington, wild young son of the wealthy worsted spinner and manufacturer Ely Titterington, who owned mills on the hill-top at Midgley, and a house called Old Ridings over-looking the Luddenden valley. James Titterington was two years older than Branwell, and always 'on the razzle'. He was also an enthusiastic member of the Luddenden Reading Society, which met at the Lord Nelson Inn in the village of Luddenden itself, a mile or so from Luddenden Foot Station. It was possibly Titterington who introduced Branwell to the other members of the Reading Society, though Branwell's name is not on the list of members. Young Titterington read a book a week, so he, at least, did not waste every evening in the bar parlour.

The Reading Society at the Lord Nelson could at least discuss the books the members read, which would give them an advantage over the boaties in the Basin. So Branwell must have thought, torn between the more rarefied climate of the Nelson and the opaque atmosphere of the Weavers Arms.

At first the Nelson held priority. The landlord, Timothy Wormold, was himself a member of the Society, as well as clerk to the church across the way. John Whitworth, manufacturer, with a mill at Longbottom by the canal and a fine home, Peel House, beyond Luddenden, and John Garnett of Holm House, another manufacturer, also belonged. These men obeyed the rules of the Society, one of which was

> that if any of the members come to the said meeting drunk so that he be offensive to the company, and not fit to do his business, he shall forfeit twopence. Swearing on oath, or using any other kind of bad language judged by a majority of the members to be offensive, also calls for a fine of twopence.

The books were a mixed collection, and perhaps the most thumbed were the volumes of the Newgate Calendar, consisting of the lives, crimes, trials and tortures of the most notorious murderers of the century. *Tales of the Genii* which was also on the shelves, would bring nostalgia to Branwell, if he was given the opportunity of borrowing it. These divinities who accompanied man through life, the one bringing happiness, the other misery, were so constantly at war in himself that the Chief Genius Brannii of childhood days had become lost somewhere between the two of them.

The pendulum of his spirits swung between high and low. High when he was with lads younger than himself, like Francis Grundy, the railway engineer – related, surely, to the Richard Grundy who first drove the Manchester train to the Calder Valley; and high, too, with William Heaton, a handloom weaver who had taught himself to read and write by copying the tombstones in Luddenden churchyard. Both men in after years remembered Branwell with affection. Grundy, bluff, hearty, wildly inaccurate, when it came to recalling dates and meetings, gave a more down-to-earth description of the Luddenden station-master than that of the restrained printer, Francis Leyland. Branwell, according to Grundy, was

almost insignificantly small – one of life's trials. He had a mass of red hair, which he wore brushed high off his forehead – to help his height, I fancy; a great, bumpy, intellectual forehead, nearly half the size of the whole facial contour; small ferrety eyes, deep, sunk, and still further hidden by the never removed spectacles; prominent nose, but weak lower features. He had a downcast look, which never varied, save for a rapid momentary glance at long intervals. Small and thin of person, he was the reverse of attractive at first sight. He took to me amazingly . . .

It is interesting to compare this description with a passage from one of Branwell's own sketches, *The Wool Is Rising*:

A colour grinder presented himself, and in answer said something in so hurried a tone that Edward could not catch its meaning. This grinder was a fellow of singular aspect. He was a lad of perhaps seventeen years of age, but from his appearance he seemed at least half-a-score years older, and his meagre freckled visage and large Roman nose, thatched by a thick mat of red hair, constantly changed and twisted themselves into an endless variety of restive movements. As he spoke, instead of looking his auditor straight in the face he turned his eyes – which were further beautified by a pair of spectacles – away from him, and while one word issued stammering from his mouth it was straight way contradicted or confused by a chaos of a strange succeeding jargon.

130

It was with Grundy that Branwell used to walk the countryside, leaving the ticket collector, William Woolven, in charge of the station and discoursing

> with wondrous knowledge upon subjects moral, intellectual, and philosophical . . . in his fits of passion driving his doubled fist through the panel of a door. At times we would drive over in a gig to Haworth and visit his people. He was then at his best, and would be eloquent and amusing, although sometimes he would burst into tears when returning, and swear that he meant to amend.

One of Grundy's most significant revelations was that Branwell had a 'habit of making use of the word "sir" when addressing even his most intimate friends', which would account for the formality of the many letters which he later wrote to Joseph Leyland.

Heaton, the self-taught poet-weaver, knew nothing of Branwell's passion. 'His temper,' he told the sculptor's brother, 'was always mild towards me. I shall never forget his love for the sublime and beautiful works of nature, and I have heard him dilate on the sweet strains of the nightingale . . . He was blithe and gay, but at times appeared downcast and sad . . .'

Like most people with Irish blood, Branwell knew how to adapt himself to an audience of one person or a dozen. Older than Grundy, he could play man-of-the-world, philosopher, to the engineer; younger than Heaton the weaver, with all the advantages of education and a more subtle mind, he could make patronage appear a gift and never a condescension. The rising young manufacturers of his acquaintance presented a tougher problem. A classical scholar was no one if he did not have brass; these men had been working in their fathers' mills and factories when Branwell was scribbling in the nursery study with his sisters. They could spend a day in the Piece Hall in Halifax on business, finish up with their clients at the

131

Talbot or the Old Cock afterwards, put away more hard liquor in a couple of hours than Branwell had been used to taking in months, and then do a stiff day's work back in the mill next morning. If the bright spark of a station-master at Luddenden Foot wanted to keep pace with these lads, then he must quit quoting Latin and Greek on every occasion, learn to hold his liquor and not be sorry later, and prove himself a man when a skirt showed round the corner.

Talk was not enough. How about action? 'You little epitome of the leavings of nature's workshop, you compound of all sorts and sexes, you little whey-faced hermaphrodite . . .' This strange outburst from Percy's friend O'Connor in an early Angrian story perhaps found echoes now in Luddenden. A letter to Grundy, written 1842, when both had left Luddenden, points to a course of conduct unknown to the engineer.

I would rather give my hand than undergo again the grovelling carelessness, the malignant yet cold debauchery, the determination to find how far mind could carry body without both being chucked into hell, which too often marked my conduct when there [at Luddenden], lost as I was to all I really liked, and seeking relief in the indulgence of feelings which form the black spot on my character.

The language is Alexander Percy's, strained, exaggerated, but not entirely false; some measure of sincerity escaped from Mr Brontë's conscience-stricken son. Though 'cold debauchery' smacks of Angrian licence, excessive drinking with the boaties in the Basin might conjure up the flames of hell to one nurtured beneath the parsonage roof. Nor were the boaties the only source of real or imagined contamination. Numbers of Liverpool Irish, despised by the local workmen, and employed by the rich mill-owners because they sold their labour cheap, herded together, squatter-fashion, near the canal at Luddenden Foot. That Branwell counted these among his aquaintances seems clear from a curious entry in his notebook at that time.

At R. Col last night with
    G. Thompson
    J. Titterington
    R. L. Col
    H. Killiner and another.
I quarrelled with J.T. about going but after a wrestle met him on the road and became friends – quarrelled almost on the subject with G. Thompson. Will have no more of it.
    August 18th, 1841.   P.B.B.

The Cols, Colls, McColls and Killiners were all Irish families, brought over to work in the mills. It was among these people that Titterington the young worsted-spinner and Thompson the corn merchant amused themselves of a summer evening, persuading the station-master, against his conscience, to do the same. Did Branwell, once involved, become enmeshed, all the Irish in him drawn to these folk who spoke with a brogue harsher than his father's yet equally familiar, who laughed and cursed and cried all in a matter of seconds, as he did himself, calling upon their Saviour and the Devil in the same breath, loving with momentary fervour and lying with equal facility?

The entries in his notebook at this time are scattered with the name of Jesu. 'Jesu . . . Jesu . . . Jesu . . .' comes at random among five shillings given to sweeps, and two-and-sixpence for cups. 'Jesu Rex' is scribbled beside the London address of the Mottet Society, whose object was the collection of ancient church music. It is easy enough to believe that the Liverpool Irish of Luddenden Foot, with their slovenly, charming ways, Catholic every one of them, were the cause of all the Jesu's and the tortured conscience too.

The truth is that Branwell Brontë, born and bred in

133

Yorkshire, was not a Yorkshireman at all. He had none of their determination, none of their strength of character; he might mimic their ways and customs, but he was not one of them. The heights of Haworth, the chimneys of Bradford and Halifax, the wheels of the Manchester trains that rattled through the Calder valley, were all fundamentally alien to his nature. He belonged, by blood and by temperament, to the first feckless group from across the water which might beckon him; to the eloquent, unpublished poets of many a Dublin side-street, to the painters with canvases untouched, to the musicians with notes unscored, to the fierce arguing politicians of the Liffeyside pubs who had failed in their exams for Trinity College. He belonged to the great company of gifted, wasted Irishmen who, in their mother country, are content to fail and dream, but transplanted to another, break in body and soul. 'Holy Jesu . . . Jesu Salvator . . .' is scattered among 'Have some curled greens for Mr Woolven' – no Cornish or Yorkshire Methodism here, but a Catholic cry for succour from Elinor McClory's grandson.

He would never have the courage to attend Mass in the Assembly room which the Irish workpeople rented on Sundays and Holy Days; the Pope was still anti-Christ to one brought up in an evangelical tradition, and Catholicism itself the Scarlet Woman. Here, perhaps, lay the deep attraction. To those Revivalists who shouted their Hallelujahs in the hills around Haworth and whom he so much despised, yes, and to his freemason brethren also, Rome was anathema. Temptation lay in those bleeding Crucifixes, those cheap, too brightly coloured statuettes of Mother and Child, the heady smell of incense, the veiled and sinister glance of the black-robed visiting priest. The squalid cabins of the Liverpool Irish had a glow to them, a glorious dirty warmth pervading Branwell's senses, clouding his intellect; whisky, lust and possibly laudanum too creating an image even more benign and merciful than that of his dead sister Maria, or of the other Mary, Percy's second wife. Years earlier, in his account of that Mary's death, Branwell had put into the mouth of her grief-stricken husband the words: 'Had'st thou never been alive, I should not now be alive.' An echo of that cry is to be found in one of his poems dating from the Luddenden Foot days:

Amid the world's wide din around,
I hear from far a solemn sound
That says, 'Remember me!
And though thy lot be widely cast
From that thou picturedst in the past
Still deem me dear to thee,
Since to thy soul some glow of heaven,
To give thy earth some glow of heaven,
And, if my beams from thee are driven,
Dark, dark, thy night will be!'
What was that sound? 'Twas not a voice
From ruby lips and sapphire eyes,
Nor echoed back from sensual joys,
Nor a forsaken fair one's sighs.
I, when I heard it, sat amid
The bustle of a town-like room
'Neath skies, with smoke-stained vapours hid –
By windows, made to show their gloom.
The desk that held my ledger book
Beneath the thundering rattle shook
Of engines passing by;
The bustle of the approaching train
Was all I hoped to rouse the brain
Or startle apathy.
And yet, as on the billow swell
A Highland exile's last farewell
Is borne o'er Scotland's sea,
And solemn as a funeral knell,
I heard that soft voice, known so well,
Cry – 'Oh remember me!'

This is only part of a poem, one among many that scatter the pages of Branwell's Luddenden notebook. None of them shows outstanding talent: they abound in 'o'er' and ''neath' and forced rhymes picked at random in the manner of William Dearden and other minor poets. Some attempt was, however, made to sketch out a series of poems on famous men. Their names were listed underneath the address of a Mr Warburton's warehouse, No. 10, Pall Mall (not London, as might be supposed, but Pall Mall, Manchester):

Alexander of Macedon
Oliver Cromwell
Samuel Johnson
Robert Burns
Horatio Nelson
Napoleon Bonaparte
Michelangelo
Scylla of Rome
Julius Caesar
Walter Scott
John Wilson
Henry Brougham
Danton
Columbus

This heterogeneous list was compiled without regard to period or claim to immortality, and the inevitable Holy Jesu was scribbled alongside. A fragment of Burns survives, allusions to Johnson in another scrap and an interminable elegy on the life and death of Nelson, which Branwell probably thought his best poem but which is quite easily his worst. If it was read aloud to the members of the Luddenden Reading Club it must have fetched loud applause and so encouraged its creator. The theme was vigorous, for Nelson was a popular hero. And lines such as:

A vessel lies in England's proudest port
Where venerating thousands oft resort . . .

would make landlord Timothy Wormold nod his head in understanding. 'Aye, that's Portsmouth!'

A prostrate form lies 'neath a double shade
By stifling smoke and blackened rafters made,
With head that backward rolls whene'er it tries
From its hard thunder-shaken bed to rise . . .

And so on and so on, until:

The guns were thundering fainter on his ear,
More, fading fast from sight that cabin drear;
The place, the hour became less clearly known;
He only felt that his great work was done,
That one brave heart was kneeling at his side,
So, murmuring 'Kiss me, Hardy' Nelson, smiling, died.

The whole of this poem was later sent for criticism to Leigh Hunt and Miss Martineau, not by Branwell himself but by his young engineer friend Grundy. 'All,' declared Grundy in his reminiscences, 'spoke in high terms of it.'

More interesting than the laboured verse are the cryptic notes and sketches; the title of a book, *Manhood, the Cause of its Preservation and Decline*; the memorandum for Sunday, October 24th, 1841 – 'Next Monday visit *The Creation* at Assembly Rooms, Halifax' (this would be a performance of Haydn's *Creation* given at the Rooms next to the Talbot Inn); the tortured profile of a long-haired man flanked by a jotting concerning three wagons for Sowerby and topped by a 'Holy Jesu'; and, most intriguing of all, the full-length sketch of a man seated cross-legged in a high-backed chair, his tall hat on his head, above him the letters:

137

ΙΩΑΝΝΕΣ ΜΥΡΓΑΤΡΟΙΔΕΣ

and below him:

ΓΗΩΡΓΕ ΡΙΧΑΡΔΣΩΝ

John Murgatroyd and George Richardson – the first a wealthy
woollen manufacturer of Oats Roy, Luddenden, thirty-two
years old and lately widowed, employer of the Liverpool Irish;
the second the wharfinger of Sowerby Bridge, controller of
the warehouses and wharfs. Why were they represented in a
composite portrait, their dual identity thinly disguised by
Greek lettering? Did they come together to the bar parlour
of the Lord Nelson Inn, or the Anchor and Shuttle, symbolizing – to the young draughtsman sketching in the opposite
corner – a single man of substance, great in power, to whom
boaties bowed and weavers touched their forelocks?

The mystery, if mystery there was, stayed hidden in the
notebook. 'Poor, brilliant, gay, moody, moping, wildly excitable,
miserable Brontë', as Grundy the engineer described him,
never disclosed it. The sketches were only doodles, perhaps,
drawn to offset a phase of growing despair, with the autumn
closing in, the trees dripping in Luddenden churchyard, so
deep in the valley that the sun never found it once October
had passed, the swollen mill-stream sounding in his ears, even
in Turn Lea cottages up the hill where he lodged, his bedroom
window looking out over the hills to those Ewood estates
once owned by poor Johnny Grimshaw.

'Once tha' carriest an angel, and now tha' carriest a devil!'
What demon, Branwell must have wondered, drove Johnny,
so soon to die, on horseback through those woods? Now they
were all dead, Grimshaws, Lockwoods, Sutcliffes, most of them
buried down in Luddenden below. Increasing apathy came
upon him, not only here at his lodging, but even down at the
Nelson, or trudging to his station work at Luddenden Foot;

for while his prospects had diminished through the months, so that he foresaw the impossibility of ever rising above the miserable status of station-master on a branch line, his weekly wage spent before it was earned, letters came from home full of high hopes and plans. There was talk of the girls running a school backed financially by his aunt, and then, when this project dimmed, a new idea of travel, Charlotte and Emily to follow the Taylor sisters to Brussels, Anne perhaps to join them later, aunt and father both in warm approval. But never a hint that he might have done the same, that he too could have travelled, escorting the girls as one of the Taylor brothers had escorted Mary and Martha, no word or suggestion that his presence would be missed. He had been given his chance in Bradford. He had failed. Now he must make do with his branch-line in a valley. It was his own choice, his own decision. The turn of his sisters had come.

The bitterness of realizing that he had failed through his own fault, through want of spirit, through lack of concentration, must somehow be blotted out, and for this whisky was the only panacea, because it temporarily turned despair into muffled ease, and drear acquaintances into jovial friends. Let the girls go to Brussels if they wanted – they would see precious little of life shut up in a pension. Whereas on the barges, or with the Irish down by the canal, or any come-by-chance companion who rolled tipsily off the Halifax coach and called for laughter, he could find the essence of all living and all pain, the zenith of twisted pleasure.

Both Branwell and Emily wrote poems on December 19th, 1841. One was at Luddenden, the other at Haworth. Neither poem is particularly good. Emily's forms part of her Gondal saga, and represents a sister speaking to a brother, both mourning their dead mother; yet the theme suggests a thought winging its way to Luddenden. Branwell's is more personal, himself at the crossroads. Emily's was headed 'A.S. to G.S. December 19th, 1841.'

I do not weep, I would not weep;
Our Mother needs no tears;
Dry thine eyes too, 'tis vain to keep
This causeless grief for years.

What though her brow be changed and cold,
Her sweet eyes closed for ever?
What though the stone – the darksome mould
Our mortal bodies sever?

What though her hand smooth ne'er again
Those silken locks of thine –
Nor through long hours of future pain
Her kind face o'er thee shine?

Remember still she is not dead,
She sees us, Gerald, now,
Laid where her angel spirit fled
'Mid heath and frozen snow.

And from that world of heavenly light
Will she not always blend,
To guide us in our lifetime's night
And guard us to the end?

Thou knowest she will, and well may'st mourn
That we are left below,
But not that she can ne'er return
To share our earthly woe.

Branwell's poem was headed 'Dec. 19, 1841, at Luddenden
Church. P.B.B.'

O God! while I in pleasure's wiles
Count hours and years as one,

140

And deem that, wrapt in pleasure's smiles,
My joys can ne'er be done.

Give me the stern sustaining power
To look into the past,
And see the darkly shadowed hour
Which I must meet at last:

The hour when I must stretch this hand
To give a last adieu
To those sad friends that round me stand,
Whom I no more must view.

For false though bright the hours that lead
My present passage on,
And when I join the silent dead
Their light will all be gone.

Then I must cease to seek the light
Which fires the evening heaven,
Since to direct through death's dark night
Some other must be given.

What is interesting about both poems is the similarity of
style, the choice of words and metres. Even the themes are
interwoven – the one could be the reflection of the other.
Both show the influence of hymn-book jingle, absorbed in
babyhood, now part of the blood-stream, though Emily's later
poems were free of it.

Now the sister, for the first time since Roe Head, was to meet
in Brussels competition in the classroom, and, better still, submit
to the discipline of the French language taught by an expert.
This, and the nine months' break from home, must have played
an incalculable part in bringing latent genius to the surface;
without such a stimulus it might have stayed fitful and immature.

141

The brother had no such opportunity. No fierce Belgian professor would run a blue pencil through his essays, or force him to read Montaigne or Racine. He had never measured his intellect against any competitor; his criterion of excellence was William Dearden. If Branwell could have had nine months' intensive concentration upon French, German or any other language under a master of perception and personality, as Charlotte and Emily experienced with Monsieur Héger in the rue d'Isabelle, the talent he possessed might have flowered instead of withered, and the brilliance that still waited, poised, to expand and glitter would not have shrunk back into a dulled exhaustion, a pitiful reminder of what might have been.

In February 1842 Charlotte and Emily left for Brussels. Anne was away as governess near York. Brothers and sisters had never been more divided and apart. It was at the end of March that Branwell was dismissed from his post as stationmaster at Luddenden Foot because of negligence.

11

Brontë the station-master and Woolven the ticket-collector were jointly responsible for the book-keeping at Luddenden Foot station. Both had to appear before the auditors of the railway company when the books were found to be at fault. There was a discrepancy in the figures entered: the price of the tickets sold did not tally with the sums received. Closer examination of the ledger showed haphazard entries, with rough sketches of the station-master's acquaintances in the margin. The ticket-collector admitted that the station-master had often been absent from duty. Neither could explain what had happened to the missing money. Theft was not proved, but careless book-keeping was.

Woolven seems to have kept his post, but Branwell's 'services' were no longer required. His inglorious tenure of office in the Leeds and Manchester railway company had come to an end. Perhaps the removal from Sowerby Bridge station to Luddenden Foot had not been promotion at all, but merely a second chance to prove himself in a smaller station where responsibility would be lighter than at the junction, though Emily, at the time, had said to Charlotte, 'It looks like getting on . . .'

Now Branwell had three failures to chalk to his record – four, if he counted non-admission to the Royal Academy schools. Lack of patronage had closed the career at Bradford, but lack of concentration too. The tutorship at Broughton-in-Furness? Almost certainly misdemeanour sent him home after six months. And now the railway . . .

A breakdown was inevitable. Branwell, in a letter to Leyland

143

on May 15th, spoke of 'severe indisposition'. The return home after facing the railway auditors, and the necessary explanation to his father and his aunt, was a bitter experience. Illness was the only answer, and the wave of depression that engulfed him was no subterfuge. If his father and his aunt could guess how he had spent his time during that year at Luddenden Foot they would be appalled – indeed, the doors of the parsonage might be closed to him forever.

Like all persons prone to hysteria, Branwell magnified his offences: he was guilty beyond redemption, he had sunk lower than the lowest. Worst of all was the shock to his own pride. He, Branwell Brontë, the brilliant versatile genius of the family, had not been able to hold down the trumpery job of station-master on a branch line.

By the end of May the pendulum had swung once more, the peace and quiet of home had mended the wounded pride and softened the sense of guilt, and Branwell's innate tendency to soar from zero to the heights was set in motion once again. Today such a rapid swing might seem ominous, the increasing susceptibility to emotional extravagance a sign of neurosis and a presage of trouble to come, but in the mid-nineteenth century the abrupt emergence from depression to elation was seen as the natural recovery of youth and vigour.

Dr Thomas Andrew, respected inhabitant of Haworth, had lately died, and it was decided to put up a monument to him, in St Michael's church, and commission Joseph Leyland to design it. Branwell was instructed to approach the sculptor, and for the first time he was able to invite his idol to Haworth, to introduce him to his father, to John Brown also, who, as stonemason, would carry out the lettering on the monument. It must have seemed to Branwell that Leyland was no longer the indulgent, amusing acquaintance of Halifax, forever surrounded by a group of hangers-on, but a personal friend, visiting Haworth at his bidding. The excitement of giving the invitation, the graciousness of Leyland's acceptance, restored

Branwell's sense of dignity and pride. The folly of Luddenden Foot could be forgotten. The disgrace of the railway episode belonged to the past.

Whatever impression the sculptor might make upon Mr Brontë and the committee in charge of putting up the monument was nothing, in Branwell's eyes, to the effect the small community would have upon his friend. He suffered all the agonies of a go-between with a foot in both societies. Eager for Leyland's goodwill, and aware that the sculptor was putting himself out to oblige him, he had the mortification of hearing members of the committee talk to the great man as if he were a common mason. Some argument, possibly, about the charge, some disagreement perhaps in wording or design, whatever it was that marred the splendour of the visit, Branwell was humiliated in consequence.

'I have not often felt more heartily ashamed,' he wrote to the sculptor on June 29th, 1842,

than when you left the committee at Haworth; but I did not like to speak on the subject then, and I trusted that you would make that allowance which you have perhaps often ere now had to do, for gothic ignorance and ill-breeding, and one or two of the persons present afterwards felt that they had left by no means an enviable impression on your mind.

Though it is but a poor compliment – I long much to see you again at Haworth, and forget for half a day the amiable society in which I am placed, where I never hear a word more musical than an ass's bray . . .

The apologies for his surroundings brought invitations in return. Branwell, who had hovered for so long on the fringe of that close group which delighted to foregather at No. 10, The Square, was now an intimate. Poems were exchanged and read aloud. Advice was given. Grundy, the engineer, to whom

145

Branwell had written in May, when he was recovering from his breakdown, asking what hopes there might be for further employment on the railway, was now told that Branwell 'had been advised to turn his attention to literature', that he would indeed be a fool, 'under present circumstances, to entertain any sanguine hopes respecting situations'.

Branwell revised some of his old poems and stories, sorting from the mixed collection such examples, minus Angrian names and allusions, as might appeal to Leyland and his friends. William Dearden challenged him to competition, but his letter to the Halifax *Guardian* describing the occasion (which has been briefly referred to in an earlier chapter) was not written until 1867, when all four Brontës were dead.

'Many years ago,' he wrote,

Patrick Brontë and I agreed that each should write a drama or a poem, the principal character in which was to have a real or imaginary existence before the Deluge; and that in a month's time, we should meet at the Cross Roads Inn, which is about half way between Keighley and Haworth, and produce the result of our lucubrations. We met at the time and place appointed, and in the presence of a mutual friend, the late J. B. Leyland, the promising sculptor, I read the first act of *The Demon Queen*, but when Branwell dived into his hat – the usual receptacle of his fugitive scraps – where he supposed he had deposited his MS. poem, he found he had by mistake placed there a number of stray leaves of a novel on which he had been trying his 'prentice hand'. Chagrined at the disappointment he had caused, he was about to return the papers to his hat, when both friends earnestly pressed him to read them, as they felt a curiosity to see how he could wield the pen of a novelist. After some hesitation, he complied with the request, and riveted our attention for about an hour, dropping each sheet, when read, into

146

his hat. The story broke off abruptly in the middle of a sentence, and he gave us the sequel 'viva voce' together with the *real names of the prototypes of his characters; but as some of these personages are still living, I refrain from pointing them out to the public.*

He said he had not yet fixed upon a title for his production, and was afraid he should never be able to meet with a publisher who would have the hardihood to usher it into the world. The scene of the fragment which Branwell read, and the characters introduced in it – so far as then developed – were the same as those in *Wuthering Heights*, which Charlotte Brontë confidently asserts was the production of her sister Emily.

The letter continued with Dearden's opinion on the published novel, and concluded with a 'poetical sketch' of his own describing how shocked both he and Leyland had been by the character of Heathcliff in the fragment read, and had earnestly advised Branwell to throw his prospective novel into the fire. Branwell refused to do so, saying his hero should 'live a little longer yet', and that one day he might fill his 'empty exchequer'. If he should suit public taste, then Branwell would produce a 'female mate' and the pair of them would propagate 'a monster race' that might 'quell the heroes and the heroines effete that strut in tinsel through the fictive world'.

'But,' said Branwell, 'let my slandered Romeo, for the nonce, sleep in the tomb of all my Capulets,' and he pointed to his hat.

The classical schoolmaster was a bad poet but no liar. If it was indeed an embryo *Wuthering Heights* that Branwell read aloud, then reason suggests that this first draft of what was later to become a world-famous novel by Emily Brontë was in fact either Branwell's own work, or the result of collaboration between brother and sister. Charlotte and Branwell collaborated in the Angrian series; Emily and Branwell could have done the same. The handwriting of all three, when they wrote in the minute script which they used for their private writings, was very similar; that of Emily and Branwell so alike as to be nearly identical. Much confusion has been caused over the right authorship of their poems for this very reason.

There remains the possibility that Branwell, short-sighted as he was, seized a manuscript believing it to be his own, and on taking it from his hat realized that it was a tale of Emily's. His love of mischief would make him read it aloud, if only to watch the effect upon Dearden and Leyland. That they were shocked, even horrified, would add to his delight. The fact that Branwell most significantly told his friends not only the *'real names of the prototypes . . . some of them existing still'* (i.e., in 1867, when Dearden penned his letter) but also the 'sequel' proves that he knew the source of the story and the course it was destined to take, thus confirming Charlotte's words, after both Branwell and Emily were dead, that *Wuthering Heights* was 'hewn in a wild workshop, with simple tools, out of homely materials'.

Those who know something of Alexander Percy and his satanic qualities, who have read the Angrian stories of Charlotte and Branwell, accept with equanimity an embryonic *Wuthering Heights* consisting of a few chapters, written either by Branwell, or by Emily, or by both in collaboration. Brother and sisters borrowed freely from one another; Angrian stories and Gondal sagas were read aloud at the parsonage and enjoyed by all four young authors.

The nineteenth-century critics, who knew nothing of the early writings and came to *Jane Eyre* and *Wuthering Heights* believing that they had sprung fresh from the minds of two secluded sisters who had never before expressed themselves on paper, must be pardoned their attacks of apopletic rage when William Dearden penned his letter to the Halifax *Guardian* in 1867. That Edward Sloane, another member of the Halifax group of friends, corroborated Dearden's story, declaring that: 'Branwell had read to him, portion by portion, the novel as it was produced at that time, insomuch that he no sooner began the perusal of *Wuthering Heights* [published in December, 1847] than he was able to anticipate the characters and incidents to be disclosed', intensified the fury of all those who admired the novel. They had no idea, any more than Dearden or Sloane, that brother and sisters had collaborated in each other's stories from early childhood.

Whoever scribbled the first draft of that world-famous story in 1842, or even earlier – for Branwell told Dearden that it was a novel on which 'some time ago' he had tried his prentice hand – the reputation of Emily, who completed and revised the whole in the autumn and winter months of 1845–46, need not suffer. To her the full credit and the glory, though the germ of the idea could have sprung from her brother.

Somewhere between the Worth and Calder valleys, somewhere between the Haworth, Stanbury and Wadsworth moors, or even sweeping to the fringes of Halifax and thence to Hebden Bridge and Hepstonstall, Emily, surely with Branwell's knowledge, sketched out the destiny of two families known to them both by hearsay – whether drawn from the many scattered Heatons nearer home, or from the heights of Ewood where the much inter-married Grimshaws lived and died, who can say? Members of these families were 'living still' when both brother and sister, buried within three months of one another, had lain nineteen years in the grave, and Joseph Leyland, who acted as judge on that memorable occasion at the Cross Roads Inn, had been dead nearly as long. Thirty-nine years old, riddled with dropsy, attended faithfully by his personal manservant and a boy, the one-time brilliant sculptor came to his tragic end in a debtors' prison in 1851, surviving Branwell by three years.

In 1842 both fatalities were remote. Leyland, with his inevitable meerschaum alight and a full glass in his hand, a sardonic smile on his heavy, handsome face, would have listened

149

while his bespectacled, red-haired little friend read aloud some chapters about the impossible owner of a remote moorland farm, and, backed by the classical schoolmaster, have advised Branwell that he had created a motiveless monster out of his own black bile.

Like Richard the Third? Nonsense! Richard the Third was born deformed, and, politically ambitious, won his throne by cunning and high intelligence. Besides, he redeemed himself at the end through courage in battle. But this hero of Brontë's did not possess one human quality. No reader would believe in him. So Heathcliff was dismissed at his first hearing.

Back at home, Branwell passed his time going over the Percy manuscripts. Not the old Percy of Angrian days, but that more modern, sardonic version conceived in 1837, and probably developed in the summer of 1840 after the Broughton-in-Furness débâcle, when the whole countryside round Haworth had been stirred by the great Revivalist meetings which swept through the district. In the story which he had written then, called *And the Weary Are At Rest*, Percy, once more backed by his old Angrian henchmates, became the unscrupulous mocker of Evangelical preachers, from McNeile of St Jude's to the Baptist Winterbotham of Haworth. No one was spared in Branwell's tirade against the hypocrisy of the disestablished churches and the false modesty of the female sex. The life of Alexander Percy, when it came to be written in its entirety, would ridicule churches, chapels, wives, daughters, the law, freemasonry and the landed gentry; no traditional order of things would escape the shafts directed with so sure a hand from the back bedroom of a Yorkshire parsonage.

On the evening of the first day of Ardmore fair, Sanctification Chapel presented to the crowd assembled about its doors a blaze of gaslight from every square-paned window. Inside, abundance of light threw a yellow glory over the rapidly filling pews and galleries, while a

150

double lustre blessed the green baize-bordered platform erected for the distinguished orators in the forthcoming missionary meeting. Men with slouched shoulders and downcast eyes assiduously trimmed the lamps or scraped discordant preludes on violins or violoncellos, and perspiring but regenerated souls buried their faces in their hands under the influence of groaning prayer. The ladies, too, crowded fast into the scene of action with a very holy fervour, though sadly carnal attraction as to dress. 'Their upturned eyes and saddened sighs' told of heaven; but their satin bonnets and white handkerchiefs smelt a little of the earth, earthly.

For a while the bare boards of the platform caused a feeling of impatience in the rapidly filling edifice, but ere long these boards were pressed by the boots of five as beautiful specimens of sinners as ever trod upon Memel timber. The Rev. H. M. M. Montmorency, the Rev. J. Simpson, the Rev. G. Gordon, the Rev. A. O'Connor, the Rev. Q. Quamina, all attired in solemn sable, took their seats amid the deepest groans among the male, and with the liveliest sympathies from the female, portion of the audience; and though the chosen presented countenances as rascally as ever faced the mob round Tyburn tree, their erect gentlemanly figures and well-whiskered manliness told well, especially with the fairer and holier portion of the audience . . .

Waiting until an obligato movement of sighs and groans had ceased, the Rev. Alexander Percy began in a distinct but calm and silvery voice:

'My brethren and sisters in Christ. I feel so much oppressed with the weight of a duty which a higher power has laid upon me that I request from you a song of prayer and praise ere we open the business of the evening. My brother Slugg, I shall give out

151

a hymn and accompany on the organ myself, so it will be quite unnecessary for my Christian friend to make any use of the instrument I see in the music seat.'

As I have alluded to Mr Percy's musical powers, I need hardly add now that when, after giving out the hymn, he took his seat at the organ, he soon sent the solemn harmony rolling through the chapel and ascending as if to Heaven. Whatever the discomfited gut-scrapers felt, they were obliged to stare at the powers of the rich converted squire, and even the Rev. S. Slugg gave a groan of astonishment when the last deep chord had died away . . .

The Rev. A. Percy, with a general bow to the enraptured audience, took his seat amid a flourish of five hundred white handkerchiefs. The male portion of the assembly groaned deeply, but the female portion felt deeply; and, if a keen observer had noticed the odd half-smile on Percy's mobile lips as he looked round after taking his seat, he would have known at once that the orator had known to whose feelings he ought to address himself and to whom he meant to feel indifference.

The advance in technique in this extract is very marked when compared with the arrival of Percy at Darkwall Hall, written in the autumn of 1837. The satirical touch is sure, and the writer knows his subject. Percy the mocker is a far more convincing figure than Percy the melancholy lover of the earlier Angrian tales.

So the summer of 1842 continued, the spasmodic additions to the Percy story interspersed with a more careful revision of past sonnets, and the monotony of the Haworth scene enlivened by growing friendship with William Weightman the curate, and varied by excursions to Halifax. Charlotte wrote cheerfully from Brussels; occasional bouts of homesickness

152

would not deter either Emily or herself from staying on another half-year at the pensionnat Héger, where they had been offered free bed and board in exchange for teaching services. This decision, incidentally, combined with Mary Taylor's statement to Ellen Nussey, in a letter dated September, 1842, that 'Charlotte and Emily are well; not only in health but in mind and hope . . . They are content with their present position and even gay and I think they do right not to return to England . . .' makes nonsense of the tradition that Emily hated Brussels and pined for Haworth.

Mary and her sister were now living *en pension* at the Château Koekelberg, in a suburb of Brussels, not far from the rue d'Isabelle and the pensionnat Héger. The intelligence of Mary, the high spirits of Martha, made a fascinating combination which perhaps even the self-sufficient Emily found it hard to resist. Familiar faces seen in new surroundings can have an unconscious charm; somewhere in Emily's imagination a turbulent, tempestuous Cathy was taking shape, a wilful, passionate Cathy who had no wish to die.

'Martha was her father's pet child,' said Ellen Nussey. 'He delighted in hearing her sing, telling her to go to the piano, with his affectionate "Patty lass". Among her school companions she was always a favourite, so piquant and fascinating were her ways. She was not in the least pretty, but something much better, full of change and variety, rudely outspoken, lively and original, producing laughter with her own good humour and affection.'

Martha was taken ill at the Château Koekelberg early in October, 1842. She died at ten o'clock at night on the 12th of the month, and her death was reported to the authorities at two a.m. the following morning by two Belgian gentlemen, 'friends of the deceased'. She was buried immediately in Koekelberg cemetery, and her sister Mary went to relatives in Brussels. The cause of her death was not stated on the official certificate. The haste with which her death was reported,

153

and not, apparently, by a doctor, suggests a bungle, or a mystery, or both; even Mary Taylor, writing to Ellen Nussey a fortnight later, said:

> You will wish to hear the history of Martha's illness – I will give you it in a few months if you have not heard it then; till then you must excuse me. A thousand times I have reviewed the minutest circumstances of it, but I cannot without great difficulty give a regular account of them. There is nothing to regret, nothing to recall – not even Martha. She is better where she is. But when I recall the sufferings that have purified her, my heart aches – I can't help it, and every trivial accident, sad or pleasant, reminds me of her and what she went through.

Strange language for one sister to use about another, especially a forthright sister like Mary Taylor. Why should twenty-three-year-old 'Patty' need purifying? And were her sufferings physical or mental? The secret lies buried beneath the old Koekelberg cemetery, now grassed over and a cemetery no more.

When Branwell heard the news of Martha Taylor's death from his sisters in Brussels, it would have seemed to him either additional proof of the utter heartlessness of God, or, more likely still, the confirmation that no God existed who heard prayer. For six weeks earlier the young curate William Weightman, playfully nicknamed Celia Amelia on his arrival in Haworth in 1840, and soon a general favourite at the parsonage – though according to Charlotte an incorrigible flirt – had been taken ill. He had died on September 6th. The cause of death was given as 'cholera and peritonitis' – a wide term in those days, suggesting anything from a ruptured appendix to summer dysentery.

Young Weightman was a year older than Branwell, and

according to Branwell's letter to the engineer Grundy, written on October 25th, 'one of my dearest friends'. Since Branwell's return to Haworth six months before, what could only have been a casual acquaintance in the Sowerby Bridge and Luddenden Foot days, with Branwell returning home for occasional afternoons, had developed into warmer feelings of affection, with the curate in and out of the parsonage every day.

Martha Taylor and William Weightman. Two young people of Branwell's age struck down within five weeks of one another, who were loved by all who knew them, who had done no wrong. If this was justice, Branwell wanted no part of it. If this was the love of God, the word was meaningless.

The long sermon that his father preached in commemoration of the curate on October 2nd might have been written especially for Branwell, sitting alone in the family pew below the pulpit.

When good men die early, in the full tide of their usefulness, there is bewildering amazement, till we read in the scriptures, that in mercy they are taken away from the evil to come. In all such cases we want faith, and strong faith too . . . This world, with its false lights, eclipses in our morbid imagination the unimaginable splendour of heaven. Honour and riches, power and fame, with long life to enjoy them, frequently occupy but too much of our attention, whilst we dread the visitation of death, the darkness of the grave, the worm of corruption, the loathsome work of decomposition, eternal separation and oblivion . . . We may easily comprehend why the wicked have a desire for life, and a dread of death and judgement; but that the followers of Christ should tremble at the last step of their journey, which will introduce them into His presence and His glory, can only be accounted for by the weakness of their faith, and the remains of sin, that would chain them down, or keep

155

them from those unspeakable pleasures which he has in reserve for them in the kingdom of their Heavenly Father.

The weakness of faith, the remains of sin – when had the son ever been strong in faith, or without sin? The voice of his father, stern in the pulpit now as it had been in Branwell's childhood, yet compassionate, too, and kind, strong in its own belief, only added to his remorse and sense of loss. Why speak of the splendours of heaven when there were no eyes to see the glories, no lips to smile, no hands to touch? Dear, warm-hearted Weightman lay beneath the cold stone. There was the blunt truth. Nothing else counted. And the same would be true of vivacious Martha, soon to be buried in Brussels, far from home.

There was to be one more test of faith – if his father cared to call it so. Branwell's aunt, now sixty-six, had given no signs of illness until she complained of pain in mid-October. On the 25th of the month, when Branwell told his friend Grundy of Weightman's death, he added: 'And now I am attending at the death-bed of my aunt, who has been for twenty years as my mother. I expect her to die in a few hours . . .' On the 29th he wrote again: 'I am incoherent, I fear, but I have been waking two nights witnessing such agonising suffering as I would not wish my worst enemy to endure; and I have now lost the guide and director of all the happy days connected with my childhood . . .'

Elizabeth Branwell had died that same day. The cause of death, 'exhaustion from constipation'. This brief statement conjures in its very brevity the full misery of illness a hundred and fifty years ago. The courageous little Cornish woman, who had left her home twenty years before to devote her life to her sister's husband and his children, was obliged, through lack of medical skill, to endure unspeakable agony and die, when today efficient treatment, or at worst an immediate operation, would have saved not only suffering but life as well.

This letter of Branwell's to Grundy is the sole witness of her last moments. Was he the only one to sit by the bedside? Did his father, powerless to help, remain below? Did little fourteen-year-old Martha, daughter of John Brown and assistant to the crippled aged Tabby, fetch and carry?

Branwell, in early childhood, had seen two sisters die. Some seven weeks since he had lost a gay and affectionate friend. Now the aunt who for twenty-two years had tried to take his mother's place had gone after a fortnight's suffering which no doctor or drug had been able to cure.

Anne returned for the funeral; Charlotte and Emily, travelling from Belgium, arrived when all was over. But to Branwell reunion with his sisters, when it came, was not enough. He had seen with his own eyes the ugliness of death. They lied who said that death was beautiful. His aunt had no wish to meet her Maker face to face. All she had demanded, had cried aloud for, was to be spared pain. And this had been denied. Prayer therefore was useless, was a mockery, and all that his aunt had lived for and sworn by and upheld deserted her when she needed it most. If he should ever come to suffer physically he would ask for no one's prayers. He would not pray himself. There was only one panacea to pain — oblivion. And oblivion could be found in whisky, gin or laudanum. These would be his gods when the time of reckoning came.

Meanwhile . . . meanwhile nothing but the memory of that suffering, the puzzled wondering face, the restless tortured eyes. And did he but know it, it was not the quiet of the parsonage that could ever comfort him, nor the familiar ticking of the clock on the stairs, nor the silent prayers of his father alone in the parlour. The natural release to Branwell's pent-up emotions would have been the keening of an Irish wake, the neighbours with veiled heads sitting beside the coffin; the wailing, the singing, the rocking to and fro, the flushed weeping faces, the comradeship, the tears.

12

Branwell was now twenty-five, without a penny to his name. The aunt who had loved him, confident of his future success when she made her will in 1833, had left her small capital to be divided between her nieces. The boy of sixteen, as her nephew had been then, with a brilliant career in front of him, would need no help from her when the time came; and the 'Japan dressing-box', which perhaps he had looked into and admired as a child, was her single bequest to the nephew she had brought up from babyhood. Branwell's erratic behaviour since he had grown to man's estate had not caused her faith in him to falter. Beliefs die hard. The boy would surely make his own way one day. The girls needed support, and not only Charlotte, Emily and Anne but a fourth niece, Elizabeth Jane Kingston, child of her remaining sister Anne.

The question facing Branwell was, what now? The reading of his poems to Leyland and the Halifax coterie had not resulted in their publication, although the sculptor's brother was a printer and bookseller. Friends on the railway gave no hope of employment. He seemed to have reached a dead end. Charlotte and Emily, who had not seen their brother for close on a year, must have noticed the change in his appearance, which could not be accounted for by grief at his aunt's death alone.

And Branwell, on his side, must have felt that Charlotte, who had always been closest to him, had changed just as greatly. For, however much she might conceal it from her family and her reasoning self, her passion for her professor

Monsieur Héger was turning from the usual pupil–master attitude to an obsession. Just as once the feelings of the highly emotional Charlotte had spent themselves in daydreams of a life shared with Ellen Nussey – only worked out of her system by a frantic writing of Angrian romances – so now they were simmering to boiling point once more, but with the added excitement of a male–female relationship, hitherto unexperienced. The stories she had written before she went to Brussels had all tended in this direction – the younger girl, the older man, and that man married. Once conceived in the imagination and put on paper, the stories had to work themselves out in reality, and Monsieur Héger, the master, was the peg on which to hang the preconceived idea. If it had not been Monsieur Héger it would have been someone else: the girl who had lived in fantasy with the Duke of Zamorna since childhood days was forced through emotional necessity to bring him alive. It did not matter if he was a 'little, black ugly being', something between 'an insane tom-cat and a delirious hyena', as she described him in a letter to Ellen; the moment had come for imagination and reality to fuse. No wonder Charlotte was determined to return to Brussels.

So before long only Emily was left at home, content to look after her father, and Branwell, too, if he cared to behave himself. But Emily's satirical essay, written in French the preceding autumn, showing Death choosing Intemperance as Viceroy above all other claimants, hardly suggests a tolerant attitude to drinking; she would never scold, but she might easily ignore, and the man who drank to win attention, or through lack of will-power, would be met with a shrug of the shoulder and possibly silence. Self-contained and detached as she was, to Emily the easily aroused emotions of others showed weakness; she had long ago resolved never herself to betray feeling. It was for this reason that she was often misunderstood and even disliked by passing acquaintances. The Misses Wheelwright, English neighbours in Brussels with whom Charlotte was friendly, described Emily as 'tall and ungainly, always looking untidy', and complained that the small Wheelwright children of ten and eight, to whom she taught music, had more than once come from their lessons in tears. But Ellen Nussey, who knew her better, said: 'Her extreme reserve seemed impenetrable, yet she was intensely lovable . . . Few people have the gift of looking and smiling, as she could look and smile – one of her rare expressive looks was something to remember through life.'

It was Anne, with her strong sense of duty combined with quiet determination and a sense of humour, who seemed best fitted at this moment to be Branwell's companion. Whether she was herself, at this time, suffering from a secret grief, which would make her especially sympathetic to the troubles of her brother, is a matter for speculation. It has been suggested that she was in love with William Weightman, and shattered by his death. But downcast looks in church and a poem to his memory are no more proof of emotional attachment than the fact that the hero of her first novel was a clergyman. The grave, quiet, plain Mr Weston of *Agnes Grey* bears small resemblance to the gay, flirtatious, light-hearted 'Celia Amelia' of Charlotte's letters. Mr Weston could just as easily be an idealized portrait of the Reverend James La Trobe, who had prayed by the sick Anne's bedside when she was a pupil at Roe Head, and who had still been minister to the Moravian congregation in Mirfield when she returned there in 1839, this time as governess to the Ingham family of Blake Hall.

Since March, 1841, Anne had been governess to the daughters of Mr and Mrs Robinson of Thorp Green Hall, near York. When she had been with them for four months she wrote in her birthday note to Emily – which would be opened, according to their private arrangements, four years later – 'I dislike the situation, and wish to change it for another'. There was nothing to prevent her, yet she had not changed it by January, 1843, and a few months after their aunt's death she even prevailed upon Branwell to accept the post of tutor to Mr Robinson's son and heir, and return with her to Thorp Green Hall. If Anne had disliked her pupils, mistrusted Mr and Mrs Robinson and felt uneasy and unhappy in her surroundings, she would never have come forward with such a suggestion, knowing as she did the peculiar weaknesses of her brother's character. The Robinsons, therefore, no matter how they had first appeared to Anne in the spring of 1841, must have developed into sympathetic friends two years later, since she risked introducing Branwell into the household.

If Anne herself made the suggestion to her employers that her brother should return as tutor, it must have shown that she had confidence in their character, and a belief that the cheerful atmosphere of Thorp Green would act as a tonic to low spirits. If it was the Robinsons who put forward the plan, then at least they made a good-natured attempt to solve a family difficulty, and showed a desire to help the governess who had endeared herself to her pupils. Perhaps the brother would prove as capable an instructor and as pleasant a companion as the sister. The Murrays of *Agnes Grey*, rich, rude, shallow, uncultured and disagreeable, yet continually and confidently held to represent the Robinsons of Thorp Green Hall, would surely have been the last people on earth to whom to introduce a highly strung, susceptible, easily led and excitable young man like Branwell. If the Murrays were in truth the Robinsons, then Anne was either a fool or a criminal to take her brother among them.

But she was neither. She had a natural gift for satire, and, like Jane Austen, she poked fun at the society in which she found herself; but the Robinsons, unlike the fictitious Murrays, must have had some kind qualities, some genuine good faith, some good-tempered jollity among them for sister and brother to remain there, as they did, two-and-a-half years before trouble broke.

Anne was a young woman of spirit and determination. She

161

would never have endured the insults and slights that Mrs Murray and her daughter Rosalie put upon Agnes Grey, nor would she have encouraged a brother who had already lost one position as tutor to take up another with people of no integrity. Those who insist that life with the Murrays of Horton Lodge is an accurate picture of life with the Robinsons of Thorp Green must follow the story through to its conclusion, and find the model for Henry Weston among the vicars or curates of Little Ouseburn, or even among those of Scarborough, where Anne was happiest of all, and which she chose as a final resting-place.

The position of Thorp Green Hall, set in a grove of trees in low, flat country, two-and-a-half miles from the village of Little Ouseburn and twelve from York, was not one calculated to appeal to Branwell, fond of 'active life' and the attractions of Halifax. This Anne knew very well. Occasional visits to York to admire the Minster and to shop with the family would be tame compared with jaunts to the Talbot and the Old Cock. She knew her brother's innate restlessness, his fretting to mix with poets, painters, sculptors. Aware of the effect which such company had upon him, she must have believed it to be harmful, and considered that the Robinsons would have an opposite effect, and that a normal family circle was what Branwell needed most. A quiet country life, a lad of eleven as companion (and Branwell was the only one of his family genuinely fond of children), a comfortable home atmosphere, with his evenings free for writing – here was the opportunity, she would reason (they must all have reasoned, discussing the plan at the parsonage), for Branwell to start life afresh and develop into the responsible adult his family wished him to become. Anne would no more have taken her brother to a house where there was constant drinking and gambling, where men ill-treated their wives, where a husband had an 'affaire' with a visiting guest under his own roof – all described in her second novel, *The Tenant of Wildfell Hall*, and again held by successive readers to be a true picture of life at Thorp Green – than she would have taken him, had she lodged at Luddenden Foot, among the Liverpool Irish or the boaties at the Weavers Arms.

Mr Edmund Robinson, forty-three years of age when Branwell became tutor to his son, was a clerk in Holy Orders but held no living. He owned a fair-sized estate which he had inherited at the age of three months from his father. Mr Robinson's maiden aunt Jane would seem to have had the control of the estate until her nephew came of age. It was she who paid the bills, dealt with the agent and wrote to the tenants; and when Edmund Robinson at twenty-four became engaged to Miss Lydia Gisborne, daughter of the Reverend Thomas Gisborne of Yoxall Lodge, Staffordshire, it was Aunt Jane who saw to the drawing up of the marriage settlement, and complained afterwards to her solicitor about 'pious, canting old Gisborne', who presumably had left Miss Robinson to pay the brunt of the lawyer's fees. Edmund's mother was taken to York to add her signature to the documents, but it was Jane who made all the arrangements for the day, and told her lawyer: 'I hope the Almighty will bless us and prosper what we are doing. I am sure my nephew deserves to prosper as he is an excellent creature.'

Her two nieces both subsequently married clergymen, and, supported as he was by these pillars of the church, watched over by his mother after his aunt died, Edmund Robinson may have been narrow-minded and unimaginative – he was certainly not corrupt. His account-book, with expenses carefully entered, shows him to have been an indulgent husband and father to his wife and four children – Lydia, Elizabeth, Mary and Edmund – during the period when Branwell Brontë was tutor to his son. The account-book tells of shawls and scarves, parasols and brooches, either with his wife's name – Lydia – beside them, or 'The Girls'.

Branwell's salary was £80 a year: 'Mr Brontë's salary. £20'

is marked on quarter days. The steward and his wife, Mr and Mrs Thomas Sewell, took a prominent part in the running of the house, and Mrs Sewell received thirty pounds as her annual wages. It could be that the Sewells lodged, as Branwell did, in the old dwelling known as the Monk's House, standing within a couple of hundred yards of Thorp Green Hall itself. Here Branwell would have had a sitting-room to himself, where he could write or sketch, and where Anne would join him in those hours when she was free.

That his first few months were not particularly happy ones is obvious from the poem entitled 'Thorp Green', dated March 30th, 1843. This is the only scrap which is known to have been written during the two-and-a-half years he lived with the Robinsons. It was scribbled in the same notebook that he had kept at Luddenden Foot, and the despondent mood is that of 1841 once more, repeating the dispirited hymn-book jingle.

> I sit, this evening, far away
> From all I used to know,
> And nought reminds my soul to-day
> Of happy long ago.
>
> Unwelcome cares, unthought-of fears,
> Around my room arise;
> I seek for suns of former years,
> But clouds o'ercast my skies.
>
> Yes – Memory, wherefore does thy voice
> Bring back old times to view,
> As thou wouldst bid me not rejoice
> In thoughts and prospects new?
>
> I'll thank thee, Memory, in the hour
> When troubled thoughts are mine –

For thou, like suns in April's shower,
On shadowy scenes will shine.

I'll thank thee when approaching death
Would quench life's feeble ember,
For thou wouldst even renew my breath
With thy sweet word 'Remember!'

Branwell, forgetting anything he had learnt from Hartley
Coleridge, and reverting instead to the Methodist hymns he
had sung at Maria's knee, was once more haunted by the spirit
of his dead sister. What was it that she asked of him? It was
like being cleft in two, one part of him longing to hold fast
to the first impressions of childhood, the faith he had learnt
from Maria and his aunt, which Anne still so earnestly held
before him as the only safeguard against despair; and the other
part of him desiring nothing so much as to be back in Halifax,
in high spirits and more than a little drunk, making his friends
laugh with his mocking descriptions of life at Thorp Green.

Leyland and Halifax were miles away: fantasy and the
infernal world, with all its joys, all its terrible consolation,
bringing alternate excitement and lassitude to the body, tension
and torpor to the mind, must be the one indulgence. Was not
Charlotte following the very same path in Brussels?

'It is a curious metaphysical fact,' she wrote to him on May
1st, 1843, 'that always in the evening when I am in the great
dormitory alone, having no other company than a number of
beds with white curtains, I always recur as fanatically as ever
to the old ideas, the old faces, and the old scenes in the world
below.'

Yes, but how deeply was she involved, how utterly
dependent? When morning came, could she concentrate on
teaching English to her French pupils? Or did she hear herself
speak at random, as he did to young Edmund, eye on lesson
book but imagination turning back to the manuscript *And the*

Weary Are At Rest, begun in the summer of 1840 but never finished, in which Maria Thurston, mistress of Darkwall Hall, fell a victim to the wily tongue and impassioned advances of Alexander Percy? In one episode Percy is a guest under the Thurstons' roof at the opening of the grouse shooting.

When, at noon-tide, the diverging groups of sportsmen and attendants met at a lonely spring, whose diamond water gushed up through deep green mosses in a knell of knee-deep heather under a semi-circle of whinstone rock, they seemed all engrossed in the display of their bags or in excusing a want of display . . . All rode triumphant over the acknowledged best shot in the party, Mr Percy.

'Well,' exclaimed Mr O'Connor, turning over Percy's single cock bird, which was minus a head from some access of fury on the part of the shooter. 'Well, gentlemen, hand me the flask. I have lived through many troubles in my time, but this is a regular extinguisher upon all! To think I have nine brace to show against half a one from the best gun between Derbyshire and Westmorland is enough to make me fancy I can pay off my debts . . . Percy, with half a bird! I say, Quamina, hand me over the flask.'

Mr Quamina replied, 'He's head over ears, O'Connor. He has bagged his bird before he donned his jacket, and Thurston had better take care of that . . .'

'Who – I? – What are you saying?' exclaimed the host furiously; but Mr Quamina, evidently astonished, swallowed all reply in another pull at his flask, and Mr Percy, not desirous of being victim of his friends' or host's revenge, tossed off his horn of mountain dew, threw his single headless bird to his old servant, and bidding him take care to bring the pony and his own skin back safe to Darkwall, he lost no time in good mornings and excuses, but dashed back across the gulley and down the long car-truck which served as a path from the peat pits to the farmsteads of a more civilised land.

I cannot be expected to dissect Mr Percy's feelings or emotions during his rapid walk to Darkwall, as I believe he scarce left time to do so himself, but with a scorn of his morning's employment, a distaste towards his morning's companions, and a revulsion of thoughts which made the whole Twelfth a day of black chalks, he sprang over the first stile and strode over the first causeway through the twenty-acre pasture of green land stolen from heather and made part and parcel of Darkwall Farm.

Percy did not make any halt in his intrusion so soon and unexpectedly upon the quietude of the Hall, which expected domestic slumber till evening brought in such visitors as might be willing to turn night into day. He made his return known to the Lady of the Mansion, and was received by her in the breakfast room . . .

During the first moments of her meeting with the unexpectedly arrived guest, no servant about the establishment could have been so dull as not to perceive the embarrassment of their usually calm and sweet-tempered Mistress. The eye which usually had a dove-like glance for all, the voice which had a gentle tone, and the steps which were so quiet, now changed into a phase of irritation in manner, trouble in the eyes, and hesitation both in voice and step; but a ready key might have been given to these changes had the observers been aware of the promise given to her furious husband and meant to be kept as faithfully as made, and the revulsion of all hospitable or ladylike feeling should she keep to the letter of her promise, as well as the still, small voice, scarce daring to whisper amid conflicting winds, which told a woman's and a lady's heart that a visitor was sheltered under her roof whose mind possessed some mettle more attractive than ebullitions of sour reproach; whose feelings had a wider, higher and deeper range than what would be exercised in attempts to ruin others or oneself; whose person likewise had animated instead of cloudy looks, gentle flexibility of tone instead of bilious snappishness, eyes of mobile imaginativeness instead of acerb ill-temper – that she might now, in fact, have hoped for one happy afternoon after so many blank or blotted ones but for the grim, threatening scowl which, from neighbouring moors, frowned upon her companionship the thunder shadows of resentment and revenge.

Just as Ellen Nussey and Mary and Martha Taylor had been ignorant of the part they played in Angrian history, so Mrs Robinson, as she went about her household tasks or sat at her embroidery frame, was unaware that she made a perfect incarnation of Mrs Thurston of Darkwall Hall; while her husband, Branwell's employer, fitted delightfully into the role of jealous, bilious Thurston, who had allowed none of his guests to pay court to the ladies of the household.

Mr and Mrs Robinson, when they invited Mr Brontë to stay for a short visit in the spring of 1843, and complimented him on the excellent characters of his son and daughter, had no more idea than their guest that the well-mannered and most respectful young man whom they had engaged as tutor enacted, during his solitary evenings at the Monk's House, scenes of seduction from the Thurston story of so daring a nature that, when he was confronted with the reality of his position the following morning, and faced with the routine of the day, he was obliged to hold himself in check in order not to destroy the image they had formed of him.

At the beginning of January, 1844, Charlotte finally returned to the parsonage from Brussels, profoundly disillusioned and wounded in spirit, her beloved Professor Héger having shown a certain degree of evasion in her presence, and his wife a marked coldness, which could only mean a united marital front in a situation threatening embarrassment. Later in the month she wrote to Ellen Nussey: 'Anne and Branwell have just left us to return to York. They are both wondrously valued in their situations.' Neither brother nor sister was mentioned again until June 23rd, five months later, when she informed Ellen:

> Anne and Branwell are now at home, and they and Emily add their request to mine that you will join us in the beginning of next week. Write and let us know what day you will come, and how – if by coach we will meet you at Keighley. Do not let your visit be later than the beginning of next week, or you will see little of A and B as their holidays are very short. They will soon have to join the family at Scarborough.

On July 16th both Charlotte and Emily were busy making shirts, presumably for Branwell to wear while escorting the Robinsons in Scarborough. This year the family arrived on July 11th, and took lodgings, as usual, in the most fashionable quarter of the town, at No. 7, Cliff. They were there certainly until August 9th, when their names disappeared from the list of Scarborough visitors.

The local newspapers of August 3rd mentioned the first appearance of the 'celebrated comedian' Robert Roxby, manager not only of the Theatre Royal, Scarborough, but also of the Royal, Manchester. Perhaps it was on this occasion that eighteen-year-old Miss Lydia, the eldest Miss Robinson, who was now 'out' and in society, saw and admired young Henry Roxby, one of the members of the actor's family, with whom she afterwards eloped.

If Miss Lydia Robinson was truly the Rosalie Murray of Anne Brontë's *Agnes Grey*, then she was a very pretty girl indeed.

She was tall and slender, but not thin, perfectly formed, exquisitely fair, but not without a brilliant, healthy bloom; her hair, which she wore in a profusion of long ringlets, was of a very light brown, strongly inclining to yellow; her eyes were pale blue, but so clear and bright, that few could wish them darker; the rest of her features were small, not quite regular, and not remarkable otherwise, but altogether you could not hesitate to pronounce her a very lovely girl . . . She was lively, light-hearted, and could be very agreeable with those who did not cross her will. Towards me, when I first came, she was cold and haughty, then insolent and overbearing; but on a further acquaintance, she gradually laid aside her airs . . . She had never been taught to moderate her desires, to control her temper or bridle her will, or to sacrifice her own pleasure for the good of others; her temper being naturally good, she was never violent or morose, but from constant indulgence and habitual scorn of reason, she was often testy and capricious; her mind had never been cultivated: her intellect at best was somewhat shallow; she possessed considerable vivacity, some quick-ness of perception, and some talent for music and the acquisition of languages.

In *Agnes Grey* Rosalie Murray flirts with every male on sight; and had the novel included a red-haired young tutor never at a loss for conversation, with a turn for imitation and a fund of amusing stories, she would doubtless have made him her willing slave in the first few months. Whatever Lydia Robinson's manner towards Branwell, whether she teased the tutor or ignored him, belongs to the realm of speculation: either mode of treatment would have contributed to his state of distress that summer and autumn. His irritability and tendency to excitement during the brief holiday at home preceding the visit to Scarborough were hinted at in a letter, months later, from Charlotte to Ellen Nussey; and in one of her many, never-answered letters to Professor Héger, written on October 24th, she said: 'My father and my sister send you their respects. My father's infirmity increases little by little. Nevertheless, he is not yet entirely blind. My sisters are well, but my poor brother is always ill.'

No clue exists to the cause of Branwell's illness, but it was evidently not serious enough to warrant his giving up his post and coming home. Had he been drinking, Anne would have noticed it and warned Charlotte, and Charlotte would have phrased her letter to M. Héger differently, or not mentioned her brother at all. She knew too well, from bitter personal experience, how soaring spirits could plunge into despair. Why had she wasted her time in Brussels, waiting day after day for a glance or a smile from her professor that, when it came, would only plunge her into deeper misery? Reason and conscience brought her home. Branwell, with autumn closing in, Mrs Robinson and Miss Lydia going out and about in a society that did not include the tutor, would ask himself the question that Charlotte must have put to herself many times. What have I to show at twenty-seven for my many talents? Am I to remain for the rest of my life a paid employee, a gentleman lackey whose only value lies in opening doors, and winding skeins of silk, and carrying parasols? The familiarity which the Robinsons would have permitted him a year before, with their oldest daughter emerging from the schoolroom, would now be frowned upon and out of place. However gracious they may have been, the division was rigid between employers and employees in the nineteenth century.

It was this attitude that so riled Charlotte, in her two posts as governess, that in unconscious revenge she created Jane Eyre, the most celebrated governess not only of the century but of all time. Anne gave her answer in *Agnes Grey*. It was not so much the people whom she attacked as the system, the snobbery of a society where birth and affluence made employers deem themselves superior to those in humbler circumstances possessing better brains and a wider range of talent.

Did this resentment seize Branwell too? And did he allow his bitterness to turn inward, proudly refusing acceptance of what he thought base humility? If so, his Percy daydream may have induced him to toy for a time with the prospect of Lydia bestowing her favour upon him. Then, snubbed for his pains, did he transfer his infatuation from daughter to mother?

This would seem the most likely explanation of what was happening to Branwell during 1844 and the first few months of 1845. Wounded emotions can swiftly transfer themselves to another object. The few lame verses which he wrote to a lady sketching a self-portait and deliberately, so it would seem, making a poor job of it may have been a first tentative attempt at a declaration, if a very different one from the bravado with which Alexander Percy advanced upon Mrs Thurston.

> Her effort shows a picture made
> To contradict its meaning:
> Where should be sunshine, painting shade,
> And smiles with sadness screening;
> Where God has given a cheerful view,
> A gloomy vista showing;
> Where heart and face are fair and true,
> A shade of doubt bestowing.
>
> Ah, Lady, if to me you give
> The power your sketch to adorn,
> How little of it shall I leave
> Save smiles that shine like morn.
> I'd keep the hue of happy light
> That shines from summer skies;

I'd drive the shades from smiles so bright
And dry such shining eyes.

I'd give a calm to one whose heart
Has banished calm from mine;
I'd brighten up God's work of art
Where thou hast dimmed its shine,
And all the wages I should ask
For such a happy toil —
I'll name them — far beyond my task —
Thy Presence and Thy Smile.

Mrs Robinson — if the poem, which is undated, was in truth addressed to her — could read the vapid lines without a blush. Perhaps the smile, and the mock bow with which she would return it to the author, were seized upon as a promise of better things to come, of a secret understanding that would make every commonplace remark hereafter fraught with a double meaning. How pleasant, after all, the meadows and the stream and the copses of Thorp Green when summer came! The discomforts of Luddenden and Sowerby were a world away.

A smile, a glance, a kindly word in conversation, received as a crumb of comfort, can become transmuted to the bread of life. Starved emotions do not accept defeat. If Branwell loved, he dared to believe himself loved in return.

These were the fantasies that Charlotte had woven around Monsieur Héger in the rue d'Isabelle, but had had the sense to check in time.

An hour hence, in my master's room,
I sat with him alone,
And told him what a dreary gloom
O'er joy had parting thrown.

He little said; the time was brief,
The ship was soon to sail;
And while I sobbed in bitter grief
My master but looked pale.

They called in haste: he bade me go,
Then snatched me back again;
He held me fast and murmured low,
'Why will they part us, Jane? . . .

'They call again: leave then my breast;
Quit thy true shelter, Jane;
But when deceived, repulsed, opprest,
Come home to me again!'

This poem was written in the exercise book which Charlotte brought back with her from Brussels. In January, 1845, when Branwell was entering upon his last months at Thorp Green, she wrote to Monsieur Héger:

Monsieur, the poor have not need of much to sustain them — they ask only for the crumbs that fall from the rich man's table. But if they are refused the crumbs they die of hunger. Nor do I, either, need much affection from those I love. I should not know what to do with a friendship entire and complete — I am not used to it. But you showed me of yore a *little* interest, when I was your pupil in Brussels, and I hold on to the maintenance of that *little* interest — I hold on to it as I would hold on to life . . .'

Branwell too held on to his little interest, but he was not content with the crumbs, nor with the small mercies of day-by-day, nor with dreams. The rich joys of his infernal world must be savoured in reality.

13

No letter survives to tell what happened in that month of July, 1845, when Branwell was dismissed from his post. All is hearsay, gossip and surmise. The few weeks preceding his dismissal contain nothing more than scraps of indirect information – slender clues which, combined with his past history, lead only to theory and supposition, never to established fact.

Mr Robinson's expense book for May gives no hint that anything was wrong. It tells us that Miss Brontë's salary of £10 was due on the 8th of the month; that Mrs Robinson and the girls were in York on the 12th, spending £1 for lodging and an additional £1 10s for soda water. On the 17th there were races at Little Ouseburn – to which Mr Robinson contributed 5s. only – but on the 21st he paid £2 for parasols for his daughters, and on the 29th £1 for their jaunt to Harrogate.

Young Edmund was given 10s. for ferrets on June 1st. On the 11th Miss Brontë was paid £3 10s., and there is a note to the effect that £20 was due to Branwell on July 21st, in six weeks' time. Beneath the word 'July' Mr Robinson drew a little line, perhaps as a reminder that the salary was to be paid in July and not in June. That Anne had already 'handed in her notice' is clear from Charlotte's letter to Ellen Nussey on June 18th: 'Branwell and Anne are both come home and Anne I am rejoined to say has decided not to return to Mr Robinson's – *her* presence at home certainly makes me feel more at liberty.'

Charlotte was trying to arrange a visit to Ellen Nussey, but she could not manage it unless her sisters were at home to look after her father, who was gradually losing his sight and was very low-spirited in consequence. On June 24th she wrote once more to her friend, still endeavouring to make plans, and adding: 'Branwell only stayed a week with us, but he is to come home again when the family go to Scarborough.'

On Monday, June 30th, Emily and Anne made a two-day excursion to York – the first journey they had ever made alone together in their lives. The original plan had been to visit Scarborough, but for some reason they changed their minds. Perhaps Anne was embarrassed that she might meet friends of the Robinsons, and so be obliged to give reasons for having left them; but the sisters could equally well have met the Robinsons themselves in York. The timing of the brief holiday was curious, for if the idea was to show Emily the Minster, an occasion when the Robinsons were safely out of the way at Scarborough might have been chosen instead.

Anne did not speak of the holiday in her four-yearly birthday note, written a month later, but Emily did, saying nothing of sight-seeing, shopping or the Minster, only that they enjoyed themselves very much, and that during the excursion they were 'Ronald Macalgin, Henry Angora, Juliet Angusteena, Rosabella Esmalden, Ella and Julian Egremont, Catharine Navarre and Cordelia Fitzaphnold, escaping from the palaces of instruction to join the Royalists, who are hard driven at present by the victorious Republicans'. This glorious feat of imagination on the part of Emily – twenty-seven the day before she wrote the note – showed that she, at any rate, had no concern with Robinsons or reality, but moved joyously and freely in her own fictitious world.

The Robinsons left for Scarborough on July 5th. This year their lodgings were No. 7a, Cliff, and Mr Robinson noted in his expense book that the journey cost £4 12s. The coach carrying four maids cost a further £1 8s., and William and five horses £1 18 11d. This was William Allison, the stud groom, to whom young Edmund – who, with six others, was tragically drowned twenty-four years later, when a ferryboat bearing the members of the York and Ainsty Hunt overturned in the River Ure – was to leave an annuity of £52 10s. for life.

Young Edmund would by now have been thirteen or fourteen years of age, and that he accompanied William and the horses part of the way seems possible from the entry of 'Edmund's whip, 17s.' in his father's expense book. A halt was evidently called at York for shopping. Mrs Robinson was presented with a brooch costing £1 8s., and three days later, having arrived at Scarborough, she was in need of a new shawl and a smelling-bottle, and on the 11th £4 10s. was spent on ruby and diamond pins.

Edmund cannot have gone on to Scarborough with the rest of the family, for his name was printed in the Scarborough *Herald* on July 24th as having joined them. Presumably he stayed on at Thorp Green until the middle of the month, for there is a note in Mr Robinson's expense book that he was given 12s. 6d. on the 16th. He would not have stayed at home without his tutor. And the significant clue to these various comings and goings is that it was on Thursday the 17th, probably just after he arrived in Scarborough, that Branwell, by now home at Haworth, received the fatal letter from Edmund's father dismissing him from his post.

This direct evidence suggests that the boy, or the servant who accompanied him – for the lad of thirteen or fourteen would hardly have travelled alone – on his arrival in Scarborough gave some account of the tutor which warranted instant action on Mr Robinson's part.

Charlotte was away from home, staying with Ellen Nussey, when the letter arrived. She returned to Haworth two days later, and was told the news. When she informed Ellen Nussey of the fact twelve days afterwards, the first shock of discovery was over. Branwell, stunned at first by the blow, then stupefied by drink to deaden shame, had been hurried off to Liverpool in the care of John Brown.

In her letter, Charlotte did not say when Branwell had returned from Thorp Green. She gave no reason for the dismissal. The words which she used to Ellen Nussey were significant.

> It was ten o'clock at night when I got home. I found Branwell ill; he is so very often owing to his own fault. I was not therefore shocked at first, but when Anne informed me of the immediate cause of his present illness, I was very greatly shocked. He had last Thursday received a note from Mr Robinson sternly dismissing him, intimating that he had discovered his proceedings, which he characterised as bad beyond expression, and charging him on pain of exposure to break off instantly and for ever all communication with every member of his family. We have had sad work with Branwell since. He thought of nothing but drowning his distress of mind. No one in the house could have rest . . .'

The words 'proceedings', 'bad beyond expression' and 'on pain of exposure' sound as if they are being quoted direct from Mr Robinson's letter. Father and sisters alike would have demanded: 'But what have you done?' Horror, shame, remorse, then half a bottle of whisky would be Branwell's first measure of protection. A man who is stupefied by alcohol cannot answer questions.

Branwell had not been with the family at Scarborough. He had committed some action either at Thorp Green or in the neighbourhood which had been revealed to his employer. If Branwell had been writing love letters to Mrs Robinson, the husband would not have threatened him with 'exposure', for to expose Branwell would also expose the lady who received the letters. Did the Robinsons keep silence for the sake of

Anne, and to spare Mr Brontë, having learnt something about Branwell which, in his father's near-blindness and uncertain state of health, might have proved a death-blow? It is possible that, left at Thorp Green with Edmund, and free from the constraining presence of his employer, he had attempted in some way to lead Edmund astray: no other 'proceedings . . . bad beyond expression' would quite seem to warrant 'pain of exposure', and a charge 'to break off instantly and for ever all communication with every member of the family'.

Luddenden and the days of 'grovelling carelessness, of malignant yet cold debauchery', were only three years distant; whatever fever of excitement, whatever desperate impulse drove Branwell Brontë, in the guise of his demon Percy, to lose control in the presence of *someone* at Thorp Green Hall or the immediate neighbourhood, he could no more help himself than any other unhappy creature in the grip of a severe neurosis. His state of shock would have been such that the necessity to forget was paramount. Percy had committed an action which Branwell would condemn, therefore the action must be blotted out; but the emotion precipitating the action must be translated into one which Branwell could himself forgive. What else could he do, when waking from his stupor to face Charlotte's accusing eyes, but stammer out a tale of love for Mrs Robinson? Surely, he thought, such a confession would bring understanding, and as he turned it over in his mind it became the truth, giving rhyme and reason for his employer's anger. Anne, whose own reason for quitting the Robinsons has never been discovered, although she could not condone her brother's behaviour would do her best to excuse it.

The contrast in attitude between Emily and Anne showed itself in the birthday notes which were written on July 31st. Speaking of the note written four years before, in 1841, Anne said: 'I was then at Thorp Green, and now I am only just escaped from it. I was wishing to leave it then, and if I had known I had four years longer to stay how wretched I should have been; but during my stay I have had some very unpleasant and undreamt-of experiences of human nature . . . Branwell has left Luddenden Foot, and been a tutor at Thorp Green, and had much tribulation and ill-health. He was very ill on Thursday, but he went with John Brown to Liverpool, where he now is, I suppose; and we hope he will be better and do better in future.' She concluded her note by admitting: 'I, for my part, cannot well be flatter or older in mind than I am now.'

The 'undreamt-of experiences of human nature' has been held to mean that Anne was a silent witness of a love affair between her brother and her employer's wife. The words fit, and yet . . . There are still missing links in that chain of evidence, some reason needed for Anne's four-year stay at Thorp Green other than care for her brother.

Emily's birthday note referred only briefly to Branwell's 'tribution': 'We are all in decent health, only that Papa has a complaint in his eyes and with the exception of B., who, I hope, will be better and do better hereafter.' She continued by 'merely desiring that everybody could be as comfortable as myself and as undesponding, and then we should have a very tolerable world of it'.

Unrequited passion had not come her way, nor undreamt-of experience. Those who suffered these afflictions were unfortunate. Emily evidently thought that too much had been made of the events at Thorp Green.

It was on Tuesday, July 29th, that Branwell had sufficiently recovered to be packed off to Liverpool with John Brown. Charlotte concluded her letter of information to Ellen Nussey on the 31st – the day her younger sisters wrote their birthday notes – by saying:

> At last we have been obliged to send him from home for a week, with someone to look after him; he has written to me this morning, expressing some sense of

contribution for his frantic folly; he promises amend-
ment on his return, but so long as he remains at home
I scarce dare hope for peace in the house. We must all,
I fear, prepare for a season of distress and disquietude.

Ellen Nussey, whose elder brother George was now in a
lunatic asylum in York after a series of breakdowns, finally
dying there, was hardly in a position to send back encour-
aging advice. Charlotte saw herself trapped, with a sightless
father and a neurotic brother. No wonder she flung herself
down on the dining-room sofa after finishing her letter, telling
Anne she hoped to find another situation, and wishing she
could go to Paris. The atmosphere at the parsonage that
Thursday afternoon drove Emily to scribble her note in the
kitchen. Tabby and Martha were better company than either
of her sisters. And Branwell, the cause of all the stress, who
had suffered 'tribulation', tried to forget his shame on
Merseyside, scene of former frolics in company with Hartley
Merrall. But boaties and sailors had lost their charm, the rough
humour of John Brown failed to distract, and he could not
forget that everyone who mattered most to him faced the
North and not the Irish Sea. An excursion by steamer to
North Wales, with a band aboard striking up *Ye Banks and
Braes* – the sort of thing that would have delighted him once,
with John to join in the chorus – only produced a greater
melancholy. He told the sculptor Leyland after he returned
home on Sunday, August 3rd:

> I found during my absence that wherever I went a
> certain woman robed in black, and calling herself
> 'MISERY', walked by my side, and leant on my arm as
> affectionately as if she were my legal wife. Like some
> other husbands I could have spared her presence.
>   I need hardly add that I shall myself be most delighted
> to see you,

181

Branwell continued in his letter to Leyland – who had once again been commissioned to design a tablet in Haworth church, this time to the memory of William Weightman –

> as God knows I have a tolerably heavy load on my mind just now, and would look to an hour spent with one like yourself as a means of at least temporarily lightening it.

That August in Scarborough Mr Robinson totted up sums in his expense book. Sixty-five guineas for a stay of five weeks. Five shillings to the band, £10 to the butcher, £1 6s. for house linen and the gift of a dog to his wife on August 7th, costing the sum of £2. As to young Edmund, to make certain he would run no risk of future contamination with undesirable characters in or about Thorp Green, he would be sent away in the care of a clergyman, the Rev. Theophilous Williams, of Charlton Mackwell, near Somerton, in Somerset – in short, as far away from Yorkshire as possible.

Young Edmund remained with Mr Williams for five years, until he was eighteen, and at his departure the clerical tutor wrote that 'few young men have passed the critical period of life at which he has arrived with more purity and innocence. His moral conduct has been exemplary, and that his mental acquirements are so very inferior is his infelicity rather than his fault.' So the stables and the woodsheds of Thorp Green had not, after all, proved his downfall, nor the influence of Branwell Brontë fatal to character.

Branwell himself, during the August and September of 1845, had sufficiently roused himself from shock to retire upstairs to his old studio and sort out his manuscripts with the intention of shaping a novel from the many fragments. Charlotte told Ellen: 'His health and consequently his temper have been somewhat better this last day or two, because he is now forced to abstain.'

'I have,' Branwell wrote to the sculptor Leyland on September 10th,

since I last saw you at Halifax, devoted my hours of time snatched from downright illness, to the composition of a three-volume novel — one volume of which is completed — and along with the two forthcoming ones has been really the result of half-a-dozen by-past years of thoughts about, and experience in, this crooked path of Life.

I felt that I must rouse myself to attempt something while roasting daily and nightly over a slow fire — to while away my torment; and I knew that in the present state of the publishing and reading world a novel is the most saleable article, so that where ten pounds would be offered for a work the production of which would require the utmost stretch of a man's intellect, two hundred pounds would be a refused offer for three volumes whose composition would require the smoking of a cigar and the humming of a tune.

My novel is the result of years of thought and if it gives a vivid picture of human feelings for good and evil — veiled by the cloak of deceit which must enwrap man and woman — if it records, as faithfully as the pages that unveil man's heart in Hamlet or Lear, the conflicting feelings and clashing pursuits in our uncertain path through life, I shall be as much gratified (and as much astonished) as I should be if in betting that I could jump over the Mersey I jumped over the Irish Sea. It would not be more pleasant to light on Dublin instead of Birkenhead than to leap from the present bathos of fictitious literature on to the firmly fixed rock honoured by the foot of a Smollett or a Fielding.

That jump I expect to take when I can model a rival to your noble Theseus, who haunted my dreams when

I slept after seeing him – but meanwhile I can try my utmost to rouse myself from almost killing cares, and that alone will be its own reward.

If this projected novel had been a continuation of the draft read to Leyland and William Dearden some years before, which his friends afterwards recognized as *Wuthering Heights*, Branwell would surely have reminded his friend of the fact. In any case, the phrases used in his letter do not suggest the passionate drama of a romantic novel. It is obvious that Branwell intended to write, in satirical vein, the life story of Alexander Percy, placed in a contemporary setting, pruned of all the old Angrian history, its wars and politics, and portraying Percy as a Yorkshire landowner flinging himself into every sort of dissipation. The long soliloquies of Percy, visiting the tomb of his dead wife Mary, would be what Branwell had in mind when he used the words 'Hamlet or Lear' in his letter to the sculptor; while the riotous fun of the same Percy, disguised as a Methodist preacher, accompanied by his band of companions, would all form part of the 'cloak of deceit', the 'conflicting feelings and clashing pursuits' which had torn Branwell himself in two during his adult years.

Whatever his intention, the novel was never completed; or if it was Branwell himself, in a fit of despair, later 'fed it to the flames' in the parsonage grate, so that it might escape a 'printer's fire', which he feared would be its fate.

His decision to shut himself up and write must have been prompted by the creative energy of all three sisters at this time. It was in the autumn of 1845 that Charlotte made her famous discovery of the book of verse in Emily's handwriting, and the three sisters, after some objection on Emily's part, agreed, in Charlotte's words, 'to arrange a small selection of our poems, and, if possible, get them printed. Averse to personal publicity, we veiled our names under those of Currer, Ellis, and Acton Bell.' The choice of pseudonyms may have been

184

picked at random, but Ellis – Emily's choice – could have been derived from Ellis Gate, the old name of Johnny Grimshaw's Ewood property on the heights beyond Luddenden, or from the Mr Elles of one of Branwell's Angrian tales.

Branwell, too, was writing scraps of poetry that autumn. Brother and sisters must all have had an intense desire to recapture the spirit of the old days when the nursery-study had been their haven, and Chief Genius Brannii the instigator of every whim and plan.

Now everything was changed. They wrote divided and apart: Charlotte in the bedroom that had been her aunt's, Emily in the old nursery that was now her room, Anne in the dining-room, Branwell in his studio. Emily alone was happy. No outward source could filter into her uncontaminated well of inspiration. Looking eastward through her window, she would see the cluster of the Pleiades in the night sky, and the horns of Taurus; and however much Charlotte might sigh for her lost professor, Anne for an idealized Weightman, Branwell for a dream Lydia, she would have her own consolation, more durable than theirs could ever be.

He comes with western winds, with evening's wandering airs,
With that clear dusk of heaven that brings the thickest stars;
Winds take a pensive tone, and stars a tender fire,
And visions rise and change which kill me with desire.

After this, the gloomy 'Penmaenmawr', Branwell's ode to the Welsh mountain written in recollection of his steamer trip from Liverpool, and the even gloomier 'Real Rest' – with its opening lines:

I see a corpse upon the waters lie,
With eyes turned, swelled and sightless, to the sky,
And arms outstretched to move, as wave on wave
Upbears it in its boundless billowy grave . . .

– are better left unquoted. Fantasy and laudanum were rapidly destroying what creative powers were still within him.

An undated sonnet entitled 'The Callousness Produced by Care' may have been written during this autumn, though more likely it belongs to an earlier year. It cannot compare with Emily's maturer work – as she increased in power so her brother declined – but it was certainly the last sonnet Branwell wrote which would have any sort of merit at all.

> Why hold young eyes the fullest fount of tears
> And why do youthful breasts the oftenest sigh
> When fancied friends forsake, or lovers fly,
> Or fancied woes and dangers waken fears?
> Ah! He who asks has seen but springtide years,
> Or Time's rough voice had long since told him why!
> Increase of days increases misery,
> And misery brings selfishness, which sears
> The heart's first feelings – mid the battle's roar
> In Death's dread gasp the soldier's eyes are blind
> To other's pains – so he whose hopes are o'er
> Turns coldly from the sufferings of mankind.
> A bleeding spirit will delight in gore –
> A tortured heart will make a Tyrant mind.

This would undoubtedly have been worth including in the small volume of poems which the three sisters were considering that autumn. It may have been that the first thought was for all four to contribute, but that when the suggestion was put to Branwell he would not agree. If this verse had no merit on its own account he would have no desire to see it bolstered by his sisters'. He had tried too often to get his verses into print. It was a waste of time and patience. They must do as they pleased, they would never find a publisher.

So Currer, Ellis and Acton Bell went quietly ahead with

186

the sorting and choosing of their own poems, leaving their brother to flourish his pseudonym Northangerland at the base of his.

On 20 October something happened to drive all thought of poetry out of Branwell's head. Anne may have expected it, sighing that such a thing was bound to happen to anyone so headstrong who had never learnt self-control; but to Branwell it must have opened up possibilities of which he had never dared to dream. A little more persuasion, a little more daring, and the prize snatched from under Mr Robinson's nose might have been his. Nineteen-year-old Lydia Robinson ran away with the actor Henry Roxby of Scarborough, and married him at Gretna Green.

14

It was not until after Lydia Robinson's elopement that Branwell declared openly, in letters to his friends, that he had been in love with Lydia's mother and she with him. The runaway marriage acted like a torch to tinder, and his imagination was on fire with possibilities.

First would come regret that he had wasted his own chances – for what did the actor possess that he lacked? – and, secondly, the new fantasy that what the daughter had done the mother could do too. Confusion between mother and daughter of the same name must have been intense to a mind that could no longer distinguish between illusion and reality. His demon Percy was in full possession now, stripping him of self-control, leaving the shell of Branwell bereft of judgement and emotionally drained – not the all-conquering Alexander of the early Angrian tales, but the aged Earl of Northangerland, who had lost wife, mistress and daughter.

Branwell must have kept silence about the daughter's runaway marriage, for no one in Haworth knew of it. Even ten or more years later, when Mrs Gaskell was collecting material for her biography of Charlotte, not a word was said to her about it. The only thing that mattered to Branwell, in the summer of 1845, was to transmute the mother's distress at her daughter's disgrace into despair at her own separation from Branwell. Here was fuel with which to feed the fire of gossip and Branwell's own obsession. This was perhaps the origin of the stories circulating in Haworth, and repeated with gusto to Mrs Gaskell, that Mrs Robinson had proposed elopement with Branwell, and met him clandestinely in Harrogate. He had no other source by which to live now but the continual tragedy of his broken heart. Here was the ultimate excuse, the valid reason for failure. If the broken heart were mended, the bleeding wound staunched, he would be nothing but a man of twenty-eight who had wasted the best years of his life.

It was to Francis Grundy, the engineer, that he first wrote his confession; and although the letter bore no date when Grundy printed it in his book, from internal evidence it appears to have been written in October. Grundy's *Pictures of the Past*, published in 1879, when Mrs Robinson – later Lady Scott – had been dead for twenty years, was probably never seen by her descendants; otherwise the offending letter, so often quoted since, might have been challenged, and the matter it contained denied. Mrs Gaskell, who in her biography of Charlotte, first published in March, 1857, called Mrs Robinson Branwell's 'paramour', and accused her of 'criminal advances', was threatened with a libel action by Mrs Robinson's solicitors, and was obliged to make a public apology, through her own lawyers, which was printed in *The Times*. Leyland the printer, reporting this when he published his own book on the Brontë family in 1886, said that 'the indignation of the injured lady knew no bounds, and that she was only dissuaded from carrying the matter to a trial by the earnest desire of her friends'. He also stated that a gentleman he had spoken to, 'who knew this lady personally, had good reason for entirely disbelieving the stories, relating to the lady in question'. Certainly Francis Leyland's own opinion was that the story had 'no foundation save in Branwell's heated imagination', and his brother the sculptor never believed it.

'For a time Branwell could talk of nothing but of the lady to whom he was attached,' said Francis Leyland.

This lady, he said, loved him to distraction. She was in a state of inconceivable agony at his loss. Her husband, cruel, brutal, and unfeeling, threatened her with his dire indignation, and deprivation of every comfort. Branwell told one friend by letter that in consequence of this persecution the suffering lady 'had placed herself under his protection', and many other stories, equally unfounded, extravagant, and impossible, were circulated. In a word, he went about among his friends, telling to each, in strict confidence, the woes under which he suffered, and painting in gloomy colours the miseries which the lady of his love had been compelled to undergo.

This is the letter which Branwell wrote to Grundy in the autumn of 1845.

I fear you will burn my present letter on recognising the handwriting; but if you will read it through, you will perhaps rather pity than spurn the distress of mind which would prompt my communication, after a silence of nearly three (to me) eventful years. While very ill and confined to my room I wrote to you two months ago, hearing that you were resident engineer of the Skipton Railway, to the inn at Skipton. I never received any reply, and as my letter asked only for one day of your society, to ease a very weary mind in the company of a friend who *always* had what I always wanted, but most want now, *cheerfulness*, I am sure you never received my letter, or your heart would have prompted an answer.

Since I last shook hands with you in Halifax, two summers ago, my life till lately has been one of apparent happiness and indulgence. You will ask, 'Why does he complain then?' I can only reply by showing the undercurrent of distress which bore my bark to a whirlpool, despite the surface waves of life that seemed floating me to peace. In a letter begun in the spring, and never finished owing to incessant attacks of illness, I tried to tell you that I was tutor to the son of

Edmund Robinson, a wealthy gentleman whose wife is sister to the wife of Mr Evans, M.P. for the county of North Derbyshire, and the cousin of Lord——. This lady (though her husband detested me) showed me a degree of kindness which, when I was deeply grieved one day at her husband's conduct, ripened into declarations of more than ordinary feeling. My admiration of her mental and personal attractions, my knowledge of her unselfish sincerity, her sweet temper, and unwearied care for others, with but unrequited return where most should have been given . . . although she is seventeen years my senior, all combined to an attachment on my part, and led to reciprocations which I had little looked for. During nearly three years I had daily 'troubled pleasure, soon chastised by fear'. Three months since I received a furious letter from my employer, threatening to shoot me if I returned from my vacation, which I was passing at home; and letters from her lady's maid and physician informed me of the outbreak, only checked by her firm courage and resolution that whatever harm came to her, none should come to me . . .

I have lain during nine long weeks utterly shattered in body and broken down in mind. The probability of her becoming free to give me herself and her estate never rose to drive away the prospect of her decline under her present grief. I dreaded, too, the wreck of my mind and body, which, God knows, during a short life have been severely tried. Eleven continuous nights of sleepless horror reduced me to almost blindness, and being taken into Wales to recover, the sweet scenery, the sea, the sound of music caused me fits of unspeakable distress. You will say, 'What a fool!' but if you knew the many causes I have for sorrow which I cannot even hint at here, you would perhaps pity as well as blame.

At the kind request of Mr Macaulay and Mr

Baines, I have striven to arouse my mind by writing something worthy of being read, but I really cannot do so. Of course you will despise the writer of all this. I can only answer that the writer does the same, and would not wish to live if he did not hope that work and change may yet restore him.

Apologising sincerely for what seems like whining egotism, and hardly daring to hint about days when in your company I could sometimes sink the thoughts which 'remind me of departed days', I fear never to return, – I remain, etc.

If Francis Grundy, whose garrulous reminiscences proclaim him an incessant chatterbox, repeated the contents of his friend's letter to his many acquaintances on the railway staff, the gist, through repetition and misrepresentation, would suggest an innocent young man in the toils of a lady of easy virtue. At the same time, the fact that Branwell's constant requests for employment, through Grundy, never seem to have reached the executive railway authorities implies that the engineer knew his friend's weaknesses too well, and, however fond of him, had no desire to recommend him for a situation. 'I believe, however, he was half mad, and could not control himself,' Grundy admitted, referring to the Luddenden year of 1841–2.

On 25 November Branwell sent his poem 'Penmaenmawr' to Joseph Leyland, asking him to forward it to the Halifax *Guardian*.

'I have no other way,' he told the sculptor,

not pregnant with danger, of communicating with one whom I cannot help loving. Printed lines with my usual signature 'Northangerland' would excite no suspicion – as my late employer shrank from the bare idea of my being able to write anything, and had a day's sickness after hearing that Macaulay had sent me a complimentary letter, so *he* won't know the name.

I sent through a private channel one letter of comfort in her great and agonising present afflictions, but I recalled it through dread of the consequences of a discovery.

The 'afflictions', of course, were the shock and anxiety of her daughter's elopement, but the sculptor was not to know this. Leyland must believe, like everyone else, that Mrs Robinson was pining for grief at his absence.

'I suffer very much,' Branwell said,

from that mental exhaustion, which arises from brooding on matters useless at present to think of, and active employment would be my greatest cure and blessing – for really, after hours of thoughts which business would have hushed, I have felt as if I could not live, and, if long continued, such a state will bring on permanent affection of the heart, which is already bothered with most uneasy palpitations.

I should like extremely to have an hour's sitting with you, and if I had the chance, I would promise to try not to be gloomy. You said you would be at Haworth ere long but that ere has doubtless changed to nc'er, so I must wish to get to Halifax sometime to see you.

I saw Murray's monument praised in the papers, and I trust you are getting on well with Beckwith's, as well as with your own personal statue of living flesh and blood. Mine, like your Theseus, has lost its hands and feet, and, I fear, its head also, for it can neither move, write or think as it once could . . .

Leyland, heavily in debt, snowed under with commitments which he could not fulfil, was still fond enough of his many friends to welcome them to his studio and listen to their woes, but Branwell and his broken heart must have been a trial to patience. Nothing is so tedious as the love affair of another when it has turned to obsession, and Branwell in despair was very different company from Branwell in exultation. Leyland, slaving away at mural tablets to meet his debts instead of at the giant figures he preferred, surely groaned inwardly when Branwell repeated, for the tenth time, the story of his love for Lydia Robinson. Leyland's own financial affairs were far more disturbing to him. Only £68 for the tablet to the Reverend John Murray in Halifax parish church, and now he was behindhand with the monument to Stephen Beckwith in York Minster, for which he was to be paid £250 and find his own material, an impossible task at the price, when the full-length recumbent figure of Dr Beckwith and the slab had both to be of pure statuary marble, the tomb of white Huddlestone stone and the cover of black polished marble. Even the £50 on account he asked for was but grudgingly allowed him by the memorial committee, which believed in treating a famous sculptor like a working mason.

Branwell, however, could not be expected to interest himself in such mundane matters.

I know a flower, whose leaves were meant to bloom
Till Death should snatch it to adorn a tomb,
Now, blanching 'neath the blight of hopeless grief,
With never blooming, and yet living leaf;
A flower on which my mind would wish to shine,
If but one beam could break from mind like mine.
I had an ear which could on accents dwell
That might as well say 'perish' as 'farewell'!
An eye which saw, far off, a tender form,
Beaten, unsheltered, by affliction's storm;
An arm – a lip – that trembled to embrace
My angel's gentle breast and sorrowing face;
A mind that clung to Ouse's fertile side
While tossing – objectless – on Menai's tide!

The sculptor, shaking his head over the lines from 'Penmaenmawr', must have sighed for the excited fellow of a few years back who, at the Cross Roads Inn, had read some pages of very different stuff. He gave the poem to his brother the printer, who was much impressed, feeling that 'the lady, whose charms had bewildered his [Branwell's] imagination, had supplied him with a subject for sorrowful recollections'. Francis Leyland, himself newly married, and about to become a Roman Catholic, had more compassion, though possibly less perception, than the sculptor, and he hoped to convert not only his unbelieving brother but his brother's erring friends.

It seems incredible that Branwell and Charlotte, so close in childhood, so understanding of one another in adolescence, should not at this moment have shared each other's troubles. Perhaps they did. No surviving letter tells us they did not.

Proof exists that Charlotte was yearning for her professor; but we have only Branwell's letters to his friends to tell us that his passion for Mrs Robinson was real.

Less than a week before Branwell wrote to his friend the sculptor of Mrs Robinson's 'agonising present afflictions', Charlotte had told Monsieur Héger:

I have done everything; I have sought occupation; I have denied myself absolutely the pleasure of speaking about you – even to Emily; but I have been able to conquer neither my regrets nor my impatience. That, indeed, is humiliating – to be unable to control one's own thoughts, to be the slave of a regret, of a memory, the slave of a fixed and dominant idea which lords it over the mind. Why cannot I have just as much friendship for you, as you for me – neither more nor less? Then should I be so tranquil, so free – I could keep silence then for ten years without effort.

195

Surely she was thinking of Branwell when she penned the words 'the slave of a fixed and dominant idea', and the possibility that she was suffering for the same reason, and with as bad a grace, was hateful to her.

'Your last letter was stay and prop to me,' she told her late professor,

> nourishment to me for half a year. Now I need another and you will give it me; not because you bear me friendship – you cannot have much – but because you are compassionate of soul and you would condemn no one to prolonged suffering to save yourself a few moments' trouble. To forbid me to write to you, to refuse to answer me, would be to tear from me my only joy on earth, to deprive me of my last privilege – a privilege I shall never consent willingly to surrender. Believe me, my master, in writing to me it is a good deed that you will do. So long as I believe you are pleased with me, so long as I have hope of receiving news from you, I can be at rest and not too sad. But when a prolonged and gloomy silence seems to threaten me with the estrangement of my master – when day by day I await a letter, and when day by day disappointment comes to fling me back in overwhelming sorrow, and the sweet delight of seeing your handwriting and reading your counsel escapes me as a vision that is vain, then fever claims me – I lose appetite and sleep – I pine away.

No sister who wrote lines such as this to a married man, years older than herself, could possibly wholly condemn a brother who vowed that he had been dismissed from his post as tutor for expressing just these sentiments. The letter which Branwell told Leyland he wrote to Mrs Robinson, and then withdrew, may even have been written at the same time as Charlotte wrote to the professor, some chord of sympathy or intuition uniting brother and sister in their common misery, just as years before they had invented and developed the same characters in the Angrian stories. For Monsieur Héger and Lydia Robinson were in truth those identical characters pegged on to living people. The infernal world had come alive for both Branwell and Charlotte, but without the old delight, the lovely solace. Figures of flesh and blood, unlike Zamorna and Mary Percy, could not be moulded as the will desired, but chose their own direction.

To Ellen Nussey, so often her confidante, Charlotte said nothing of Monsieur Héger or of the manuscript she was adapting, which she would call *The Professor*, or of the poems she was collecting and intended to have published. But she could at least complain of Branwell, if only because a sick and erring brother was the one thing in the world Ellen would understand, with one of her own being nursed at home and another in an asylum.

'Branwell offers no prospect of hope – he professes to be too ill to think of seeking for employment – he makes comfort scant at home,' she told Ellen on January 23rd, 1846, which was the very date that Emily began a poem with the lines:

No coward soul is mine,
 No trembler in the world's storm-troubled sphere;
I see Heaven's glories shine,
And Faith shines equal, arming me from Fear.

What a blessed relief it must have been for Emily to stride away over the moors with her dog, and put aside, if only for an hour on a winter's afternoon, the memory of her brother humped on his bed thinking of his Lydia, and her sister crouched on the dining-room sofa brooding on her professor. Meanwhile Branwell, too listless to walk with her as he would have done once, too obsessed with his own image to collaborate in

Earnshaw history, sat up in the bleak studio finishing the poem to a corpse which he had started back in the autumn.

> I have an outward frame, unlike to thine,
> Warm with young life – not cold in death's decline;
> An eye that sees the sunny light of Heaven –
> A heart by pleasure thrilled, by anguish riven –
> But, in exchange for thy untroubled calm,
> Thy gift of cold oblivion's healing balm,
> I'd give my youth, my health, my life to come,
> And share thy slumbers in thy ocean tomb.

Beside the last lines of another undated poem, entitled 'Juan Fernandez', he scribbled 'Lydia' in Greek.

> Tossed overboard, my perished crew
> Of Hopes and Joys sink, one by one,
> To where their fellow-thoughts have gone
> Where past gales breathed or tempests blew
> Each last fond look ere sight declines
> To where my own Fernandez shines,
> Without one hope that they may e'er
> Storm-worn, recline in sunshine there.

March was an evil month, cold and grey, and, with Charlotte away from home on her first snatched visit to Ellen Nussey since last July, Branwell could persuade his father into giving him a sovereign. A little store of gin and laudanum could thus be obtained. What blessed release it gave from pain and misery, what a blotting-out of feeling, and before full oblivion set in such strange and wandering images filled the room, the two Lydias beside him, mother and daughter in one, their shining faces sometimes turning into his own mother and sister, the two Marias.

'I went into the room where Branwell was, to speak to

him, about an hour after I got home,' wrote Charlotte to Ellen Nussey on March 3rd.

It was very forced work to address him. I might have spared myself the trouble, as he took no notice, and made no reply; he was stupefied. My fears were not in vain. Emily tells me that he got a sovereign from Papa while I have been away, under the pretence of paying a pressing debt; he went immediately and changed it at a public-house, and has employed it as was to be expected. She concluded her account by saying he was a 'hopeless being'; it is too true. In his present state it is scarcely possible to stay in the room where he is. What the future has in store I do not know.

She wrote on the same day to Messrs Aylott & Jones, sending them a draft for £31 10s. to cover the cost of the printing of the poems by Currer, Ellis and Acton Bell. Her aunt's legacy could be well employed. How providential, she may have thought, that none of it had been left to Branwell – he would only have spent it on drink.

On March 28th Charlotte requested the publishers to send all proofs and letters in future to Miss Brontë rather than C. Brontë Esq., a little mistake having occurred the day before. Did Branwell open the packet, and see what his sisters were about? If they wanted to print poems at their own expense, let them. They could afford to do so. He could not. Nevertheless, they need not think themselves the only poets in the household. Six days later he composed an 'Epistle From a Father to a Child in Her Grave', inspired, possibly, by some earlier Percy poem, and now interwoven with fantasies of what might have been. Perhaps he was thinking of Mrs Robinson's baby Georgiana, who had died as an infant before he ever went to Thorp Green, or of some other young child laid to rest in Haworth churchyard. Hartley and Harriet Merrall's little

199

William Edwin, possibly, buried five years ago, in April, during his first year of life:

If then thoud'st seen, upon a summer sea,
One, once in features, as in blood, like thee,
On skies of azure blue and waters green,
Melting to mist amid the summer sheen,
In troubles gazing – ever hesitating
'Twixt miseries each new dread creating,
And joys – whate'er they cost – still doubly dear,
Those 'troubled pleasures soon chastised by fear';
If thou hadst seen him, thou would'st ne'er believe
That thou had'st yet known what it was to live!

Thine eyes could only see thy mother's breast;
Thy feelings only wished on that to rest;
That was thy world; thy food and sleep it gave,
And slight the change 'twixt it and childhood's grave.
Thou saw'st this world like one who, prone, reposes,
Upon a plain, and in a bed of roses,
With nought in sight save marbled skies above,
Nought heard but breezes whispering in the grove:
I – thy life's source – was like a wanderer breasting
Keen mountain winds, and on a summit resting,

Whose rough rocks rose above the grassy mead,
With sleet and north winds howling overhead,
And Nature, like a map, beneath him spread;
Far winding river, tree, and tower and town,
Shadow and sunlight, 'neath his gaze marked down
By that mysterious hand which graves the plan
Of that drear country called 'The Life of Man' . . .

The poem's interest lies in the images conjured by certain lines. The 'skies of azure blue and water's green', the 'bed of roses', the 'marbled skies', the 'wanderer breasting keen mountain winds, and on a summit resting' – all these are successive dream-pictures, while the dead child is not only Branwell himself who, prone, reposes' but also his other wandering self poised on the heights above.

The sensation of being, as it were, 'out of the body', looking down upon the other self, is a well-known sign of the mental disorder known today as schizophrenia. The taking of alcohol or laudanum would inevitably increase Branwell's susceptibility to images both horrific and beautiful, leaving him suggestible to any impulse, and therefore a potential danger to those about him. The tales of upset candles, burning bedclothes, concealed carving-knives, all common chat in Haworth later, and repeated to successive visitors, must have dated from this period, when Branwell, aware of heightened imagination and failing concentration, was obliged to enact, in some outward fashion, the promptings of the demon within. If Emily read aloud to her brother, as she did to her sisters, the scenes in *Wuthering Heights* which, according to Charlotte, 'banished sleep by night and disturbed mental peace by day', then the identification of himself with Hindley Earnshaw was very possible.

He would have seen all three sisters working on their novels during these months. Their method of writing was known to him, the way they set about it, the unvarying routine. Had he not been their leader once, and Genius Brannii? It was on April 6th, 1846, that Charlotte wrote once more to Aylott & Jones, who were printing the poems, to ask advice about a 'work of fiction, consisting of three distinct and unconnected tales', which 'C., E. and A. Bell' were 'preparing for the Press'. Branwell knew all three 'tales'. The early part of Charlotte's *The Professor* had been worked up from their Angrian stories of Alexander Percy's sons; *Wuthering Heights* was the final Heathcliff narrative, completed with the second generation; and *Agnes Grey* the 'Passages in the Life of an Individual' which

Anne had been struggling with at Thorp Green. He would not believe that a publisher would risk his money and reputation by printing novels or poems by unknown authors, but if the girls cared to try their luck it was their own affair. Certainly they would not receive any encouragement from him.

His own plan was more ambitious. He would write an epic about an ancestral connection of Leyland's, the beautiful Anne Leyland of Morley Hall near Lancaster, eldest daughter of stern Sir Thomas Leyland. Anne fell in love with one Edward Tyldesley, and, notwithstanding her father's anger and disapproval, eloped one night and fled to her lover's moated home. About her waist was a rope, and she threw the loose end to her waiting lover on the farther side of the water, so that he was able to draw it to shore, and his loved one with it. The legend was the more remarkable because, although the irate father had a son and heir, the manor house of Morley passed to the Tyldesley family through this clandestine marriage. The resemblance between this story and Lydia Robinson's elopement is too close to be pure accident.

'You ask if we are more comfortable,' wrote Charlotte to Ellen on April 14th.

I wish I could say anything favourable – but how can we be more comfortable so long as Branwell stays at home and degenerates instead of improving? It has lately been intimated to him that he would be received again on the same railroad where he was formerly stationed if he would behave more steadily, but he refuses to make an effort, he will not work – and at home he is a drain on every resource – an impediment to all happiness. But there's no use complaining.

No use at all. All the same, Charlotte must have complained of his conduct. Cold looks and nagging tongues, or, worse

202

still, a stony silence and a swift covering-up of conversation if he did choose to enter the dining-room, encouraged him to escape over to Halifax, and fling himself on Leyland's mercy.

The three hours he had intended to stay stretched into three days. The shake-down at No. 10, The Square, was better than the back bedroom at the parsonage, especially when the sculptor fed him with nips of whisky or gin to steady his brain. The letter of thanks which Branwell wrote the sculptor on April 28th implied that the change of air and company had done him nothing but good, giving him new initiative and hope.

My dear Sir, – As I am anxious – though my return
for your kindness will be like giving sixpence back for
a sovereign lent – to do my best in my intended lines
on 'Morley', I want answers to the following questions.
1st. (As I cannot find it on the map or Gazetteer) In
       what district of Lancashire is Morley situated?
2nd. Has the Hall a particular name?
3rd. Do you know the family name of its owners
       when the circumstances happened which I
       ought to dwell on?
4th. Can you tell in what century it happened?
5th. What, told in the fewest words, was the nature of
       the leading occurrences?
    If I learn these facts I'll do my best, but in all I try
to write I desire to stick to probabilities and local
characteristics.
    Now, after troubling you so much, I doubt not that
you will drive your fist through that damned medallion
in your studio, as being the effigy of a thorough bore.
    I cannot, without a smile at myself, think of my
stay for three days in Halifax on a business which
need not have occupied three hours; but in truth

when I fall back *on* myself I suffer so much wretchedness that I cannot withstand my temptations to get *out*
of myself – and for that reason I am prosecuting
enquiries about situations suitable to me whereby I
could have a voyage abroad. The quietude of home,
and the inability to make my family aware of the
nature of my sufferings makes me write –

> Home thoughts are not, with me,
>   Bright, as of yore;
> Joys are forgot by me,
>   Taught to deplore!
> My home has taken rest
> In an afflicted breast
> Which I have often pressed,
>   But – may no more!

Troubles never come alone – and I have some little
troubles astride the shoulders of the big one.

Literary exertion would seem a resource, but the
depression attendant on it, and the almost hopelessness
of bursting through the barriers of literary circles, and
getting a hearing among publishers, make me
disheartened and indifferent; for I cannot write what
would be thrown, unread, into a library fire.
Otherwise I have the materials for a respectably sized
volume, and if I were in London personally I might
perhaps try Henry Moxon – a patroniser of the sons
of rhyme; though I dare say the poor man often
smarts for his liberality in publishing hideous trash.

As I know that, while here, I might send a
manuscript to London and say goodbye to it, I feel it
folly to feed the flames of a printer's fire.

So much for egotism!

I enclose a horrible ill-drawn daub done to while away the time this morning. I meant it to represent a very rough figure in stone.

When all our cheerful hours seem gone for ever,
　All lost that caused the body or the mind
　To nourish love or friendship for our kind,
And Charon's boat, prepared o'er Lethe's river
Our souls to waft, and all our thoughts to sever
　From what was once life's light, still there may be
　Some well-loved bosom to whose pillow we
Could heartily our utter self deliver:
And if toward her grave – Death's weary road
　Our darling's feet should tread, each step by her
Would draw our own steps to the same abode,
　And make a festival of sepulture;
For what gave joy, and joy to us had owed,
　Should Death affright us from, when he would her restore?
　　　　　　　Yours most sincerely,
　　　　　　　　　P. B. Brontë

Branwell enclosed the sketch of a woman, with bowed head, her face hidden by her streaming hair. Above it he had written 'Our Lady of Grief' and 'Nuestra Senora de la pena'.

Perhaps those three days with Leyland had brought religious discussion too, argument as to whether the sculptor's brother was saving his soul or selling it by taking instruction in the Catholic faith. The sculptor, hitherto supreme among the mockers, had been impressed by the printer's sincerity, and Branwell would remember the plaster madonnas and the dripping candles in the homes of the Liverpool Irish at Luddenden Foot. But he himself was past salvation. He was as much a castaway as the subject of Cowper's poem, and the corpse in his own:

Not time, but ocean, thins its flowing hair;
Decay, not sorrow, lays its forehead bare;
Its members move, but not in thankless toil,
For seas are milder than this world's turmoil;
Corruption robs its lips and cheeks of red,
But wounded vanity grieves not the dead.

The answer was to get right away from his family, from Haworth, from everything that reminded him of the immediate past. Those 'little troubles astride the shoulders of the big one' were doubtless debts, loans made to him at Thorp Green or Little Ouseburn by a tenant or a member of the Robinson staff, or by his friends in Haworth. Was it in Liverpool that he 'prosecuted his inquiries about situations where he could have a voyage abroad', as he had mentioned in his letter to Leyland? The only way to escape creditors would be to leave the country. The only way to put aside the whole miserable mess of life was to start all over again. But how? And where?

He was certain of one thing, and that was 'the hopelessness of bursting through the barriers of literary circles'. At the end of May, 1846, a small volume of poems by Currer, Ellis and Acton Bell, published at their own expense, appeared from the press of Aylott & Jones, 8 Paternoster Row, London. In the year that followed exactly two copies were sold. Branwell may or may not have known of the luckless venture. On publication day he would hardly have cared had Aylott & Jones reported an advance sale of a thousand copies. For news had come from Thorp Green that Mr Edmund Robinson, his late employer, had died on May 26th.

Mr Edmund Robinson was forty-six years old when he died on May 26th, and the cause of his death was stated in the certificate to be 'Dyspepsia many years Phthisis 3 months'. The local newspapers, reporting the death, said that Mr Robinson, 'was greatly esteemed by his parishioners', and that 'he died, as he lived, in a firm and humble trust in his Saviour'.

That his wife Lydia was devoted to her husband is very evident from the jottings in the small cash-book during May and June. On May 29th she noted £18 'paid to Old Servants', and in brackets 'for my Angel'. On June 7th the poor of Great Ouseburn were given £5 in cash, and two in the parish of Little Ouseburn £10. Mr Lascelles, the vicar of Little Ouseburn, was paid £5 for taking the funeral ceremony, the six bearers, the clerk and sexton a further £6, the singers 6s., and 'Joe and Braggs, too old to help', another £1. On June 17th 'Taylors Funeral Bill' – doubtless the undertakers – of £30 9s. was paid, and on the blotting paper opposite his widow wrote 'My Angel Edmund'.

Here, finally and forever, is the proof that Lydia Robinson was devoted to her husband.

Edmund Robinson had altered his will (originally drafted in 1825 and 1831) on January 2nd, 1846, less than three months after his eldest daughter Lydia had made her runaway marriage, and four months before his own death. The reason for the new draft was to make certain that his daughter and her actor husband should not benefit from his own marriage settlement, which they would have done had the 1831 will stood unaltered.

Under the terms of the new will, all Mr Robinson's money and other possessions were left to his wife, to his son and heir Edmund, and to his daughters Elizabeth and Mary. His wife was left guardian of the children. The daughter Lydia was not even named. Nor, contrary to the story which Branwell put about, was there a clause under which Mrs Robinson would forfeit her inheritance if she remarried.

The memorial tablet to Edmund Robinson in St Mary's, Little Ouseburn, says:

Precious in the sight of the Lord is the death of his saints.
When the shore is won at last
Who will count the billows past?

Such was the exemplary character of the worthy gentleman who, according to Branwell, had threatened to shoot him. Dyspeptic his death certificate proves him to have been, but the tell-tale cash-book records for posterity that he was also his wife's 'Angel Edmund'.

Whether Branwell first heard the news of his employer's death through a newspaper, through a letter from one of the staff at Thorp Green, or from the visit of the Robinson's coachman, is hard to disentangle from the ensuing Haworth gossip. It was evidently unexpected, and almost as great a shock as his dismissal. The talk in Haworth at the news of Mr Robinson's death, the chit-chat repeated at the Black Bull to Mrs Gaskell and others years afterwards – that Branwell, after an interview with one of the Robinson servants in a private room at the inn, was found 'in a kind of fit', the man having paid his bill and ridden away – suggests that whatever news the servant brought had produced an attack of epilepsy, unrecognized by the people at the inn or any of Branwell's family. Those outside the room, said Mrs Gaskell, 'heard a noise like the bleating of a calf' – a recognizable description of the cry of an epileptic, caused not by terror or pain, but by the convulsive action of the muscles of the larynx.

Somehow Branwell had to fabricate a reason for not going to the widow immediately to offer his condolences. His family, his friends, all expected that he would marry her after a suitable period of mourning. Had he not told everyone that his love for Mrs Robinson had been returned? He must, whatever the cost, cling to his story.

Francis Grundy was one of the first to hear the news. Branwell asked for employment at the same time, which showed that he was still determined to find himself some sort of situation. Unfortunately, although the engineer mentions this request, in his *Pictures of the Past* he only printed part of Branwell's letter, leaving out the beginning, in which the plea for work was made.

The gentleman with whom I have been is dead. His property is left in trust for the family, provided I do not see the widow; and if I do, it reverts to the executing trustees, with ruin to her. She is now distracted with sorrows and agonies; and the statement of her case, as given me by her coachman, who has come to see me at Haworth, fills me with inexpressible grief. Her mind is distracted to the verge of insanity, and mine is so wearied that I wish I were in my grave.

Leyland the sculptor received a longer letter.

My dear Sir,
I should have sent you 'Morley Hall' ere now, but I am unable to finish it at present from agony to which the grave would be far preferable.
Mr Robinson of Thorp Green is dead, and he has left his widow in a dreadful state of health. She sent the coachman over to see me yesterday, and the account which he gave of her sufferings was enough to burst my heart.

209

Through the will she is left quite powerless, and her eldest daughter who married imprudently is cut off without a shilling.

The Executing Trustees detest me, and one declares that if he sees me he will shoot me.

These things I do not care about, but I do care for the life of one who suffers even more than I do. Her coachman said that it was a pity to see her, for she was only able to kneel in her bedroom in bitter tears and prayers. She has worn herself out in attendance on him, and his conduct during the few days before his death was exceedingly mild and repentant, but that only distressed her doubly. Her conscience has helped to agonize her, and that misery I am saved from.

You, though not much older than myself, have known life. I now know it with a vengeance – for four nights I have not slept – for three days I have not tasted food – and when I think of the state of her I love best on earth, I could wish that my head was as cold and stupid as the medallion which lies in your studio.

I write very egotistically but it is because my mind is crowded with one set of thoughts, and I long for one sentence from a friend.

What I shall do I know not – I am too hard to die, and too wretched to live. My wretchedness is not about castles in the air, but about stern realities; my hardihood lies in bodily vigour: but, dear Sir, my mind sees only a dreary future which I as little wish to enter on as could a martyr to be bound to the stake.

I sincerely trust that you are well, and hope that this wretched scrawl will not make me appear a worthless fool, or a thorough bore.

Believe me,

Yours most sincerely,

P. B. Brontë.

Another undated letter followed closely in the wake of the first.

Well, my dear Sir, I have got my finishing stroke at last − and I feel stunned to marble by the blow.

I have this morning received a long, kind and faithful letter from the medical gentleman who attended Mr R. in his last illness and who has since had an interview with one whom I can never forget.

He knows me *well*, and he pities my case most sincerely for he declares that, though used to the rough ups and downs of this weary world, he shed tears when he saw the state of that lady and knew what I should feel.

When he mentioned my name − she stared at him and fainted. When she recovered she in turn dwelt on her inextinguishable love for me − her horror at having been the first to delude me into wretchedness, and her agony at having been the cause of the death of her husband who, in his last hours, bitterly repented of his treatment of her.

Her sensitive mind was totally wrecked. She wandered into talking of entering a nunnery: and the Doctor fairly debars me from hope in the future.

It's hard work for me, dear Sir: I would bear it − but my health is so bad that the body seems as if it could not bear the mental shock.

I never cared one bit about the property. I cared about herself − and always shall do.

May God bless her, but I wish I had never known her!

My appetite is lost; my nights are dreadful, and having nothing to do makes me dwell on past scenes − on her own self, her voice, her person, her thoughts, till I could be glad if God took me. In the next world I could not be worse than I am in this.

I am not a whiner, dear Sir, but when a young man like myself has fixed his soul on a being worthy of all love – and who, for years, has given him all love, pardon him for boring a friend with a misery that has only one black end.

I fully expected a change in the will, and difficulties placed in my way by powerful and wealthy men, but I hardly expected the hopeless ruin of the mind that I loved even more than its body.

Excuse my egotism, and believe me,

Dear Sir,

Yours,

P. B. Brontë.

The 'change in the will' was now his alibi, and the 'executing trustees' were able to take the place of Mr Robinson as formidable foes holding his lady completely in their power. Thus he would save face, not only before his friends but in his own eyes too. The astonishing thing was that his family believed him.

'The death of Mr Robinson, which took place about three weeks or a month ago,' Charlotte wrote to Ellen Nussey on June 17th,

served Branwell for a pretext to throw all about him into hubbub and confusion with his emotions, etc., etc. Shortly afterwards, came news from all hands that Mr Robinson had altered his will before he died and effectually prevented all chance of a marriage between his widow and Branwell, by stipulating that she should not have a shilling if she ever ventured to reopen any communication with him. Of course, he then became intolerable. To papa he allows rest neither day nor night, and he is continually screwing money out of him, sometimes threatening that he will kill himself if it is withheld from him. He says that Mrs Robinson is now insane; that her mind is a complete wreck owing to remorse for her conduct towards Mr Robinson (whose end it appears was hastened by distress of mind) and grief for having lost him. I do not know how much to believe of what he says, but I fear she is very ill. Branwell declares that he neither can nor will do anything for himself, good situations have been offered him more than once, for which, by a fortnight's work, he might have qualified himself, but he will do nothing, except drink and make us all wretched.

Branwell was undoubtedly drinking, but he continued to ask Francis Grundy for work, which was something, perhaps, he did not tell his sister. He also repeated the tale of Mrs Robinson's illness.

Since I saw Mr George Gooch, I have suffered much from the account of the declining health of her whom I love most in this world, and who, for my fault, suffers sorrows which surely were never her due. My father, too, is now quite blind, and from such causes literary pursuits have become matters I have no heart to wield. If I could see you it would be a sincere pleasure, but . . .

In the midst of all this Currer Bell, alias Charlotte Brontë, undaunted by the ill-success of the poems, had written on July 4th to another publisher, Mr Henry Colburn, asking whether she might send him the completed manuscripts of *The Professor*, *Wuthering Heights* and *Agnes Grey*. These three novels, which the sisters had 'prepared for the press' during winter and spring, were now to set forth on their wearisome round of one publishing house after another. At some point Branwell must have seen the return of the rejected packages, which would confirm him in his fixed opinion that it was useless for an unknown writer to attempt an entry into the literary world.

He hoped to accept an invitation to visit Grundy on July 31st, but the distance of seventeen miles must have been too much for him, for he never turned up, and shortly afterwards Grundy went over to Haworth instead.

Grundy's notion of time was extremely vague. In his *Pictures of the Past*, published thirty years later, he post-dated all the events of 1846 to 1848. The matter contained in Branwell's letters proves them, however, to have been written in 1846, and indicates that his particular visit to Haworth was probably made in August. Grundy was shocked at Branwell's wrecked and wretched appearance. 'Yet he still craved for an appointment of any kind, in order that he might try the excitement of change; of course uselessly. I now heard his painful history from his own lips — his happiness, his misery, and the sad story which was the end. He was miserable.'

If it was indeed in August that Grundy paid his visit to Branwell, then very possibly Charlotte and her father had already left for Manchester, where Mr Brontë was to undergo an operation for cataract. Branwell, always more at ease these days when Charlotte, once his inseparable companion, was out of the way, would have invited Grundy to the parsonage.

'Patrick Brontë declared to me,' said Grundy in 1879, 'and what his sister said bore out the assertion, that he wrote a great portion of *Wuthering Heights* himself.'

This statement, howled at by critics at the time, as William Dearden's had been some twelve years earlier, could have had the simplest possible origin. Branwell, in the presence of either Emily or Anne, may have told his friend that all four members of the family had collaborated on tales at varying times. Such a remark, dropped at random, would have lingered at the back of Grundy's mind, and when he came to read *Wuthering Heights* he would immediately connect the story with the 'weird fancies of diseased genius' of Luddenden Foot days, and the remark of Branwell's about early collaboration.

Charlotte and Mr Brontë were a month in Manchester, and the operation was successful. During their absence Branwell gave no trouble. It might well be that the two members of the family who had always held the highest hopes of his success in the world were the very people whose presence he could now least bear about him. He had failed the father who well-nigh worshipped him, and failed the sister who had been his boyhood's dearest companion. It was these two whose unuttered reproaches and weary sighs nagged his conscience most. Anne was at least a link with Thorp Green, and Emily . . . Emily neither sympathized nor condemned, she had the supreme tact to let him be.

John Brown remained as staunch as ever, and when the atmosphere at the parsonage became too much for him Branwell could always go down the lane to John and be sure of a welcome, or to William either, for that matter; neither Mary, John's wife, nor Anne, the wife of William, gave him the looks he got at home.

Freemasonry was a thing of the past, though. He never attended a meeting now. Sometimes he may have remembered the old vows of initiation and the various ceremonies, and the threat that, if he betrayed them, retribution of a fearful kind would overtake him. It was easy to laugh, in retrospect, but what if all the misery of his life had come about through some sort of betrayal? It was beyond his memory now to recall whether he had ever revealed the secrets of freemasonry to anyone. But the possibility that he might have done so when in his cups, and that one day the Devil himself would call for him, was not the least of his fears during moments of tension.

The success of his father's operation quietened Branwell's conscience for a time. The sight of that near-blinded figure, sitting so patiently in the parlour, waited on by the girls, and more especially by Charlotte, had added gall to his own bitterness; but now he had recovered his sight, and was likely to do duty again before long, one anxiety had been lifted – the fear of his father's death or total blindness being somehow laid at his door, not through his sisters' reproaches, but by his own accusing self.

His friend Leyland, as usual overwhelmed with work, was farming some of it out to John Brown, and early in October Branwell was well enough to act as go-between for this particular commitment.

> My dear Sir, – Mr John Brown wishes me to tell you that if, by return of post, you can tell him the nature of his intended work, and the time it will probably occupy in execution, either himself or his brother, or both, will wait on you *early* next week.
>
> He has only delayed answering your communication from his unavoidable absence in a pilgrimage from 'Rochdale on the Rhine' to 'The Land of Ham' and from thence to Gehenna, Tophet, Golgotha, Erebus, the Styx and to the place he now occupies called Tartarus where he along with Sisyphus, Tantalus, Theseus, and Ixion, lodge and board together.
>
> However, I hope that when he meets you he will join the company of Moses, Elias and the twelve prophets, 'singing psalms sitting on a wet cloud', as an acquaintance of mine described the occupation of the blest.

Why Tophet – which in masonic language means 'wanting understanding' – and Golgotha, the 'expansion of the five senses through the human skull, particularly on the forehead', should come to be allied with Erebus, one of the gods of Hades, son of Chaos, and Tartarus, an inner region of hell where only the exceptionally depraved were sent, Branwell and possibly Leyland alone understood. Doubtless John Brown would have laughed at the allusion and the sketch of himself, glass in hand, tables flying, which graced the head of the writing paper.

'Morley Hall is in the eighth month of her pregnancy,' Branwell continued, 'and expects ere long to be delivered of a fine thumping boy whom its father means to christen *Homer* at the least, though the mother suggests that "Poetaster" would be more suitable, but that sounds too aristocratic.

'Is the medallion cracked that Thorwaldsen executed of August Caesar?'

Here Branwell drew his own head on a coin, with the emperor's name around it. Thorwaldsen, the Danish sculptor, who had died two years before, was presumably Leyland's temporary nickname.

> I wish I could see you, and as Haworth fair is held on Monday after the ensuing one, your presence there would gratify one of the FALLEN. [Here he showed himself, plunging head foremost into a gulf.]
> In my own register of transactions during my nights and days I find no matter worthy of extraction for your perusal. All is yet with me clouds and darkness. I hope you have at least blue sky and sunshine.
> Constant and unavoidable depression of mind and body sadly shackle me in even trying to go on with any mental effort which might rescue me from the fate of a dry toast soaked six hours in a glass of cold water, and intended to be given to an old maid's squeamish cat.
> Is there really such a thing as the 'Risus Sardonicus' – the sardonic laugh? Did a man ever laugh the morning he was to be hanged?

The sketch of a gallows, and a hand holding out a rope to a smiling John Brown, concluded the letter. The victim being his friend the sexton and not himself suggests that the reason for John Brown's absence was not simply a drinking bout but a masonic initiation ceremony, possibly to pass the degree of Royal Arch Mason. John Brown, as candidate, would be prepared with a cable-tow – not round the neck, but round the waist; the gallows would be Branwell's own mocking salute to the occasion.

As to the epic *Morley Hall*, in the 'eighth month of her pregnancy', the only piece that survives consists of a fragment which constitutes part of the introduction, and gives no hint of the romance to come. The lame couplets, hammered out by Branwell during heaven knows how many laborious hours, were simply an echo of his own weary thoughts. The 'thumping boy' was mere bravado, for the sculptor, remembering Branwell's rapid composition in the past, would hardly credit such a long gestation period for lines so few and so lament-ably lacking in inspiration. The poem was written in Branwell's upright hand on four pages of an exercise book, and was unsigned and undated.

Morley Hall
Leigh – Lancashire

When life's youth, overcast by gathering clouds
Of cares, that come like funeral-following crowds,
Wearying of that which is, and cannot see
A sunbeam burst upon futurity,
It tries to cast away the woes that are
And borrows further joys from times afar.
For, what our feet may tread may have been a road
By horses' hoofs pressed, 'neath a camel's load,
But, what we ran across, in childhood's hours
Were fields, presenting June with Mayday flowers
So what was done, and born, if long ago,
Will satisfy our heart though stained by tears of woe.

When present sorrows every thought employ
Our father's woes may take the garb of joy,
And, knowing what our sires have undergone,
Ourselves can smile, though weary, wondering on.
For if our youth a thundercloud o'ershadows,
Changing to barren swamps life's flowering meadows,
We know that fiery flash and bursting peal
Others, like us, were forced to hear and feel.
And while they moulder in a quiet grave,
Robbed of all havings — worthless all they have —
We still with face erect behold the sun —
Have bright examples in what has been done
By head or hand — and in the times to come
May tread bright pathways to our gate of doom . . .

And so on for another thirty interminable couplets. It ends
abruptly — and none too soon, Leyland must have thought,
when the pages were sent to him as a sample of what was to
come. Nothing could show more clearly the disastrous decline
in imagery and thought than these poor lines from Branwell's
pen. Compared with the sonnets of a few years back, and the
facility of expression he managed to achieve when translating
the Odes of Horace, *Morley Hall* was fourth-rate stuff, an
amateur effort that might have come from one of Branwell's
railway acquaintances at Luddenden Foot.

Not that the supreme poet of the family, Emily, was doing
so very much better. Her masterpiece, 'No Coward Soul Is
Mine', had been written in the January of that same year,
1846. After this, silence until September 14th, when she began
revising an earlier ballad, the rhyming couplets certainly more
spirited than her brother's, but lacking both the fire and the
vision of her earlier work. Perhaps the ill-success of the
published poems had disillusioned her, or she had spent herself
in the writing of *Wuthering Heights*, still going the dreary round
of publishing houses. The ballad, like *Morley Hall*, was never

finished; indeed, no later poem of hers has ever been found, except a revised scrap of this same poem dated May 13th, 1848.

There has never been an explanation of Emily's silence. Anne, with less talent, was writing steadily and well, and in the early summer of 1848 her second novel, *The Tenant of Wildfell Hall*, was published. It has been suggested that Emily did in fact write further poems and another novel, but destroyed them, for some reason, before she died. If this was so, why did she not destroy all her earlier unpublished poems and fragments? Why leave anything at all for posterity?

Possibly, once she saw the poems in print, and unwanted, a curious distaste came upon her for the whole business, a reluctance ever again to unmask herself, even under a pseudonym. Charlotte, impelled by her emotions to express herself – and already at Manchester she had been working furiously on *Jane Eyre* – and Anne, equally impelled by a sense of duty to portray society, were stimulated by the names Currer and Acton Bell on the printed page. Not so Ellis. The undercurrent of cynicism in her nature, which had first betrayed itself in the French essays she had written at Brussels, now rose to the surface; not only were 'the thousand creeds that move men's hearts unutterably vain', but the hopes and the ambitions too.

In December, 1846, Branwell suffered a further humiliation. Whoever it was he owed money to at Great or Little Ouseburn, or at Thorp Green itself, the creditor showed no mercy. A sheriff's officer arrived at the parsonage from York to serve a writ; either the money must be paid or Branwell return with him to prison. The debts were paid – by his father, his sisters, or both. And not, it would seem, for the first time.

'It is not agreeable to lose money time after time in this way,' Charlotte wrote to Ellen Nussey on December 13th. 'But it is ten times worse to witness the shabbiness of his behaviour on such occasions.'

Shabbiness . . . The word conjures in its very forcefulness the wretched figure Branwell must have cut on the occasion.

At first surprise, perhaps indignation, at the appearance of the sheriff's officer, swiftly followed by denial of responsibility. Then, when the hopelessness of the situation had sunk in, blaming the mess upon other shoulders. Companions had led him astray, he had been misled, those he had imagined his friends had proved enemies; and after a tirade of abuse against whoever it was near York who now demanded repayment of the debt there would come the collapse, the gasps for breath, the excuse of illness, complaints of misunderstanding and even ill-treatment by all around him, and finally tears, abject, miserable tears, the utter loss of any remaining self-control.

And so, finally, to bed. Not to the studio, where he might do some damage to himself, but to his father's bedroom, which he had shared as a little boy, and must now, in shame and humiliation, share again. Mr Brontë, his sight recovered, could still watch over his beloved son by night, listen to blasphemy, and pray.

This would be the period when Grundy, the engineer, came to Haworth for the last time, and invited Branwell to dinner at the Black Bull.

Presently the door opened cautiously, and a head appeared. It was a mass of red, unkempt, uncut hair, wildly floating around a great, gaunt forehead; the cheeks yellow and hollow, the mouth fallen, the thin white lips not trembling but shaking, the sunken eyes, once small, now glaring with the light of madness − all told the sad tale but too surely. I hastened to my friend, greeted him in my gayest manner, and, as I knew he best liked, drew him quickly into the room, and forced upon him a stiff glass of hot brandy. Under its influence, and that of the bright, cheerful surroundings, he looked frightened − frightened of himself. He glanced at me a moment, and muttered something of leaving a warm bed to come out into the cold night. Another glass of brandy, and returning warmth gradually brought him back to something like the Brontë of old. He even ate some dinner, a thing which he said he had not done for long; so our last interview was pleasant, though grave. I never knew his intellect clearer. He described himself as waiting anxiously for death – indeed, longing for it, and happy, in these his sane moments, to think it was so near. He once again declared that death would be due to the story I knew, and to nothing else.

When at last I was compelled to leave, he quietly drew from his coat sleeve a carving-knife, placed it on the table, and holding me by both hands, said that, having given up all thoughts of ever seeing me again, he imagined when my message came that it was a call from Satan. Dressing himself, he took the knife, which he had long secreted, and came to the inn, with a full determination to rush into the room and stab the occupant. In the excited state of his mind he did not recognise me when he opened the door, but my voice and manner conquered him, and 'brought him home to himself', as he expressed it. I left him standing bare-headed in the road, with bowed form and drooping tears.

The bluff, kind-hearted Grundy, his dates all wrong, declared in his reminiscences that Branwell died a few days later. He did nothing of the sort. But the tumblers of brandy probably put him to bed for a further fortnight. The weary effort of weaning him off alcohol would begin all over again, and Dr Wheelhouse, who had the unenviable task of forbidding every form of intoxicant, would become for Branwell the most hated figure in Haworth. He might deny Branwell alcohol, but he could not keep pen and paper from him.

While holy Wheelhouse far above
In heaven's unclouded light of love,
Looks down with a benignant smile
That heaven and hell might reconcile,
And shouts to Satan, 'Thou'art a funny'un,
Give him sauce as well as onion.'
You bloody bugger, ram him, jam him,
And with a forty horse-power damn him,
Or if your work you don't do well
By God I'll take your place in hell.
Say Doctor Wheelhouse is a jewel
Or you and I must fight a duel.
Say that his guts are all his hitches,
And I shall call you sons of bitches.
Say that he longed like me for woman
And I and all will call you No Man.

16

Mr Brontë, turning to his volume of *Modern Domestic Medicine*, jotted down a few further notes under the heading 'Insanity'.

'There is also delirium tremens brought on sometimes by intoxication — the patient thinks himself haunted by demons, sees luminous substances in his imagination, has frequent trembling of the limbs, if intoxication be left off this madness will in general diminish.'

It is doubtful whether Branwell ever suffered from delirium tremens. Dr Wheelhouse may have called it this, but the trouble is just as likely to have been fits to which Branwell was subject. Though they were undoubtedly excited by the smallest amount of alcohol, at the same time they seem to have been quite unpredictable. Weeks might pass without an attack. His intellect was sound, and indeed, according to Grundy, never clearer than on that winter's evening when they dined together at the Black Bull.

If Branwell had made a nuisance of himself as a drunkard in the streets of Haworth, complaints of his conduct would have reached his father. Sterner action would have been necessary. But no one outside the family ever seems to have been aware that anything was seriously wrong with him. Martha Brown, John Brown's daughter, who worked at the parsonage, told Francis Leyland that Branwell was never as bad as he was made out to be.

Branwell was well enough to meet his friends in Halifax without ill-effect. This was because the atmosphere was neutral; there was no emotion. At home he must always have been aware of condemnation, which fed his own resentment; and seeing his three sisters content in each other's company – the happy circle which he had once completed – his bitterness turned inward, and he felt himself thrust out, abandoned, the veritable castaway who had haunted him as a child. And, like a child, he used a child's weapons. If they withdrew their love from him, he must behave violently to win attention. Better be hated than ignored. Once, long ago, he had been undisputed leader at home. His every whim had been law. If he showed gaiety, so did they all. If he wept, then they comforted him. Now, rejected and despised, he would gain his ends by other means – by wounding their spirits, mocking their beliefs, destroying their ideals. If a peaceful household would not include him, then there should be no peace.

The knowledge, too, that all three of his sisters had 'means'; that should their father die the girls could, in fact, afford to live – through their aunt's legacy – while he would still be penniless, was a bitter-tasting pill, ever present to poison the relationship between them.

Eighteen-year-old Martha could hardly be aware of the subtleties of such an atmosphere. The kitchen, with Emily in charge, was a more casual, easy-going place than the dining-room, which was also the sisters' living-room, and presumably Branwell's too.

He would read over the old Percy annals, and Zenobia, Percy's third wife, must have seemed to him, nowadays, to have many characteristics of the middle-aged yet still beautiful Lydia, whose image filled his dreams and his waking hours. Once more he sat down to write a letter to her, signing it perhaps Northangerland to prove his identity. It found its way to Little Ouseburn and back again, as the following letter to Leyland bears witness.

'I am going to write a scrawl,' he told the sculptor on January 24th, 1847, for the querulous egotism of which I must entreat your mercy, but, when I look *upon* my past, present and future, and then *into* my own self, I find much, however unpleasant, that yearns for utterance.

This last week an honest and kindly friend has warned me that concealed hopes about one lady should be given up, let the effort to do so cost what it may. He is the family medical attendant, and was commanded by Mr Evans MP for North Derbyshire, to return me, unopened, a letter which I addressed to Thorp Green and which the lady was not permitted to see. She too, surrounded by powerful persons who hate me like hell, has sunk into religious melancholy, believes that her weight of sorrow is God's punishment, and hopelessly resigns herself to her doom. God only knows what it does cost, and will, hereafter, cost me to tear from my heart and remembrances the thousand recollections that rush upon me at the thought of four years gone by. Like ideas of sunlight to a man who has lost his sight they must be bright phantoms not to be realised again.

I had reason to hope that ere very long I should be the husband of a lady whom I loved best in the world, and with whom, in more than competence, I might live at leisure to try to make myself a name in the world of posterity, without being pestered by the small but countless botherments, which like mosquitoes sting us in the world of work-day toil. That hope, and herself, are *gone* – *she* to wither into patiently pining decline – *it* to make room for drudgery falling on one now ill-fitted to bear it.

That ill-fittedness rises from causes which I should find myself able partially to overcome had I bodily strength, but with the want of that, and with the presence of daily lacerated nerves, the task is not easy.

I have been in truth too much petted through life, and in my last situation I was so much master, and gave myself so much up to enjoyment, that now when the cloud of ill-health and adversity has come upon me it will be a disheartening job to work myself up again through a new life's battle, from the position of five years ago to which I have been compelled to retreat with heavy loss and no gain. My army stands now where it did then, but mourning the slaughter of youth, hope, and both mental and physical elasticity.

The last two losses are indeed important to one who once built his hopes of rising in the world on the possession of them. Noble writings, works of art, music or poetry, now, instead of rousing my imagination, cause a whirlwind of blighting sorrow that sweeps over my mind with unspeakable dreariness, and if I sit down and try to write all ideas that used to come clothed in sunlight now press round me in funeral black; for nearly every pleasurable excitement that I used to know has changed to insipidity or pain.

I shall never be able to realise the too sanguine hopes of my friends, for at twenty-eight [he was really twenty-nine] I am a thoroughly *old man* – mentally and bodily. Far more so, indeed, than I am willing to express. God knows I do not scribble like a poetaster when I quote Byron's terrible truthful words:

> No more, no more, oh! never more on me
> The freshness of the heart shall fall like dew,
> Which, out of all the lovely things we see
> Extracts emotions beautiful and new!

I used to think that if I could have for a week the free range of the British Museum – the Library included – I could feel as though I were placed for seven days in Paradise; but now, really, dear sir, my eyes would roam over the Elgin marbles, the Egyptian saloon and the most treasured volumes like the eyes of a dead codfish.

My rude rough acquaintances here ascribe my unhappiness solely to causes produced by my sometimes irregular life, because they have known no other pains than those resulting from excess or want of ready cash. They do not know that I would rather want a shirt than want a springy mind, and that my total want of happiness, were I to step into York Minster now, would be far, far worse than their want of a hundred pounds when they might happen to need it, and that if half a dozen glasses or a bottle of wine drives off their cares, such cures only make me outwardly passable in company but *never* drive off mine.

I know only that it is time for me to be something when I am nothing. That my father cannot have long to live, and that when he dies my evening, which is already twilight, will become night – that I shall then have a constitution still so strong that it will keep me years in torture and despair when I should every hour pray that I might die.

I know that I am avoiding, while I write, one greatest cause of my utter despair – but by God, sir, it is nearly too bitter for me to allude to it!

For four years (including one year of absence) a lady intensely loved me as I did her, and each sacrificed to that love all we had to sacrifice, and held out to each other HOPE for our guide to the future. She was all I could wish for in a woman, and vastly above me in rank, and she loved me even better than I did her. Now what is the result of these four years? UTTER WRECK. The 'Great Britain' is not so thoroughly stranded as I am.

I have received to-day since I began my scrawl, a note from her maid Miss Ann Marshall, and I *know* from it that she has been terrified by vows which she was forced to swear to, on her husband's deathbed (with every addition of terror which the ghastly dying eye could inflict upon a keenly sensitive and almost *worried* woman's mind), a complete severance from him in whom lay her whole heart's feelings. When that husband was scarce cold in his grave her relations, who controlled the whole property, overwhelmed her with their tongues, and I am *quite conscious* that she has succumbed in terror to what they have said.

It is questionable whether Ann Marshall, Mrs Robinson's maid, can have been in a position to describe happenings in the Robinson family during the early months of 1847, for on April 16th she died of consumption, away from Thorp Green. It may even be that the 'religious melancholy' and 'patiently pining decline' which Branwell imputes to Mrs Robinson were in fact borne by the maid and not the mistress.

Branwell concludes his letter:

To no one living have I said what I now say to you, and I should not bother yourself with my incoherent account did I not believe that you would be able to understand something of what I meant – though *not all*, sir – for he who is without hope, and knows that his clock is at twelve at night, cannot communicate his feelings to one who finds *his* at twelve at noon.

I long to be able to see you, and I shall try to do so on Friday next – the 29th inst., or on Saturday, if I am at all able to take the journey.

Till then, I am, Dear Sir,
Yours sincerely,
P. B. Brontë.

It is almost certain that this very long letter was preceded by a much shorter one, undated, which Branwell had written to the sculptor, expressing a wish that Mr Thos. Nicholson of the Old Cock would send in his bill, as 'the moment that I receive my outlaid cash, or any sum which may fall into my hands through the hands of one whom I may never see again, I shall settle it. That settlement, I have some reason to hope, will be *shortly*.'

J. B. Leyland, therefore, on receiving the two letters, would be under the impression – as would anyone else – that his friend had expected a sum of money from the lady whom he had once hoped to marry, with which he would be able to pay off his debts; and that the complete extinction of these hopes now made any question of financial help impossible. The last part of the long letter makes the case quite clear. 'Thoroughly stranded' is the expression a young woman would use who, after a four years' betrothal, and wedding preparations which have let her in for some expense, is rudely flouted by the bridegroom's relatives. The jilted one turns to her remaining friends, not only for sympathy, but for assistance also; and Branwell, who knew Leyland's generosity, must have hoped that the letter to Leyland would touch his friend's pocket as well as his heart.

Branwell was not the only friend the sculptor helped. Joseph Leyland also paid the debts of Wilson Anderson, another of the studio hangers-on, who owed money to Mrs Crowther of the Commercial Inn, near Northgate, Halifax, despite the fact that he hardly knew where to turn for money himself. His father, Roberts Leyland, printer and bookseller, was ill; the monument to Beckwith in York Minster was not yet finished; yet the sculptor, harried and bothered at every turn, still kept an ever-open purse.

When, in early May, Charlotte told Ellen Nussey that 'Branwell is quieter now and for a good reason; he has got to the end of a considerable sum of money of which he

230

became possessed in the spring, and consequently is obliged to restrict himself in some degree', she probably thought, as did her father and sisters, and anyone else in Haworth who happened to notice, that Branwell's source of income lay in Thorp Green. He would certainly tell them so. It is much more likely that J. B. Leyland had shown the same generosity to Branwell that he showed to his other friends. Nor would the sculptor necessarily be the only person whom Branwell asked for help. The woollen manufacturers of the Luddenden neighbourhood regularly 'put up' at the Talbot and the Old Cock in Halifax, when they did business at the Piece Hall. They were friendly and open-hearted. John Garnett, one of the members of the Reading Club which met at the Lord Nelson, Luddenden, always went to the Cock. James Titterington would also be in Halifax, and several others who had shown hospitality in the days when Branwell had been station-master at Luddenden Foot. A ready smile, followed by a story of wretched health and atrocious ill-luck, would surely be worth a sovereign or two for old times' sake.

In the second fortnight of February, 1847, the two younger Robinson girls, Elizabeth and Mary, had suddenly begun writing to Anne again, resuming a correspondence which, apparently, they had ceased for six months after their father's death. Their letters, Charlotte told Ellen Nussey, were 'crammed with warm protestations of endless esteem and gratitude – they speak with great affection of their Mother – and never make any allusion intimating acquaintance with her errors. It is to be hoped they are and always will remain in ignorance on that point, especially since, I think, she has bitterly repented them. We take special care that Branwell does not know of their writing to Anne.'

Charlotte's use of the word 'errors' suggests that Branwell had given his family to understand that he had been encouraged by Mrs Robinson, and indeed owed his downfall to her. The story he put about at Haworth was thus different from the one he told his friends. To Grundy, to Leyland, the lady of his heart was a model of unselfishness, of piety, neglected by a boor of a husband who also ill-treated her. The impression he gave at home was otherwise.

It was during this year that Anne was working on *The Tenant of Wildfell Hall*. This novel consists of two separate stories, most cleverly combined in one. The first sixteen chapters, and the last nine, are narrated by a young man, and tell of his admiration and growing love for a mysterious and charming new neighbour – the tenant of Wildfell Hall – whom he takes to be a widow, as she is dressed in mourning and appears to be in sole charge of her young son. Friendship ripens, and the narrator grows jealous of another frequent visitor to the Hall. At last his rage and jealousy become so great that he assaults this supposed rival. At this point the widow thrusts a manuscript into the hands of the bewildered and angry young man, and the second story begins.

This tale, which forms the middle part of the book, is the life story of the mysterious tenant, told by herself, and recounts the wretched history of her marriage to rich, handsome Arthur Huntingdon, and her bitter disillusionment at the drunken, dissolute behaviour of her husband and his friends. Finally, after experiences too hard to bear, she runs away from him and seeks shelter at Wildfell Hall, to be near her brother – who is no lover at all, but the mysterious rival of the first sixteen chapters.

The last nine chapters, once again narrated in the first person by the young man of the first story, bring everything to a satisfactory conclusion; the dissolute husband falls ill and makes a death-bed repentance, and at the finish the young narrator and the widow live happily ever after.

How much did Branwell read – or have read to him – of the two interwoven stories? The young narrator of the first story, Gilbert Markham, is so like Lockwood, the cocky young narrator of the opening chapters of *Wuthering Heights*, with his utter confidence in his powers of attracting the opposite sex, that the character was surely modelled on Branwell at twenty-five; and Markham's infatuation for the widow of Wildfell Hall, his geniality to her child, could have been an unconscious drawing of the true situation of Anne's brother when he went, full of hope and good intentions, to tutor Mrs Robinson's young son in 1843.

The second narrative, the story of the fatal marriage, and the terrible decline of the husband, may have been written as a warning to Branwell as well as to the world; but the erring, neglectful husband, the pious, praying wife, are uncannily like the version of the Robinson ménage that Branwell put about to his friends in 1846 – which was surely the very last thing that Anne, the writer, had in mind. Sometimes the cap can be made to fit the head least intended to wear it; Branwell, far from picturing Huntingdon's death-bed as a prophetic picture of his own, clapped the image on to his late dyspeptic employer, Mr Robinson, with the sorrowing, tortured Lydia in the rôle of Helen Huntingdon. In former years he had shared in his sisters' writings; somehow he must continue to live out their characters in the world of his imagination. Hindley Earnshaw and the carving knife, Heathcliff dashing his head against a tree and howling like a savage beast, were all part of Branwell's infernal world. They had no business in a publisher's office, to be thumbed over by some half-witted clerk.

Anne was the more encouraged to proceed upon her work when *Agnes Grey* and *Wuthering Heights* were accepted for publication, in one volume, by a firm called Newby, of Mortimer Street, London. The publisher expected Ellis and Acton Bell to share in the cost of publication, but at least the acceptance would prove them genuine authors at last. The only embarrassment was that *The Professor* had no similar success. It was still going the rounds. And Charlotte had been the instigator of the whole business. This time the truth was surely kept from Branwell. For Emily and Anne to have novels accepted, and for Charlotte's to be refused – this would have made the brother's jibe too easy.

Charlotte, undaunted by failure, was still hard at work on *Jane Eyre*, though, for all she knew, it would meet with no greater success than *The Professor*. Ellen Nussey, the confidante, who had been told nothing of the many stories her friend had written both as child and as growing girl during their long and unwavering friendship, was still kept in ignorance. Anonymity was the cloak, the safeguard that masked the three sisters from the deriding, suspicious world. Only 'Northangerland', their brother, did not want it; and, turning over his old manuscripts while Charlotte wove hers into a masterpiece, he chose one to send to Leyland.

> I could not bear the thoughts which rose
> Of what *had* been, and what *must* be,
> And still the dark night would disclose
> Its sorrow-pictured prophecy;
> Still saw I – miserable me –
> Long, long nights else, in lonely gloom,
> With time-bleached locks and trembling knee –
> Walk aidless, hopeless, to my tomb.
>
> Still, still that tomb's eternal shade
> Oppressed my heart with sickening fear,
> When I could see its shadow spread
> Over each dreary future year,
> Whose vale of tears woke such despair
> That, with the sweat-drops on my brow,
> I wildly raised my hands in prayer
> That Death would come and take me now;
>
> Then stopped to hear an answer given –
> So much had madness warped my mind –

When, sudden, through the midnight heaven,
With long howl woke the Winter's wind;
And roused in me, though undefined,
A rushing thought of tumbling seas
Whose wild waves wandered unconfined,
And, far-off, surging, whispered, 'Peace.'

I cannot speak the feeling strange,
Which showed that vast December sea,
Nor tell whence came that sudden change
From aidless, hopeless misery;
But somehow it revealed to me
A life – when things I loved were gone –
Whose solitary liberty
Might suit me wandering tombward on . . .

'I only enclose the accompanying fragment', Branwell
wrote, 'which is so soiled that I would have transcribed it if
I had the heart to exert myself, in order to get from you as
to whether, when finished, it would be worth sending to some
respectable periodical like *Blackwood's Magazine*.'

Blackwood's was still his Mecca. Twelve years before, aged
eighteen, he had demanded of the editor: 'Sir – Read what I
write,' and concluded: 'You have lost an able writer in James Hogg,
and God grant you may gain one in Patrick Branwell Brontë.'

The poem, and the letter of 1847, were put away with all
the other bits and pieces filling the shelves of Leyland's studio:
the broken plaster casts, the limbless Theseus, the unfinished
tablets, the beautiful recumbent Stephen Beckwith which
would one day grace York Minister, carried thither in a wagon
by no less a person than John Brown. In the summer of 1847
it was still unfinished, like the poems of his friend, which
would probably never be read by any eye but his own, and
who, even in mid-July, seemed no nearer to forgetting the
cause of all his grief.

'For myself,' said Branwell on the 16th of that month,

after a fit of horror inexpressible, and violent palpitation of the heart, I have taken care of myself bodily, but to what good? The best health will not kill *acute* and *not ideal*, mental agony.

Cheerful company does me good till some bitter truth blazes through my brain, and then the present of a bullet would be received with thanks.

I wish I could flee to writing as a refuge, but I cannot, and as to *slumber*, my mind, whether awake or asleep, has been in incessant action for several weeks.

Leyland, so long the uncrowned king of the little group of mocking, drinking friends, must have looked round his studio at the tumbled statuary that had once, long since, promised him fame and fortune. Stung, perhaps, by the strange, devout ways of his brother the printer, he spared himself a moment from his unfinished work and the sheaf of unpaid bills to compose a prayer, which he may even have showed, in a shy, shame-faced manner, to his pathetic red-haired friend when Branwell next called upon him.

The Prayer of Leyland the Sculptor.

O God, thou who made the worlds, I pray to thee, all merciful. In the morning of my life, thou gavest unto me many talents. I have been wayward and wicked, and have sorely abused these thy good and gracious gifts. And now, in this dark hour of my life, I humbly turn to thee. For the sake of thy Blessed Son, sweet Jesus of Nazareth, and for the sake of his Mother, the Holy and Immaculate Virgin, the Tower of Mary, grant unto me mental rest.

The stern granite rocks, on the everlasting hills, and

on solemn moorlands, lift up their heads to thee. Thou hast, with thy glorious hand, girt them round about with wild flowers; nay, thou hast also made them cling to the foreheads of these thy starry children, even as a love token of the divine mark.

Do thou, O Good and Gracious God, therefore, if it be thy will, give me the power to place around my stony heart the flowers of thy grace, albeit as a token of forgiveness. Amen.

17

On October 16th, 1847, a novel by an unknown author was published by Smith, Elder and Co. of Cornhill, London. They had already turned down a previous work by the same writer, but when the second manuscript reached them at the end of August they were so impressed by the remarkable story-telling powers of its creator – Mr Smith having read the tale at a sitting between breakfast and evening, not pausing for luncheon or dinner – that they wrote accepting the manuscript the following day, and set about producing proofs immediately, in order to have the book ready for early autumn publication.

The book, *Jane Eyre*, was an instant success, the talk not only of literary London but of the whole reading public throughout the country, and the name, Currer Bell, was on everybody's lips. Who was it? Man or woman? Not even the publishers knew.

The mask of anonymity, hiding Charlotte from all the world but her two sisters – whose novels, with a rival publisher, were not yet past the proof stage – was also intended to conceal the authorship of the book from the brother with whom, long ago, she had shared every ambition, every writing secret, every whispered dream. Her father could know later, when the first furore had settled, but, unless he discovered it for himself, the brother must never be told.

When the letters and the reviews poured in, and she knew that the book was being read and praised by writers like Thackeray and critics such as George H. Lewes, and when a second edition was sent to press, perhaps – for a brief moment

– she thought of her one and only collaborator; the boy who had sat beside her in the old nursery study, creating, for her delight and future inspiration, those Angrian characters from the infernal world. Was not Jane Eyre's Rochester their own Byronic, melancholy Zamorna, with his one-time mistress and her child living under his own roof? Would not Branwell recognize every altered individual, every house disguised – above all, those pages that were true to life and not imagined, her own early schooldays at Cowan Bridge, with the characters of their dead sisters Maria and Elizabeth fusing to make the Helen Burns of this new novel?

No 'Currer Bell' would hide her identity from Northangerland, should the book fall into his hands. Words, phrases, style, all were as familiar to him as if they had been his own.

Once they had plotted and created together. Once the minute handwriting, disapproved of by their elders, had hidden their shared manuscripts from prying eyes. What looks between them, what secret smiles, what muffled laughter. How the boy Branwell would have rejoiced in her success . . . But not the man. The man must not be told. He must have no part in it.

The day before *Jane Eyre* was published Charlotte wrote to Ellen Nussey: 'We are getting on here the same as usual – only that Branwell has been more than ordinarily troublesome and annoying of late; he leads Papa a wretched life.'

What did they discuss, the seventy-year-old father and the thirty-year-old son, alone together in that front bedroom which looked out upon the graves? Did the father pray long at night, and the son watch, and then, with candle extinguished, both wait for sleep and temporary oblivion?

Long ago, his soldier clasped in his hand, or made to march upon the counterpane, the boy had heard his father mourn his own loss, grieve for his own wasted manhood; now it was the father, frail, white-haired against his pillows, who must watch the grown son, tormented by images that might have been his own once, in days gone by, and were now lost in the labyrinth of an old man's memories. Mary Burder, Maria Branwell, they had been flesh and blood, vivid and compelling for Mr Brontë; the first a sweetheart he had never possessed, the second a warm and loving wife. Bereft of both he had come, in time, to terms with loneliness. At what cost, he did not now remember. Except that over and over again he must have told himself it was God's will. And this his son, tossing and turning on his bed, could not accept.

Branwell would not pray with his father. He did not believe in prayer. Prayer had never been answered. What had to be endured would be endured, but with anger, with rebellion, with mockery; if he must be damned, let it be with justification, so that, like Lucifer, he would go defiant to perdition. And yet . . . When morning came, and his father had dressed, and gone down to the parlour, and set about the daily round, something of the murmured midnight conversation would remain with Branwell, to dwell in confusion with his own half-formed regrets; still unwashed and undressed, he would go to the old back-room studio where he kept his papers, and look for one of Percy's poems, written to his second wife Mary before she died.

There was so much disorder among his manuscripts now that he could hardly tell one from the other. Some had been sent to Leyland and never returned. Others had become muddled with Charlotte's in the days when they had written in turn, chapter by chapter, an Angrian tale. Stumbling back to his bed with loose sheets of paper, soothed possibly by a last drop of laudanum secreted in a phial, he would read once more of Mary Percy as she lay on her death-bed. How fully now he was able to enter into the thoughts and see the visions of the dying woman he had once described: what the boy had written then, the man experienced now, the dying woman the link between past and future, the imagined and the real.

Nor could she wake her drowsy thoughts to care
For day, or hour, or what was, or where:
Thus – lost in dreams, although debarred from sleep,
While through her limbs, a feverish heat would creep,
A weariness, a listlessness, that hung
About her vigour, and Life's powers unstrung –
She did not feel the iron gripe of pain,
But *thought* felt irksome to her heated brain;
Sometimes the stately woods would float before her,
Commingled with the cloud-piles brightening o'er her,
Then changed to scenes for ever lost to view,
Or mock with phantoms which she never knew:
Sometimes her soul seemed brooding on to-day,
And then it wildly wandered far away,
Snatching short glimpses of her infancy,
Or lost in day-dreams of what yet might be.

Yet – through the labyrinth-like course of thought –
Whate'er might be remembered or forgot,
Howe'er diseased the dream might be, or dim,
Still seemed the Future through each change to swim,
All indefinable, but pointing on
To what would welcome her when Life was gone;
She felt as if – to all she knew so well –
Its voice was whispering her to say 'farewell';
Was bidding her forget her happy home;
Was farther fleeting still – still beckoning her to come . . .

   Meanwhile there was the day to be faced, the hours to be
gone through, the averted glances to be endured, with all the
mysterious coming and going of letters and packages, and the
bright smiles and chatter which froze the instant he entered
a room.
   He had become accustomed to Charlotte's correspondence.
Shutting herself away upstairs in the bedroom she shared with

Anne – his aunt's old room – there was endless scratching of pens, and low murmuring and sometimes laughter when the sisters were together. Then in mid-December a parcel of books came for Emily and Anne, and, as usual, no word about the contents, no hint of what was happening. Rejected manuscripts perhaps again. If they had no wish to tell him, he would ask no questions.

'*Wuthering Heights* is, I suppose, at length published,' wrote Charlotte to Mr Williams of Smith and Elder, on December 14th,

> at least, Mr Newby has sent the authors their six
> copies. I wonder how it will be received. I should say
> it merits the epithets of 'vigorous' and 'original' much
> more decidedly than *Jane Eyre* did. *Agnes Grey* should
> please such critics as Mr Lewes, for it is 'true' and
> 'unexaggerated' enough. The books are not well got
> up – they abound in errors of the press. On a former
> occasion I expressed myself with perhaps too little
> reserve regarding Mr Newby, yet I cannot but feel,
> and feel painfully, that Ellis and Acton have not had
> the justice at his hands that I have had at those of
> Messrs. Smith and Elder.

The novels of Emily and Anne did not receive the same praise from the critics or the public as *Jane Eyre* had won. Currer Bell's novel had become what a modern newspaper would call 'a best-seller overnight'; *Wuthering Heights* and *Agnes Grey* made comparatively little impact.

The publisher, Newby, printed only two hundred and fifty copies, and he hoped to sell them by letting word get about that they were earlier works by the now famous Currer Bell. This did no good for himself or for his authors. *Jane Eyre* and its creator, Currer Bell, totally eclipsed any fame or success that the other two novels might have had, and for this the sharing of the same pseudonym was partially responsible.

One or two critics recognized the originality and the power of *Wuthering Heights*, but in the main they were nonplussed, and the general reader found the story unbelievable, the characters disagreeable. Even Charlotte and Emily's intelligent girlhood friend, Mary Taylor, who had gone to live in New Zealand, and had read all three of the sisters' books by July of 1848, called Emily's novel 'that strange thing *Wuthering Heights*', and suggested that it had been written with the idea of shocking a certain class of reader.

Anne, undeterred by the scant notice of her own quite admirable *Agnes Grey*, was still hard at work on *The Tenant of Wildfell Hall* – despite adverse criticism from both her sisters – while Charlotte was pondering a new novel, *Shirley*. Emily, the enigma, with no more birthday notes to tell posterity how her mind had developed since July of 1845, alone was silent. As far as Emily knew her only novel had failed, her poems also. Charlotte was the success of the family.

'*Jane Eyre* has got down into Yorkshire,' Charlotte told her now constant correspondent, Mr Williams, of Smith and Elder, in January 1848.

A copy has even penetrated into this neighbourhood: I saw an elderly clergyman reading it the other day, and had the satisfaction of hearing him exclaim 'Why – they have got — school, and Mr — here, I declare! and Miss — [naming the originals of Lowood, Mr Brocklehurst and Miss Temple]. He had known them all: I wondered whether he would recognise the portraits, and was gratified to find that he did and that moreover he pronounced them faithful and just – he said too that Mr — [Brocklehurst] deserved the chastisement he had got'.

He did not recognise Currer Bell. What author would be without the advantage of being able to walk

243

invisible? One is thereby enabled to keep such a quiet mind. I make this small observation in confidence.

If a neighbouring clergyman had read *Jane Eyre*, it meant that the novel was being discussed perhaps in Haworth itself. Certainly in Halifax and Bradford. It would not be long before the title of the book that was on everybody's lips was mentioned, in all ignorance, before Mr Brontë himself. Charlotte, persuaded by her sisters, decided to tell her father of her success, and swear him to secrecy. Whatever the cost, though, Branwell must not know.

'My unhappy brother never knew what his sisters had done in literature,' Charlotte told Mr Williams after Branwell's death, 'he was not aware that they had ever published a line. We could not tell him of our efforts for fear of causing him too deep a pang of remorse for his own time misspent, and talents misapplied. Now he will *never* know.'

If the sisters could keep a secret, so could the brother . . . sometimes. The evidence that he did know the identity of Currer Bell, and through pride and bitterness kept the knowledge from his family, would seem self-evident not only from his increasing despair after 1847, but through the evidence of George Searle Phillips, critic, writer and one-time editor of the Leeds *Times*, who, as an outside observer, would have no reason to lie. Phillips, who wrote under the pseudonym of January Searle, and had previously met Branwell in Halifax or Bradford, wrote a scathing review of *Jane Eyre* in the *Mirror* of December, 1847. Charlotte, very rightly, considered the review unjust, but was principally concerned because the critic mentioned a former work, supposedly by Currer Bell, which he declared 'quite as bold, quite as daring, quite as much distinguished for its insidious tendency, as the present volume'. Whether he was alluding to *Wuthering Heights*, which was published in December, in the mistaken belief that it was an earlier work of Currer Bell's, Phillips never said. Charlotte may have known the identity of the critic, but she possibly had no idea that he had been an acquaintance of her brother's.

According to Searle Phillips – who, like Francis Grundy, wrote his recollections of Branwell Brontë many years later – he visited Haworth soon after *Jane Eyre* had been published and his own view had been written (that is, some time between December, 1847, and September, 1848), and there, in the Black Bull, discussed Charlotte's novel with Branwell himself. The interview almost certainly took place in a private room, for no word of Currer Bell's true identity escaped to Haworth as a result of it.

'Branwell,' said Searle Phillips,

> though altered for the worse in appearance since earlier days, was by no means a sot; his eyes were bright, and his whole manner gave indication of intense enjoyment.
>
> He described some of the characters in the novels, and talked much about his sisters, especially Charlotte, whose celebrity, he said, had already attracted more strangers to the village than had been known before.

Now this statement of Branwell's was, of course, untrue, for no one yet knew who had written *Jane Eyre*. The mask of Currer Bell was still a mask. Just as he had not hesitated to tell his own friends of Mrs Robinson, so now, when Searle Phillips questioned him as to the identity of Currer Bell, Branwell hid rancour with a smile, and pretended full knowledge of the secret.

All men like a mystery. Searle Phillips, too, would be sworn to secrecy. And the strange professor who, said the critic, suddenly appeared during the conversation and demanded to shake Branwell by the hand, even offering him money if he would introduce him to his sister – he also would be hushed to silence over a glass of brandy, Branwell, for the first and last time in his life, playing the small part of brother to a celebrity.

'Poor Branwell,' said the critic,

> spoke of his sister in most affectionate terms, such as
> none but a man of deep feeling could utter. He knew
> her power, and what tremendous depths of passion
> and pathos lay in her great surging heart, long before
> she gave expression to them in *Jane Eyre*.

'I know,' said Branwell, after speaking of Charlotte's talents,

> that I also had stuff enough in me to make popular
> stories; but the failure of the Academy plan ruined
> me. I was felled, like a tree in the forest, by a sudden
> and strong wind, to rise no more. Fancy me, with my
> education, and those early dreams, which had almost
> ripened into realities, turning counter-jumper, or a
> clerk in a railway office, which last was, you know, my
> occupation for some time. It simply degraded me in
> my own eyes, and broke my heart.

The visiting professor, who taught Greek at London
University, had been persuaded into reading *Jane Eyre* by
Williams of Smith and Elder, and, like Mr Smith himself, had
read it at a sitting. But he could not cajole Branwell into
introducing him to Charlotte.

This would surely prove the authenticity of the encounter.
If Searle Phillips had fabricated the interview in after years,
he would most certainly have said that not only the London
professor, but he himself, had gone to the parsonage and shaken
the famous Charlotte Brontë by the hand. Instead, Branwell
'fought shy of the proposition'. And very naturally. Neither
Charlotte, nor any member of his family, knew that he shared
their secret. He was not going to give them the satisfaction
of finding out the truth.

Both the professor and Searle Phillips stayed overnight at the Black Bull. Before they left the following day Branwell kept up his deception, telling the critic that he had made both Charlotte and his other two sisters laugh at the story of a professor sitting up all night to read *Jane Eyre*. Searle Phillips could not have invented this final touch. Branwell most obviously did. And when the professor had driven away, and the critic too, and the mystery and pother were over, Branwell would return to the empty room at the Black Bull and reflect that face had been saved, if nothing else. No man on earth would believe him if he told the truth. The truth being that the author of *Jane Eyre* had not shared her secret with her brother.

'I was not intoxicated when I saw you last, dear Sir', Branwell wrote Leyland early in January, 1848,

> but I was so much broken down and embittered in heart that it did not need much extra stimulus to make me experience the fainting fit I had, after you left, at the Talbot, and another, more severe, at Mr Crowthers – the Commercial Inn near the Northgate.
>
> When you return to me the manuscript volume which I placed in your hands, will you (if you can easily lay your hands on it) enclose that MS called 'Caroline' – left with you many months since – and which I should not care about any more than about the volume, only I have no copies of either . . .

The allusion to his manuscripts, coming immediately after he had admitted bitterness of heart, was significant. Branwell's three sisters were now all established authors – one of them famous – but his poems and stories were lying in the forgotten drawers of his friends.

'When I feel a little better than I do at present,' he concluded, 'I will write you a letter telling you more of my mind than I dare at present do, and leaving you to notice it or destroy it as you choose.'

Branwell illustrated his letter with two sketches. The first showed himself in profile, wearing dark-tinted spectacles, and a halter round his neck. Francis Leyland, the sculptor's brother, who kept the letter, believed that this sketch represented Branwell in the guise of an old-time martyr. More likely the draughtsman drew his likeness with memories of a masonic initiation.

The second sketch, immediately below the first, was of five companions carousing round a table, named respectively Sugdeniensis, Draco the Fire Drake, St John in the wilderness (with a devil's forked tail), Phidias, and St Patrick alias Lord Peter. Beneath the drawing, Branwell had scribbled 'The rescue of the punch bowl. A scene in the Talbot'. The characters almost certainly represented Dan Sugden, the conductor, who had died the previous July, and of whom Leyland had designed a memorial bust which later crashed to pieces; Joe Drake, the gilder and carver, an intimate friend of Leyland's; John Brown, out of his usual milieu, perhaps, and thus dubbed 'in the wilderness'; Leyland the sculptor as Phidias; and Branwell himself St Patrick – though the alias of 'Lord Peter' is harder to identify. It could be that at one time the five, or possibly the four, excluding John Brown, had formed among themselves an imitative Hell-Fire Club, after the fashion of Sir John Dashwood and his Mad Monks at High Wycombe – certainly one of the books at the Luddenden Library in the Lord Nelson Inn had several chapters on that subject – and Lord Peter may have been Branwell's title on these occasions.

That he was fearful the sketches might be seen by other eyes than the sculptor's own was evident from the warning in the letter: 'I send you herewith two scrawls on the beforehand page, which you had better burn the moment you see them.' The drawings, amusing and harmless enough to the ignorant, obviously conveyed a very opposite meaning to the initiated.

It is possible that the character 'Sugdeniensis' did not represent the dead conductor, but a relative of the landlady of the Talbot Inn, herself a Mrs Sugden. 'I was really far enough from well when I saw you last week at Halifax,' Branwell wrote at the beginning of his letter, 'and if you should happen shortly to see Mrs Sugden of the Talbot you would greatly oblige me by telling her that I consider her conduct towards me as most kind and motherly, and that if I did anything, during my temporary illness, to offend her I deeply regret it, and beg her to take my regret as my apology till I see her again, which I trust will be ere long.'

The fits, then, were coming more frequently than before. They could not be foreseen, nor could they be controlled, and Branwell himself, aware from past and bitter experience that he was not responsible for his own actions before an attack, endeavoured to disarm possible hostility by apology, and protect his reputation at the same time. Not even the sculptor realized the nature of the illness. The falls, the sudden excitement, followed by a lapse of consciousness, were charged to excessive drinking, and nothing else.

'We have not been very comfortable here at home lately,' Charlotte told Ellen Nussey on January 11th,

far from it, indeed. Branwell has contrived by some means to get money from the old quarter, and has led us a sad life with his absurd and often intolerable conduct. Papa is harassed day and night – we have little peace – he is always sick, has two or three times fallen down in fits – what will be the ultimate end God knows . . .

It did not occur to Charlotte or any of the family that there was only one course to take, and that a consultation with the best medical opinion of the day was imperative if Branwell's life and reason were to be saved. Charlotte and

Emily had not hesitated to go to Manchester two years before to arrange about the operation for their father's cataract, and after Branwell's death, when Emily was dying and refused all treatment, Charlotte did at least write to a London specialist, asking for advice. No such action was taken for her brother. Dr Wheelhouse of Haworth suggested abstention from alcohol, and nothing more. The rapid loss of weight, the continuing cough, the appalling insomnia, were left to take their course. If Branwell was ill, he was ill through his own fault. There was no remedy.

News of the Robinsons must have been filtering through to the parsonage continuously during the past twelve months. Some months before Charlotte had told Ellen Nussey how the two younger girls had written to Anne, speaking 'with great affection of their mother'. Now, in January 1848, the situation had apparently changed.

'The Misses Robinson,' said Charlotte on January 28th,

still amaze me by the continued frequency and constancy of their correspondence. Poor girls! they still complain of their mother's proceedings; that woman is a hopeless being; calculated to bring a curse wherever she goes by the mixture of weakness, perversion and deceit in her nature. Sir Edward Scott's wife is said to be dying; if she goes I suppose they will marry, that is if Mrs R. *can* marry. She affirmed her husband's will bound her to remain single, but I do not believe anything she says.

This denouncement of Mrs Robinson, both by Charlotte and by Mrs Robinson's own daughters, comes as news to the reader, but obviously not to Ellen Nussey, who received the letter. Many years later, after Charlotte's death, Ellen Nussey admitted to destroying a great number of Charlotte's letters. In some of these a closer account may have been given of the ups and downs of Robinson family life. Certainly Lydia Robinson would seem by now to have recovered from her 'angel Edmund's' death, and be spending some of her time visiting her father's old home, Yoxall Lodge, and Barr Hall, Staffordshire, the country estate of a seventy-two-year-old baronet, Sir Edward Dolman Scott, whose wife was a cousin of hers. A letter which she wrote to the estate agent of Thorp Green, Mr Daniel Seaton, although undated, must have been sent at about the time her daughters wrote to Anne.

My dear Sir,

   I wrote to you the other day and I dare say I shall soon hear from you. But I write to beg you now to arrange with my son about his journey. He is coming to Yoxall Lodge next Saturday for a few days on his way back to Mr Williams, and I wish you would supply him with travelling money. I think Edmund will know about what it will cost, but at all events I fancy about £5 or £6 will pay for himself. But I must give him I think £5 for pocket money (as he takes in no few books and smaller expenses at Mr W's) and I hope you will kindly arrange this for me. I am *very* anxious about my son.

   I am greatly mortified at the illness of Lady Scott which has changed all our holiday plans.

Yrs
L. Robinson.

Lady Scott, whose illness upset the holiday plans, was to die the following August, and Sir Edward married Lydia Robinson on November 8th, 1848, exactly three months later, only to die himself in two years' time and leave her once more a widow. The elderly husband was no less fond of her than his predecessor, for he left her £600 a year and his house in Bryanston Square, London, with all the furniture, for her lifetime, as well as the family diamonds which would pass, at her death, to his heir by his first wife.

Here was the Lady Scott whom Mrs Gaskell would hear of 'in London drawing-rooms . . . flaunting about to this day in respectable society; a showy woman for her age; kept afloat by her reputed wealth . . .'

Ministering angel or seductive siren? Branwell would have said the first, his family the second; posterity, with no proof either way, must hold the balance. Certainly Lydia Robinson's descendants never heard anything to her discredit. A great-granddaughter living in Derbyshire was told as a child that one of the Brontë sisters had taught her grandmother Elizabeth, but knew nothing of any tutor. Descendants of Charles Thorp – Mr Robinson's brother-in-law – heard the same story. No word of scandal penetrated to the second and third generation. The fatal charm of Lydia Robinson may have had no foundation save in the imagination of a young man who had long sought an enchantress in his infernal world.

Lydia Robinson, afterwards Lady Scott, died at No. 5, Curzon Street, London, on June 19th, 1859, aged fifty-nine. The cause of her death was given as a disease of the liver, with diarrhoea lasting for ten days. Such was the sad and unromantic end of the lady who had unwittingly caused so much sorrow. She left all her possessions to her son Edmund – who was to survive her by only ten years – with the exception of her jewellery, which was to be divided between all three of her married daughters, proving that the mother, at any rate, had forgiven her runaway namesake. The will ended with a touching request to be buried at Thorp Green, 'if not inconvenient to my son to do so (and quite privately) otherwise I wish to be buried wherever I may die'.

Young Edmund never married. He sold his estate of Thorp Green to a neighbour, Henry Stephen Thompson of Kirby Hall, three years before the tragic accident in which he was drowned. He left his runaway sister, Lydia Roxby, an annuity of £500 for life, and £6,000 each to her two sons when they reached the age of twenty-one. His sister Mary Pocock had £20,000 for her own use, and, apart from one or two bequests, the remainder of his estate went to his sister Elizabeth on trust, all a proof that the Robinson family was a united one.

One of the executors of his will was his uncle, Charles Thorp – the gentleman who, Branwell told Leyland, 'detested him, and threatened to shoot him'. Mr Thorp lived at Alnwick, Northumberland, and Alnwick was also the home, in so many Angrian tales, of Alexander Percy, Earl of Northangerland. This was a coincidence that must have struck Branwell very forcibly when he went to Thorp Green, and may even have touched off the first spark of that feverish imagination which ultimately led to conflagration.

This was all in the future. In that summer of 1848, before Mrs Robinson had become Lady Scott, her one-time tutor was slowly dying on his feet. The landlord of the Old Cock, Halifax, was pressing him for settlement of an outstanding bill, and had written to Mr Brontë demanding payment, under penalty of a court summons. Once again Branwell wrote to Leyland asking him to see the landlord, Nicholson, as well as Mrs Sugden of the Talbot, and inform them both that the money would shortly be paid. Dr Crosby of Great Ouseburn, Branwell said, would forward the advance. The receipt of money, through him, was 'morally certain'. Was this true or false? What pressure could Branwell possibly bring to bear upon a country practitioner, other than that of pity; unless the doctor did, in fact, carry the plea back to Mrs Robinson, who, touched in her turn by the wretched tale of ill-health, sent money through his hands?

'If he [Nicholson] refuses my offer and presses me with law,' Branwell told the sculptor,

I am RUINED. I have had five months of such utter sleeplessness, violent cough and frightful agony of mind that jail would destroy me for ever . . .

Excuse this scrawl. Long have I resolved to write to you a letter of five or six pages, but intolerable mental wretchedness and corporeal weakness have utterly prevented me.

Leyland, who only three years later would himself die in a debtors' prison, most assuredly paid these debts for his friend. Dr Crosby, to the sculptor, was just a name, and, for all he knew, as fictitious as many others.

The letter to Leyland was written on June 22nd. A week or so earlier Anne's second novel, *The Tenant of Wildfell Hall*, had been published by Newby of Mortimer Street. It caught the attention of the public far more than either *Wuthering Heights* or *Agnes Grey* had done.

Newby had put it about that the author of all the books was in reality Currer Bell, who had written the notorious *Jane Eyre*, and he had even forwarded proofs of Anne's new novel to an American publisher, telling him the same story. This tissue of lies, reported to Charlotte's publishers Smith and Elder, who reported it in turn, with some annoyance, to the mysterious 'Currer Bell' – whom they had never seen – determined Anne and Charlotte to visit London forthwith. They took the train from Keighley to Leeds, and so through the night to London, the very day the letter from the publishers had reached them, on Friday, July 7th.

The three days they spent in London, meeting both Charlotte's publishers and Anne's as well, the visits to the Opera, the Academy and the National Gallery, the astonishment of Mr Smith and Mr Williams to discover that Currer Bell and his brother Acton were two quietly dressed young women, is, of course, literary history. Posterity has never been told what excuse Charlotte and Anne made at home – not to their father, who presumably had been briefed for the occasion, but to Tabitha, young Martha Brown and, above all, to Branwell.

Affairs of business? What business? Rumours that the small railway shares they held were doing badly? A sudden whim to visit the sights of London, and leave Haworth in the middle of a summer storm? That the London visit must be connected with books and publishing, Branwell could not doubt. He would feign indifference; he might not even deign to ask questions. But he knew his sisters too well to be fobbed off with some tale of sight-seeing or finance.

A fortnight or so after her return from London, Charlotte told Ellen: 'Branwell is the same in conduct as ever; his constitution seems much shattered. Papa, and sometimes all of us, have sad nights with him. He sleeps most of the day, and consequently will lie awake at night.'

Early in August Sir Edward Scott's invalid wife died. Even before her death, Branwell must have heard from some informant in Little Ouseburn – Dr Crosby, or some local acquaintance – of the preoccupation of his own lost Lydia with her cousin's elderly husband. Now Sir Edward was at last a widower, and Charlotte wrote to Ellen: 'Mrs Robinson is anxious to get her daughters husbands of any kind, that they may be off her hands, and that she may be free to marry Sir Edward Scott, whose infatuated slave, it would appear, she now is.'

It was useless for Branwell to pretend any longer that Lydia Robinson was pining for him, or had gone into a nunnery. Such a fable would be received at home with scorn and derision. Even his friends in Halifax would not believe it. The end had come. Fantasy was over.

An undated scrap of paper, scribbled to Leyland with his right hand but addressed with his left, and written from the commercial room in the Old Cock, New Market, Halifax, was afterwards found among the sculptor's letters.

For mercy's sake come and see me, for I have sought for you till I dare not risk my knee and my eyesight any more this evening.

255

I shall have a bad evening and night if I do not see you, but I hardly know where to send the bearer of this note so as to enable him to catch you.

On Friday, September 22nd, Branwell went down into the village of Haworth. No record states where to. Perhaps to the post office. There might even now have been a letter from a Leeds or Halifax newspaper, accepting a poem.

William Brown found him halfway up the lane between the church and the parsonage. He was exhausted, and unable to walk the few yards home alone. William Brown helped him through the garden gate, and up the steps into the house. Branwell never left it again. In two days he was dead.

18

The cause of Branwell's death was stated in the death certificate to be chronic bronchitis and marasmus (wasting of the body).

The effect which it had upon his family, and on Charlotte in particular, was expressed in the letter which she wrote to W. S. Williams, of Smith and Elder, on October 6th, 1848:

When I looked on the noble face and forehead of my dead brother (Nature had favoured him with a fairer outside, as well as a finer constitution than his sisters) and asked myself what had made him go ever wrong, tend ever downwards, when he had so many gifts to induce to, and aid in, an upward course, I seemed to receive an oppressive revelation of the feebleness of humanity; of the inadequacy of even genius to lead to true greatness if unaided by religion and principle. In the value, or even the reality of these two things he would never believe till within a few days of his end, and then all at once he seemed to open his heart to a conviction of their existence and worth. The remembrance of this strange change now comforts my poor Father greatly. I myself, with painful, mournful joy, heard him praying softly in his dying moments, and to the last prayer which my father offered up at his bedside, he added 'amen'. How unusual that word appeared from his lips, of course you, who did not know him, cannot conceive. Akin to this alteration was that in his feelings towards his relatives, all bitterness seemed gone.

When the struggle was over and a marble calm began to succeed the last dread agony, I felt, as I had never felt before, that there was peace and forgiveness for him in Heaven. All his errors – to speak plainly, all his vices – seemed nothing to me in that moment; every wrong he had done, every pain he has caused, vanished; his sufferings only were remembered; the wrench to the natural affections only was felt. If Man can thus experience total oblivion of his fellow's imperfections – how much more can the Eternal Being, who made man, forgive his creature?

Had his sins been scarlet in their dye, I believe now they are white as wool. He is at rest, and that comforts us all. Long before he quitted this world Life had no happiness for him . . .

F. A. Leyland, in his biography *The Brontë Family*, published in 1885, denied a certain assertion made by Mrs Gaskell, and spoke briefly of the deaths of Emily and Anne:

Amongst Mrs Gaskell's other statements regarding him, there is one, relating even to his death, which cannot be passed over in silence . . . The statement was to the effect that, when Branwell died, his pockets were filled with the letters of the lady whom he had admired. To this bold statement Martha Brown gave to me a flat contradiction, declaring that she was employed in the sick-room at the time, and had personal knowledge that not one letter, nor a vestige of one, from the lady in question was so found. The letters were mostly from a gentleman of Branwell's acquaintance, then living near the place of his former employment. Martha was indignant at the misrepresentation.

It may not be amiss here, in the briefest possible way, to give an outline of the subsequent history of the Brontë family. Emily's health began rapidly to fail after Branwell's death, which was a great shock to her, and she never left the house alive after the Sunday succeeding it. Her cough was very obstinate, and she was troubled with shortness of breath. Charlotte saw the danger, but could do nothing to ward it off, for Emily was silent and reserved, gave no answers to questions, and took no remedies that were prescribed. She grew weaker daily, and the end came on Tuesday, December 19th.

At the same time Anne was slowly failing, but she lingered longer . . . Unlike Emily, she looked for sympathy, took medicines, and did her best to get well. It was arranged at last that Charlotte and she should go to Scarborough, hoping the change of air might invigorate her, and they left the parsonage on May 24th, 1849. But the change had no beneficial effect, and Anne died on May 28th, at Scarborough, where she was buried.

Charlotte herself, writing once again to Mr Williams on June 25th, 1849, after the successive deaths of Emily and Anne, left a lasting impression of loneliness and grief, which Branwell's undated sonnet, *Peaceful Death and Happy Life*, redrafted from the original *Percy's Last Sonnet* of 1837, so poignantly foreshadowed:

I am now again at home, where I returned last Thursday. I call it *home* still – much as London would be called London if an earthquake should shake its streets to ruins. But let me not be ungrateful: Haworth parsonage is still a home for me, and not quite a ruined or desolate home either. Papa is there, and two most affectionate and faithful servants, and two old dogs, in their way as faithful and affectionate – Emily's large house-dog, which lay at the foot of her dying bed, and followed her funeral to the vault, lying in the pew crouched at our feet while the burial service was being read, and Anne's little spaniel. The ecstasy of these poor animals when I came in was something singular; at former returns from brief absence they always welcomed me, warmly, but not in that strange, heart-touching way. I am certain they thought that, as I was returned, my sisters were not far behind – but here my sisters will come no more. Keeper may visit Emily's little bedroom as he still does day by day, and Flossy may look wistfully round for Anne; they will never see them again; nor shall I – at least the human part of me. I must not write so sadly, but how can I help thinking, and feeling, sadly? In the daytime effort and occupation aid me, but when evening darkens something within my heart revolts against the burden of solitude; the sense of loss and want grows almost too much for me. I am not good or amiable in such moments – I am rebellious – and it is only the thoughts of my dear Father in the next room, or of the kind servants in the kitchen, or some caress of the poor dogs, which restores me to softer sentiments and more rational views. As to the night – could I do without bed, I would never seek it. Waking I think, sleeping I dream of them – and I cannot recall them as they were in health; still they appear to me in sickness and suffering. Still my nights were worse after the first shock of Branwell's death. They were terrible then, and the impressions experienced on waking were at that time such as we do not put into language . . .

Peaceful Death and Happy Life

Why dost thou sorrow for the happy dead
    For if their life be lost, their toils are o'er
    And woe and want shall trouble them no more,

Nor ever slept they in an earthly bed
    So sound as now they sleep while dreamless, laid
In the dark chambers of that unknown shore
    Where Night and Silence seal each guarded door:
So turn from such as these thy drooping head
    And mourn the '*dead alive*' – whose spirit flies –
    Whose life departs before his death has come –
Who finds no Heaven beyond Life's gloomy skies,
    Who sees no Hope to brighten up that gloom;
    Tis HE who feels the worm that never dies –
The REAL death and darkness of the tomb.

'Northangerland.'

Notes

CHAPTER 1

SOURCES

The Brontë Family: F. A. Leyland

The Life of Charlotte Brontë: E. C. Gaskell

The Leyland Manuscripts: J. A. Symington

The Leyland Family: Mary Leyland

The Miscellaneous Works of Charlotte and Patrick Branwell Brontë (Shakespeare Head)

The Brontës' Web of Childhood: F. E. Ratchford

Letter from Charlotte Brontë to W. S. Williams October 6th, 1848

Extract from *And the Weary Are At Rest* by P. B. Brontë

Extract from *Speech of Alexander Percy* by P. B. Brontë (MS. in the Brotherton Collection)

CHAPTER 2

SOURCES

The Life of Charlotte Brontë: E. C. Gaskell

Shakespeare Head Brontë. Vol. I

In the Footsteps of the Brontës: E. H. Chadwick

Brontë Papers: C. M. Edgerley

Brontëana: The Collected Works of the Rev Patrick Brontë: J. Horsfall Turner

Extract from the poem *Caroline* by P. B. Brontë (Shakespeare Head)

Nancy and Sarah Garrs were sisters. Nancy was nurse to the children at Thornton and went with them when they moved to Haworth. Sarah came later to help.

Mary Burder. Mr Brontë's first love, to whom he became attached at Wethersfield, Essex, during his first curacy. She left that neighbourhood and he never saw her again, but wrote to her two years after his wife died, expressing the hope that she might become his second wife.

CHAPTER 3

SOURCES

The Life of Charlotte Brontë: E. C. Gaskell
Shakespeare Head Brontë. Vol. I
The Brontës' Web of Childhood: F. E. Ratchford
Shakespeare Head Brontë, Misc. Works. Vol. I
A Brontë Moorland Village and Its People: A History of Stanbury:
    J. Craven
The Heaton Records
The Brontë Family: F. A. Leyland
Extract from *History of the Young Men* by P. B. Brontë
Extract from *Letters from an Englishman* by P. B. Brontë

CHAPTER 4

SOURCES

The Life of Charlotte Brontë: E. C. Gaskell
Shakespeare Head Brontë. Vol. I
In the Footsteps of the Brontës: E. H. Chadwick
The Brontës' Web of Childhood: F. E. Ratchford
The Miscellaneous Works of Charlotte and Patrick Branwell Brontë
    (Shakespeare Head) Vol. I
Noctes Ambrosianae. 4 vols.: Professor Wilson
The Heaton Records
The Brontë Family: F. A. Leyland

A Leaf from an Unopened Volume (an early Brontë story printed in *Derby Day and Other Adventures:* A. E. Newton)

Morning Chronicle, December 2nd, 1834

Extract from *A Peep into a Picture Book:* Misc. works of Charlotte Brontë

Extract from *The Wool Is Rising:* P. B. Brontë

Extract from *Lines Written During a Period of Insanity:* William Cowper

Private Memoirs and Confessions of a Justified Sinner: James Hogg

Extract from *Death of Mary Percy* by P. B. Brontë (Brotherton Collection)

Ellen Nussey, 1817–1897. Twelfth and youngest child of John and Ellen Nussey. Lived at Rydings, Birtall. Educated at Roe Head with Charlotte Brontë, and became her dearest friend. Almost every description of the Brontës and life at the parsonage, compiled by Mrs Gaskell, came from Ellen Nussey's pen.

Mary Taylor, 1817–1893. Elder daughter of Joshua and Anne Taylor, of the Red House, Gomersal. Educated at Roe Head with Charlotte Brontë, and her closest friend next to Ellen Nussey. She was in Brussels at the same time as Charlotte. Emigrated to New Zealand in 1845 and returned to England in 1860. In 1890 she wrote a novel, *Miss Miles*.

Noctes Ambrosianae. These appeared month by month in *Blackwood's Magazine*, the old numbers of which would have been kept at the parsonage. The number of May, 1830, contains a discussion on Lord and Lady Byron, and on Moore's *Life of Byron*, between the four 'conversationalists' of the *Noctes*: Christopher North (Professor Wilson), 'the Shepherd' (James Hogg), 'the Opium Eater' (de Quincey) and 'Tickler'.

J. B. Leyland, 1811–1851. Joseph Bentley, elder son of Roberts Leyland, bookseller and printer of Halifax, began to sculpt at the age of sixteen. In 1832 his 'Spartacus' was exhibited in Manchester. He studied in London under Haydon. His 'Satan' was exhibited at Leeds in 1834. His best-known extant monument is that to Dr Stephen Beckwith in York Minster. There is no trace today of 'Satan' or 'Spartacus' or of other sculptures which were famous in their day – 'Kilmeny', 'African Bloodhounds', etc. – nor of his plaster bust of 'Thracian Falconer', though the bronze is at Hollins, Warley. He became insolvent in 1850, and this, coupled with grief at his mother's death and ill-health from excessive drinking, led to his death in Manor Gaol, of dropsy, on January 28th, 1851.

James Hogg, 1770–1835. The Ettrick shepherd, Scottish poet and storyteller. Wrote for *Blackwood's Magazine*. His *Confessions of a Justified Sinner* was published by Longmans in 1824. The many tales by him which originally appeared in *Blackwood's* are of a particularly horrifying nature, likely to appeal to Branwell and Emily Brontë – e.g., *The Mysterious Bride*, *The Spanish Professor*, *Expedition to Hell*, *The Marvellous Doctor*, etc., etc.

CHAPTER 5

SOURCES

Shakespeare Head Brontë. Vol. I

The Life of Charlotte Brontë: E. C. Gaskell

The Queen's Wake: James Hogg

The Brontë Family: F. A. Leyland

Extract from *The Adventures of Charles Wentworth* by P. B. Brontë

In the Footsteps of the Brontës: E. H. Chadwick

A Brontë Moorland Village and Its People: J. Craven

A Spring Time Saunter: Whiteley Turner

The Heaton Records

The Life of William Grimshaw: John Newton

Freemasonry in Airedale in the Early Nineteenth Century: Lecture
by Wade Hustwick
Manual of Freemasonry: Richard Carlile

Kilmeny. The sinless maid, the subject of one of the most
popular of James Hogg's poems, which appeared in *The Queen's
Wake.*

Rev William Grimshaw, 1708–1763. Famous evangelical
preacher. Vicar at Haworth from 1742 until his death. He was
a friend of Wesley, and 'had visions'. At his own wish he was
buried at Luddenden, next to his first wife.

CHAPTER 6

SOURCES

The Miscellaneous Works of Charlotte and Patrick Branwell Brontë
(Shakespeare Head) Vols. I and II
Extract from *A New Year's Story* by P. B. Brontë
Extract from MS. in Brotherton Collection
Extracts from the poems *Caroline, Harriet I* and *Harriet II* by
P. B. Brontë
A Leaf from an Unopened Volume by Charlotte Brontë
Poems of Emily Brontë
Shakespeare Head Brontë. Vol. I
Poem 'However young . . .' by P. B. Brontë
Extract from *Letters of an Englishman* by P. B. Brontë
In the Footsteps of the Brontës: E. H. Chadwick
Anne Brontë: Winifred Gérin
Minutes of the Three Graces Lodge
MS. *Percy* by P. B. Brontë
Brontë Society Transactions, Part 8, Vol. 1

Alexander Percy, Earl of Northangerland, Branwell's fictitious
hero. He was born in 1792, son of Edward Percy of Raiswick

Hall, Northumberland, and of Lady Helen Beresford. Mr Percy, Sr, settled in Arthurstown, Africa, and bought an estate which he called Percy Hall, where Alexander was born. Alexander married, 1st, Augusta di Segovia, an Italian countess; 2nd, Mary Henrietta Wharton, by whom he had Edward, William and Mary Henrietta; 3rd, Lady Zenobia Ellrington. He also had an illegitimate daughter, Caroline, by a French mistress. His daughter Mary married the Duke of Zamorna, against whom Northangerland led a rebellion, but they finally made peace and became friends again.

Angrian Tales. More details of Alexander Percy's youth are given in a story *Zamorna*, attributed to Charlotte, relating to letters between Alexander Percy and Harriet O'Connor. Harriet later married H. M. M. Montmorency, a barrister, committed adultery with Percy, ran away with him, and died in solitude. The MS. relating this has not been traced, but the event is alluded to in Branwell's poems and in various Angrian stories.

Gondal Saga. The many poems written by Emily Brontë between 1836 and 1846 concern the inhabitants of an imaginary kingdom named Gondal – the rival kings, queens, princesses, nobles, etc. The narrative ballad style shows the strong influence which *The Queen's Wake*, *The Queen's Hynde* and *The Pilgrims of the Sun*, all by James Hogg, which had appeared in *Blackwood's*, must have made upon Emily when she first read them.

Martha Taylor, 1819–1842. Younger sister of Charlotte's friend Mary. Ellen Nussey gave a vivid description of her. Both the Taylor sisters were described from life in Charlotte Brontë's *Shirley* as the Yorke sisters, but in the Angrian tales they were very likely the originals of Mary Percy (Percy's legitimate daughter) and Caroline Vernon (his illegitimate daughter). Martha also bears a resemblance to the two Cathys in *Wuthering Heights*.

CHAPTER 7

SOURCES

Brontë Society Transactions, Part 3, Vol. 1, Parts 62 and 63, Vol. 12, Part 68, Vol. 13

The Brontë Family: F. A. Leyland

Shakespeare Head Brontë. Vol. I

The Leyland Family: Mary Leyland

Poems of Patrick Branwell Brontë (Shakespeare Head)

Lines to an African Bloodhound: William Dearden

MS. *Percy* by P. B. Brontë

Zamorna by Charlotte Brontë

Caroline Vernon by Charlotte Brontë, transcribed in *Legends of Angria* by F. E. Ratchford

A Brontë Moorland Village and Its People: J. Craven

The Heaton Records

Azrael by P. B. Brontë (Shakespeare Head Brontë and Brontë Society Transactions, Part 43, Vol. 8)

Arthur Bell Nicholls, 1818–1906. Born in County Antrim, entered Trinity College, Dublin, and became curate to Mr Brontë in 1845. Married Charlotte on June 29th, 1854, after much opposition on the part of her father. Charlotte died the following year, and Mr Nicholls remained with Mr Brontë as curate, sharing his house, until Mr Brontë died in 1861. He then returned to Ireland, and in August, 1864, married his cousin, Miss Bell. He disliked all publicity concerning his first wife, and kept the many unpublished MSS. of all four Brontës hidden away, possibly destroying some. Charlotte, in 1847, had remarked to Ellen Nussey on his 'narrowness of mind', but in 1855, when she lay dying, she whispered, 'I'm not going to die, am I? We have been so happy.'

F. A. Leyland, 1813–1894. Younger brother of J. B. Leyland. He entered the printing and bookselling firm of his father, from whom he also inherited antiquarian tastes. He became a Roman Catholic, and in 1845 married Ann Brierley, who died in 1849. He was devoted to his brother, and administered his belongings after his death. His book, *The Brontë Family*, endeavoured to atone for Mrs Gaskell's treatment of Branwell.

William Dearden, 1805–1888. Son of John Dearden, tailor and clothier of Hebden Bridge. Educated at Heptonstall Grammar School, and taught at Keighley and Huddersfield. He was principal of Warley Grammar School for many years from 1847. He was author of *The Star Seer* and many other local poems.

Scattering of Pennies. Branwell's 'largesse' to the children of Haworth was recounted by a descendant of one of the children to Miss Bates of Sowerby Bridge.

CHAPTER 8

SOURCES

Modern Domestic Medicine: T. J. Graham

Shakespeare Head Brontë. Vol. I

Extract from the poem *Harriet* by P. B. Brontë (Shakespeare Head)

Wuthering Heights by Emily Brontë

The Brontë Family: F. A. Leyland

Poems of Emily Brontë

Confessions of an Opium Eater by de Quincey

Life of Francis Thompson by J. C. Reid

Extract from sermon on 'anti-Christ' by the Rev Hugh McNeile, at St Jude's, Liverpool

Transactions of the Halifax Antiquarian Society

The Leyland Family: Mary Leyland

Boaties. Almost every scrap of information about the old days in Sowerby Bridge, Luddenden and Luddenden Foot has been received from Miss Dorothy Bates of Sowerby Bridge, who made exhaustive inquiries among friends, relatives and others in the district. The bargees were invariably called 'boaties'.

The Rev. Hugh McNeile, 1795–1879. Born in Ballycastle, son of the sheriff of Antrim. Appointed perpetual curate to St Jude's, Liverpool, in 1834. Canon of Chester Cathedral, 1845, and Dean of Ripon, 1868. Married Ann, daughter of Archbishop Magee. He held strongly evangelical views, and was implacably opposed to Rome. He wrote innumerable sermons.

'The Gentry'. It seems certain that the young Brontës must have based many of their Angrian tales on the lives and genealogy of local and nearby 'big' families. The Heatons of Ponden would take pride of place, but 'Johnny' Grimshaw, son of Mr Brontë's predecessor, would excite their interest as heir to the vast estates at Ewood of his mother, Sarah Lockwood, which he inherited at the age of twelve. At twenty he married Grace Gibson, who was six years older than himself. A great drinker, he died childless, leaving his estates to a maternal cousin, William Lockwood. An intriguing piece of intermarriage was that his widow Grace, an ardent Methodist, subsequently married, first, another Lockwood brother, and, secondly, John Sutcliffe, whose first wife had been a sister-in-law of the Rev William Grimshaw. Thus she found herself married to her ex-father-in-law's brother-in-law! Into this complicated tale of intermarriage come many names which students of *Wuthering Heights* might note – Ellis, Grimshaw, Lockwood, Sutcliffe, Scaitcliffe.

CHAPTER 9

Sources
The Brontë Family: F. A. Leyland
The Heaton Records
History of the Three Graces Lodge: Wade Hustwick

Shakespeare Head Brontë. Vol. I

Wuthering Heights by Emily Brontë

Poems of Hartley Coleridge, with a Memoir by his brother Derwent Coleridge

Odes of Horace by P. B. Brontë (Shakespeare Head Misc. Works)

Fragment of poem, *Amelia*, by P. B. Brontë

The Devil's Thumb, etc. Local inhabitants of present-day Haworth might find amusement in tracing these disguised gentlemen from lists of the Conservative Committee in 1837 and from members of the Three Graces Lodge.

Conservative Committee (June 27th, 1837)	*Three Graces Lodge* (Sept. 11th, 1837)
William Hartley	John Brown
William Garnett	William Hartley
John Sutcliffe	John Bland
John Heaton	John Roper

Conservative Committee (June 27th, 1837)	*Three Graces Lodge* (Sept. 11th, 1837)
Enoch Thomas	Jas. Akroyd
John Brown	P. B. Brontë
William Sutcliffe	W. C. Greenwood
	John Feather
	Jas. Brown
	W. Mosley
	W. Brown
	John Greenwood

CHAPTER 10

SOURCES

Shakespeare Head Brontë. Vol. I

Letters from Miss Bates of Sowerby Bridge

The Brontë Family: F. A. Leyland
The Leyland Family: Mary Leyland
Sowerby and Luddenden Directories
List of members of the Luddenden Library in 1840
Pictures of the Past: F. A. Grundy
Extract from *The Wool Is Rising* by P. B. Brontë
Luddenden Notebook of P. B. Brontë
Poems of Patrick Branwell Brontë (Shakespeare Head)
Poems of Emily Brontë
It Happened Here: Arthur Porritt

'Whey-Faced Hermaphrodite'. This curious dialogue in *Corner Dishes*, attributed to Charlotte Brontë, is much more likely to have been Branwell's invention. A further sentence is: 'I've heard him swear many a time till questionable company has been raised like a cock in the very midst of us.' An eighteen-year-old girl would hardly use such a phrase, but her seventeen-year-old brother might easily do so.

Monsieur Héger, 1809–1896. It was Constantin Héger's second wife who started the school in the rue d'Isabelle. M. Héger took charge of the upper French classes. According to Miss Wheelwright, one of his pupils, his keen intelligence amounted to genius. His heavy black hair and black moustache made him a striking figure. He originally tore up all Charlotte's letters, and threw them in a wastepaper basket. They were retrieved by his wife, who put them away in her jewel-case. Mrs Gaskell was shown some of them when she interviewed M. Héger during her research for Charlotte's biography, but kept silent about their subject matter. In 1913 the Hégers' son and daughter, whose parents were long since dead, presented the letters to the British Museum.

CHAPTER 11

Sources

The Brontë Family: F. A. Leyland

Charlotte Brontë E. F. Benson

The Leyland Manuscripts

Shakespeare Head Brontë. Vol. I

Letter from William Dearden to Halifax *Guardian*

Extract from *And the Weary Are At Rest* by P. B. Brontë

Brontëana: The Collected Works of the Rev Patrick Brontë J. Horsfall
  Turner

And The Weary Are At Rest. There is no date to this manuscript, which is housed in the Berg Collection, New York.
The curator writes: 'There are fifty-seven pages in the MS.
Changes occur in the tone, but not colour of ink and point
of pen. The paper is apparently a copy-book from which the
covers have been stripped. There is nothing indicating an
appreciable time elapsed in the writing of this MS. It is quite
possible it is a slightly corrected fair copy of an earlier MS.'

CHAPTER 12

Sources

Shakespeare Head Brontë. Vols. I and II

The Brontë Family: F. A. Leyland

In the Footsteps of the Brontës: E. H. Chadwick

Letters from Mrs MacLeary, granddaughter of James La Trobe

Agnes Grey by Anne Brontë

Anne Brontë by Winifred Gêrin

Brontë Society Transactions. Part 64, Vol. 12

Robinson Deed Box

Scarborough newspapers

Luddenden Notebook of P. B. Brontë

Extract from *And the Weary Are At Rest* by P. B. Brontë

Poems of Charlotte Brontë (Shakespeare Head)

CHAPTER 13

SOURCES

Shakespeare Head Brontë. Vol. II

Scarborough newspapers

Agnes Grey by Anne Brontë

Wuthering Heights by Emily Brontë

Poems of Charlotte and Patrick Branwell Brontë (Shakespeare Head)

Robinson Deed Box

The Leyland Manuscripts

The Brontë Family: F. A. Leyland

Poems of Emily Brontë

Sonnet, *The Callousness Produced by Care* by P. B. Brontë

Brontë Society Transactions. Part 67, Vol. 13

CHAPTER 14

SOURCES

The Leyland Manuscripts

The Brontë Family: F. A. Leyland

Pictures of the Past: F. A. Grundy

Poems of Patrick Branwell Brontë (Shakespeare Head)

Shakespeare Head Brontë. Vol. II

Extract from poem by Emily Brontë

The Wool Is Rising by P. B. Brontë

The Professor by Charlotte Brontë

The Leyland Family: Mary Leyland

The Life of Charlotte Brontë: E. C. Gaskell

CHAPTER 15

SOURCES

Robinson Deed Box

Scarborough and York newspapers

The Leyland Manuscripts

Pictures of the Past: F. A. Grundy
The Life of Charlotte Brontë E. C. Gaskell
Shakespeare Head Brontë. Vol. II
Manual of Freemasonry: R. Carlile
Morley Hall, poem by P. B. Brontë
Poems of Patrick Branwell Brontë (Shakespeare Head)

CHAPTER 16

SOURCES

Modern Domestic Medicine: T. J. Graham
The Brontë Family: F. A. Leyland
MS. *Percy* by P. B. Brontë
The Leyland Manuscripts
Shakespeare Head Brontë. Vol. II
Robinson Deed Box
The Tenant of Wildfell Hall by Anne Brontë
Poems by Patrick Branwell Brontë (Shakespeare Head)
Prayer of Leyland the Sculptor (by courtesy of Miss Mary Leyland)

The Professor. Charlotte Brontë's *The Professor* did not find favour with her publishers during her lifetime. It was published posthumously in 1856. Comparison of the early chapters with Branwell Brontë's *The Wool Is Rising* (written when he was seventeen) is fascinating. Even the names are identical. The two brothers, Edward and William, and the clerk, Steighton, figure in both stories.

Wuthering Heights and *The Tenant of Wildfell Hall.* G. Elsie Harrison, in her *Clue to the Brontës*, puts forward the very intersting theory that both Emily's and Anne's books, as well as Branwell's and Charlotte's Angrian stories, were largely influenced by the tales which their father and aunt told them of early Methodist individuals, in particular Selina, Lady Huntingdon. She was the founder of a Calvinist sect, and was the daughter of the 2nd Earl Shirley Ferrers and cousin of the notorious 4th Earl Ferrers, who was tried for murder in 1760 and hanged at Tyburn. Selina married the 9th Earl Huntingdon, half-brother to the noted philanthropist, Lady Elizabeth Hastings. Note once more the coincidence of these names in Brontë unpublished and published works.

CHAPTER 17

SOURCES

The Life of Charlotte Brontë E. C. Gaskell
Shakespeare Head Brontë. Vol. II
The Brontë Family: F. A. Leyland
Poems of Patrick Branwell Brontë (Shakespeare Head)
Review from *The Mirror* of December 1847
Robinson Deed Box
The Leyland Manuscripts
York newspapers

George Searle Phillips, 1815–1889. Miscellaneous writer. Went to America and wrote for the New York *World and Herald.* Edited *Leeds Times,* 1845. Secretary of the People's College, Huddersfield, 1846. Became insane in 1873, when in America, and died in an asylum in New Jersey. In his review of *Jane Eyre* he said that the author 'knows how to overstep conventional usages – how, in fact, to trample upon customs respected by our forefathers . . . The clergyman in *Jane Eyre* is all that is mean, despicable, and uncharitable . . . On every occasion a blow is sought to be struck at true religion . . . The heroine herself is a specimen of the bold daring young ladies who delight in overstepping conventional rules . . . The foundation of the story is bad, the characters ill-drawn, and the feelings false and unnatural. If our readers be induced by our remarks to peruse the novel before us they are welcome to undertake the task, and much good it may do them.'

Appendix

A LIST OF THE MANUSCRIPTS OF
PATRICK BRANWELL BRONTË

History of the Rebellion in My Army. 1828.	Brontë Museum
The Young Men's Magazine. 1829.	Ashley Library, British Museum
A Collection of Poems by Young Soult the Rhymer. 1829.	Brontë Museum
Lausanne. A Dramatic Poem by Young Soult the Rhymer. 1829.	Bonnell Collection, Brontë Museum
The Revenge. A Tragedy in Three Acts, by Young Soult. 1830.	Brontë Museum
Caractacus: A Dramatic Poem. 1830.	Brotherton Collection, Leeds.
The History of the Young Men From Their First Settlement to the Present Time. December 1830 to May 1831.	Ashley Library, British Museum
Letters From An Englishman to His Relative in London. In six volumes. 1830–1832.	Brotherton Collection, Leeds
The Fate of Regina. 1832.	Brontë Museum
Ode on the Celebration of the Great African Games. 1832.	Brontë Museum

The Pass of Thermopylae. 1833.	Brontë Museum
The Pirate. February, 1833.	Bonnell Collection, Brontë Museum
The Monthly Intelligencer. (Newspaper.) 1833.	Brontë Museum
The Politics in Verdopolis. A Tale by John Flower, M.P. November 1833.	Bonnell Collection, Brontë Museum
Fragment relating to the death of Mary Percy. 1833.	Brotherton Collection, Leeds
Fragment relating to events before establishment of Kingdom of Angria. 1834.	Brotherton Collection, Leeds
Northangerland's Address to the Angrians. 1834.	Brotherton Collection, Leeds
The Wool Is Rising. June 1834.	Ashley Library, British Museum
Coronation. June–September 1834.	Brotherton Collection, Leeds
Northangerland's Letter to the Angrians. September 1834.	Brotherton Collection, Leeds
The Angrian Welcome. September to October 1834.	Brotherton Collection, Leeds
An Hour's Musings. November 1834.	Brontë Museum
The Massacre of Dongola. December 1834–January 1835.	Brotherton Collection, Leeds

The History of Angria. I. June–July 1835.	Originally Symington collection, now sold
The History of Angria. II. January 1836.	MS. scattered
A New Year Story. January–August 1836.	Ashley Library, British Museum
History of Angria. IV. May 1836.	Ashley Library, British Museum; four pages in the Brotherton Collection, Leeds
History of Angria. V. May 1836.	Brotherton Collection, Leeds
History of Angria. VI. June 1836.	Brotherton Collection, Leeds
History of Angria. VII. June 1836.	Brotherton Collection, Leeds
History of Angria. VIII. July 1836.	Brotherton Collection, Leeds
History of Angria. VIII (cont.) August 1836.	Ashley Library, British Museum and Bonnell Collection, Brontë Museum
History of Angria. IX. November–December 1836.	Bonnell Collection, Brontë Museum, and Brotherton Collection, Leeds

Fragment about Zamorna. Early 1837.   Brontë Museum

Fragment about Henry Hastings. January 1837.   Brontë Museum

Fragment about Henry Hastings. July 1837.   Brontë Museum

Percy, including fragments of three separate tales   Brontë Museum
    bound together, relating to (*a*) Percy and his third
    wife Zenobia; (*b*) Percy on a visit to W. Thurston
    of Darkwall Hall; (*c*) Henry Hastings and Mr Elles
    at an Inn. October to December 1837.

Life of Warner Howard Warner. February 1838.   Bonnell Collection,
                                                        Brontë Museum

Love and Warfare. (Fragments bound together)   Bonnell Collection,
    December 1838–April 1839.   Brontë Museum

Odes of Horace. Book One. 1840.   Brotherton

Notebook written at Luddenden Foot. 1841–1842.   Collection, Leeds
                                                        Brontë Museum

Seven sheets of Notebook as above.   Brotherton
                                                        Collection, Leeds

And the Weary Are At Rest. 1842?   Mr Harry B. Smith,
                                                        New York

The Leyland Manuscripts. (Original letters from   Brotherton
    P. B. Brontë to J. B. Leyland, 1842–1848.)   Collection, Leeds

Facsimiles of many of Branwell Brontë's manuscripts in
both prose and verse, and extracts from each, are to be found
in the Shakespeare Head edition of the *Miscellaneous Works of
Charlotte and Branwell Brontë*, in two volumes, edited by T. J.
Wise and J. A. Symington, published by Basil Blackwell,

Oxford, 1934. *The Poems of Charlotte and Patrick Branwell Brontë* have been collected in a separate volume of the Shakespeare Head edition, edited by T. J. Wise and J. A. Symington, 1934.

The Odes of Horace, privately printed for John Drinkwater in 1923, are included in the *Shakespeare Head Miscellaneous Works*.

The Leyland Manuscripts, privately printed for the Brontë Society in 1925, are included in the four volumes of the Shakespeare Head edition of *The Brontës. Their Lives, Friendships and Correspondence*, edited by T. J. Wise and J. A. Symington, 1932.

And the Weary Are At Rest was privately printed for J. A. Symington in 1924.

Branwell's Copy Book, in the Brontë Museum, proves that many of his poems, which he transcribed himself at a later date, were first written between 1834–1838. *The Doubter's Hymn*, for instance ('Life is a passing sleep . . .') was written in November, 1835, and transcribed in May, 1837. *Azrael* was written on April 30th, 1838, and transcribed on May 12th, 1838, yet in the Shakespeare Head edition of the *Poems* the date is given as 1842.

The long poem *The Wanderer*, dated Bradford, 1838 (manuscript in the Ashley Library, British Museum), was entitled *Sir Henry Tunstall* in September 1842, and sent by Branwell to *Blackwood's Magazine*. It was printed in *Annals of a Publishing House: William Blackwood and His Sons* by Mrs Oliphant, 1897.

The manuscripts of *Morley Hall* (fragment only), the poem *Landseer's Painting* ('The Shepherd's Chief Mourned' – a dog keeping watch at twilight over its master's grave), and the two sonnets *The Callousness Produced by Care* and *Peaceful Death and Happy Life*, all undated, are in the possession of the present writer.

Bibliography of
Manuscripts and Works
Studied

PRINTED BOOKS AND MSS.
bought by the author from the library of J. A. Symington

The Shakespeare Head Brontë. 19 Vols. Edited by T. J. Wise and J. A. Symington. Basil Blackwell, 1932–1934.

The Brontë Society Transactions from Parts 1 to 59.

The Leyland Manuscripts. Privately printed.

And the Weary Are At Rest by P. B. Brontë. Privately printed.

Brontëana: The Collected Works of the Rev Patrick Brontë by J. Horsfall Turner. Bingley, 1898.

The Brontë Papers by C. M. Edgerley. Published as a Memorial Tribute by the Brontë Society. Caxton Press, Shipley, 1951.

Charlotte Brontë by E. F. Benson. Longmans, Green, 1932. (Proof copy, with marginal notes by J. A. Symington.)

The Bookman. Double Number. 'The Brontës'. October 1904. Hodder & Stoughton.

'Who Wrote Wuthering Heights?' Letter from William Dearden to the Halifax *Guardian*, June 15th, 1867.

Four original manuscript poems of Branwell Brontë and many proof pages of material used in compiling *Letters from an Englishman* and other miscellaneous works of Branwell Brontë in the Shakespeare Head edition.

other than those bought from the library of J. A. Symington

Emily Brontë by Jacques Blondel. Presses Universitaires de France, 1955.

Manual of Freemasonry by Richard Carlile. William Reeves.

In the Footsteps of the Brontës by Ellis H. Chadwick. Pitman, 1914.

Poems by Hartley Coleridge, with a Memoir by his brother. 2 Vols. Edward Moxton, 1851.

A Brontë Moorland Village and Its People: A History of Stanbury by Joseph Craven. The Rydal Press, 1907.

Passionate Search: A Life of Charlotte Brontë by Margaret Crompton. Cassell, 1955.

The Death of Leyland's African Bloodhound by William Dearden. Longmans, 1837.

The Brontës: Their Lives Recorded by Their Contemporaries by E. M. Delafield. Hogarth Press, 1935.

Ewood in Midgley by G. Dent. Transactions of the Halifax Antiquarian Society. February 7th, 1839.

The Life of Charlotte Brontë by E. C. Gaskell. Introduction and Notes by Temple Scott and B. W. Willett. John Grant, Edinburgh, 1924.

Anne Brontë: A Biography by Winifred Gérin. Thomas Nelson, 1959.

Pictures of the Past by Francis H. Grundy. Griffith & Farrar, 1879.

Anne Brontë: Her Life and Work by Ada Harrison and Derek Stanford. Methuen, 1959.

The Clue to the Brontës by G. Elsie Harrison. Methuen, 1948.

The Complete Poems of Emily Jane Brontë. Edited by C. W. Hatfield. Oxford University Press, 1941.

The Brontës: Charlotte and Emily by Laura L. Hinckley. Hammond, Hammond, 1947.

The Complete Works of James Hogg: Poems and Prose. Blackie, 1863.

A History of the Three Graces Lodge. Compiled in 1931 to mark the centenary of its present Charter from the Grand Lodge of England. By favour of Mr Wade Hustwick, Bradford.

The Brontë Story by Margaret Lane. Heinemann, 1953.

Patrick Branwell Brontë by Alice Law. A. M. Philpot Ltd, 1925.

The Brontë Family, with Special Reference to P. B. Brontë by Francis Leyland. Hurst and Blackett, 1886.

The Leyland Family by Mary Leyland. Transactions of the Halifax Antiquarian Society. April 6th, 1954.

The Poetical Works of William Cowper. Edited by H. S. Milford. Oxford University Press, 1934.

A Leaf from an Unopened Volume. An Angrian story transcribed in 'Derby Day and Other Adventures' by A. Edward Newton. Little Brown & Co., 1934.

The Life of William Grimshaw by John Newton. London, 1799.

It Happened Here by Arthur Porritt. 1st and 2nd Series. Fawcett, Greenwood, Halifax, 1955 and 1959.

The Brontës' Web of Childhood by Fannie Elizabeth Ratchford. Columbia University Press, 1941.

Legends of Angria. Edited by Fannie E. Ratchford. Yale, 1933.

The Confessions of an English Opium Eater by Thomas de Quincey. John Lane, the Bodley Head, 1930.

The Brontës and Their Circle by Clement K. Shorter. J. M. Dent, 1914.

Emily Brontë by M. Spark and D. Stanford. Peter Owen, 1953.

Haworth, Past and Present by J. Horsfall Turner. Brighouse, 1879.

A Spring Time Saunter by Whiteley Turner. Halifax, 1913.

The Brontës by Irene Cooper Willis. Duckworth, 1913.

The Complete Works of Professor Wilson: Poems and Prose.
    William Blackwood, 1855.

MANUSCRIPTS BY PATRICK BRANWELL BRONTË
other than those bought from the library of J. A. Symington

A New Year's Story. (Transcript for the purpose made by Mrs
    D'Arcy Hart and Miss O'Farrell by permission of the
    British Museum.)
The Wool Is Rising. (Transcript for the purpose made by Mrs
    D'Arcy Hart, Miss O'Farrell and Mrs St George
    Saunders by permission of the British Museum.)
Percy. (Photostat supplied by the Brontë Society. Transcript
    made by Mrs St George Saunders.)
Various prose works and poems in the Brontë Museum and
    Bonnell Collection. (Manuscripts and transcripts shown
    to the author by kindness of the custodian, Mr Harold
    Mitchell.)
Various prose works and poems, including Branwell Brontë's
    Luddenden Notebook, in the Brotherton Collection,
    Leeds. (Manuscripts and transcripts shown to the author
    by kindness of the keeper of the Brotherton Collection,
    Mr B. S. Page, and of Mr David Masson, Sub-Librarian.)

NEWSPAPERS, PERIODICALS, ETC.
The Athenaeum, May 3rd, May 24th and May 29th, 1879.
The Mirror, December 1847.
The Press (Christchurch, New Zealand), August 2nd, 1935.
T.P.'s Weekly, July 1903.
The Saturday Review, January 2nd, 1886.
The Scarborough Gazette and *The Scarborough Herald* for the
    months of June, July and August, 1843, 1844 and 1845.
Morning Chronicle, December 2nd, 1834.

Walkers Directory for 1845.

Directories for Luddenden and Sowerby. 1840.

Freemasonry in Airedale in the Early Nineteenth Century, with particular reference to the Three Graces Lodge. Lecture by Mr Wade Hustwick given in Bradford on February 20th, 1956.

Brochure and Guide to Haworth. Edited by A. H. Preston.

Sowerby Bridge Official Guide.

Sowerby Bridge Centenary, 1856–1956. Illustrated Souvenir.

OTHER DOCUMENTS

List of members of the Luddenden Library (established in 1781) and some of the volumes, once at the Lord Nelson Inn and now at the Public Library, Sowerby Bridge (Shown to the author by kindness of the Librarian, Mr S. Robinson.)

The Heaton Family Records (Cartwright Memorial Hall, Bradford. Letters and extracts from these records sent to the author by kindness of Mr Wilfred Robertshaw, President, Cartwright Memorial Hall.)

The Robinson Family Records. (Permission to inspect deed-box containing letters, documents and cash-books kindly given by Messrs Brown & Elmhurst. Transcript made by Miss Elizabeth Brunskill.)

Death Certificates of Patrick Branwell Brontë, Elizabeth Branwell, J. B. Leyland, Ann Marshall, Edmund Robinson, Sr, Edmund Robinson, Jr, Lydia Scott and William Weightman (all obtained from Somerset House) and of Martha Taylor (obtained from Commune de Koekelberg).

Poll lists for Sowerby in 1838.

Wills of Edmund Robinson, Sr, Edmund Robinson, Jr, Lady Scott and Sir Edward Dolman Scott.

Administration of effects of J. B. Leyland.

Coloured pictorial historical map of Halifax and district, by kindness of the artist, Mr Geoffrey Coning.

Index

Pickles, Jonas, 51

Piece Hall, Halifax, 131, 231

Pocock, Mary, 253

Ponden Hall, 29, 36, 37, 52, 87, 108

Postlethwaite, Robert, 105, 110–11

Priestley, George, 125

Priestley family, of White Windows, 103

Rawson, Christopher, 39, 98, 103

Redman, Mr, 29

Richardson, George, 126, 138

Roberson, Rev. Hammond, 31

Robinson, Edmund, of Thorp Green Hall, 160–3, 168, 175–9, 182, 206, 207–8, 209–12

Robinson, Edmund (son of above), 177–9, 182, 191, 252

Robinson, Harriet, 80

Robinson, Lydia (Mrs Edmund Robinson; later Lady Scott), 160–3, 168–73, 175–9, 188–98, 207–13, 229, 231–2, 250–5

Robinson, Lydia (daughter of above; later Mrs Roxby), 169–72, 187, 188, 252

Robinson, of Leeds (drawing-master), 37–8, 45–6, 47, 74

Robinson, Mrs (widow of drawing-master), 101

Roe Head school, 31–3, 45, 46, 51, 64, 65, 73, 160

Roxby, Henry, 169, 187

Roxby, Robert, 169

Royal Academy, Branwell's efforts to enter, 45–7, 49, 50, 97

Royd House, Oxenhope, 29, 37

Saunders, Rev. Moses, 73

Scaitcliffe Hall, 103

Scarborough *Herald*, 177

Scott, Sir Edward Dolman, 251, 255

Scott, Lady. *See* Robinson, Lydia

Seaton, Daniel, 251

Sewell, Mr and Mrs Thomas, 164

Shackleton, John, 51

Sheep Hole, 108

Sidgwick, Mrs, 97, 101

Silver Hill, 108

Sladen Beck, 52

Slippery Ford, 108

Sloane, Edward, 148–9

Smith, Elder & Co., 238, 242, 243, 246, 254

Southey, Robert, 66, 104, 113

Sowdens, 52, 53

Sowerby Bridge, 103 122, 127

Stanbury Moor, 51, 87

Stonegappe, 97

Story, Robert, 79

Stuart-Wortley, John (Lord Wharncliffe), 46

Sugden, Mrs, 249, 253

Sunderland, Jonas, 51

Sunderland, Mr (schoolmaster), 29, 34

Sutcliffe brothers, 29

Swan Hotel, Halifax, 103

www.virago.co.uk

To find out more about Daphne du Maurier and
other Virago authors, visit
www.virago.co.uk

Visit the Virago website for:

- News of author events and forthcoming titles
- Interviews with authors, including Margaret
  Atwood, Maya Angelou, Sarah Waters, Nina
  Bawden and Gillian Slovo
- Free extracts from a wide range of titles
- Discounts on new publications
- Competitions
- Exclusive signed copies

PLUS
Subscribe to our free monthly newsletter

THE DU MAURIERS

Daphne du Maurier

With an Introduction by Michael Holroyd

When Daphne du Maurier wrote this book she was only thirty years old and had already established herself as a biographer, with the acclaimed *Gerald: A Portrait*, and a novelist. *The Du Mauriers* was written during a vintage period of her career, between two of her best-loved novels: *Jamaica Inn* and *Rebecca*. Her aim was to write her family biography 'so that it reads like a novel'. It was due to du Maurier's remarkable imaginative gifts that she was able to breathe life into the characters and depict with affection and wit the relatives she never knew, including her grandfather George du Maurier, the famous Victorian artist and *Punch* cartoonist – and creator of *Trilby*.

'Miss du Maurier creates on the grand scale; she runs through the generations, giving her family unity and reality . . . a rich vein of humour and satire . . . observation, sympathy, courage, a sense of the romantic, are here' *Observer*

MARY ANNE

Daphne du Maurier

With an Introduction by Lisa Hilton

In Regency London, the only way for a women to succeed is to beat men at their own game. So when Mary Anne Clarke seeks an escape from her squalid surroundings in Bowling Inn Alley, she ventures first into the scurrilous world of the pamphleteers. Her personal charms are such, however, that before long she comes to the notice of the Duke of York.

With her taste for luxury and power, Mary Anne, now a royal mistress, must aim higher. Her lofty connections allow her to establish a thriving trade in military commissions, provoking a scandal that rocks the government – and brings personal disgrace.

A vivid portrait of overweening ambition, *Mary Anne* is set during the Napoleonic Wars and based on du Maurier's own great-great-grandmother.

'With unfailing du Maurier skill, the author has coupled family interest with dramatic sense'   Elizabeth Bowen, *Tatler*

FRENCHMAN'S CREEK

Daphne du Maurier

With an Introduction by Julie Myerson

Lady Dona St Columb is beautiful, headstrong – and bored. Desperate to escape the pomp and ritual of the Restoration Court, she retreats to the hidden creeks and secret woods of the family estate at Navron, in Cornwall. Though renowned for her passionate engagement with life, privately she yearns for freedom, integrity and love – whatever the cost.

The peace Lady Dona craves, however, eludes her from the moment she stumbles across the mooring-place of a white-sailed ship that plunders the Cornish coast. And as she becomes embroiled in a plot to steal another ship from under the nose of the English authorities, she realises that her own heart is under seige from the French philosopher-pirate, Jean Aubrey . . .

'A storyteller of cunning and genius'   Sally Beauman

Now you can order superb titles directly from Virago

❑ The Du Mauriers	Daphne du Maurier	£7.99
❑ Mary Anne	Daphne du Maurier	£6.99
❑ Frenchman's Creek	Daphne du Maurier	£6.99
❑ The Birds and Other Stories	Daphne du Maurier	£6.99
❑ Gerald: A Portrait	Daphne du Maurier	£7.99
❑ The Glass-Blowers	Daphne du Maurier	£7.99
❑ The House on the Strand	Daphne du Maurier	£6.99
❑ Julius	Daphne du Maurier	£7.99
❑ The Loving Spirit	Daphne du Maurier	£7.99
❑ Myself When Young	Daphne du Maurier	£7.99
❑ Rebecca	Daphne du Maurier	£7.99
❑ Rebecca's Tale	Sally Beauman	£6.99
❑ Rule Britannia	Daphne du Maurier	£7.99
❑ The Scapegoat	Daphne du Maurier	£7.99

Please allow for postage and packing: **Free UK delivery**.
Europe; add 25% of retail price; Rest of World; 45% of retail price.

To order any of the above or any other Virago titles, please call our credit card orderline or fill in this coupon and send/fax it to:

Virago, P.O. Box 121, Kettering, Northants NN14 4ZQ
Tel: 01832 737526 Fax: 01832 733076. Email: aspenhouse@FSBDial.co.uk

❑ I enclose a UK bank cheque made payable to Virago for £..............
❑ Please charge £.............. to my Access, Visa, Delta, Switch Card No.

❑❑❑❑❑❑❑❑❑❑❑❑❑❑❑❑❑❑❑❑❑

Expiry Date ❑❑❑❑ Switch Issue No. ❑❑

NAME (Block Letters please) _____
ADDRESS _____
_____

Postcode:_____ Telephone: _____
Signature:_____

Please allow 28 days for delivery within the UK. Offer subject to price and availability.

Please do not send any further mailings from companies carefully selected by Virago ❑

Daphne du maurier

Daphne du maurier

Daphne du maurier

Daphne du maurier

Daphne du maurier

Daphne du maurier

Daphne du maurier

Daphne du maurier

Daphne du maurier

Daphne du maurier

Daphne du maurier

maurier

Daphne du mau

Daphne du maurier

maurier

Daphne du mau

Daphne du maurier

maurier

Daphne du mau